W9-BLZ-410

PSYCHOLOGICAL BASES OF WAR

PSYCHOLOGICAL BASES OF WAR

EDITED BY

HEINRICH Z. WINNIK

RAFAEL MOSES

MORTIMER OSTOW

Quadrangle / The New York Times Book Co.

JERUSALEM ACADEMIC PRESS

Distribution of this book is being handled by the following publishers:

For the USA and Canada
Quadrangle Books, Inc.
330 Madison Avenue
New York, New York 10017

For all remaining areas
Jerusalem Academic Press
P.O. Box 2390
Jerusalem, Israel

Library of Congress Card Number: **72-91382**
ISBN: **0-8129-0328-5**

וְכִתְּתוּ חַרְבוֹתָם לְאִתִּים וַחֲנִיתוֹתֵיהֶם

לְמַזְמֵרוֹת לֹא־יִשָּׂא גוֹי אֶל־גּוֹי חֶרֶב

וְלֹא־יִלְמְדוּ עוֹד מִלְחָמָה.

ישעיה ב, ד

And they shall beat their swords into plowshares, and their spears into pruning hooks: nation shall not lift up sword against nation, neither shall they learn war any more.

Isaiah II, 4

CONTENTS

Preface, *M. Ostow*, M. D.   9

Introduction, *H. Z. Winnik*, *M. D.*   13

Aggression in Nations, *Shimon Peres*   15

The Subjectivity of Israeli Psychoanalysts in Discussing War,
    Vicky Bental, *M. D.* (*Haifa*)   17

Another View, *Edith Buxbaum*, *M. D.* (*Seattle, Wash.*)   23

Vicissitudes of Aggression Viewed Developmentally,
    Peter B. Neubauer, *M. D.* (*New York*)   27

Another View, *Dov R. Aleksandrowicz*, *M. D.* (*Tel Aviv*)   39

Woman's Role in Aggression, *Lizzi Rosenberger*, *M. D.*   43
    (*Tel Aviv*)

Another View, *Judith S. Kestenberg*, *M. D.* (*New York*)   59

The Individual, the Group and War, *Bryant Wedge*, *M. D.*
    (*Washington D. C.*)   65

Another View, *J. A. Schossberger*, *M. D.* (*Jerusalem*)   83

Psychoanalytic Implications of Reactions of Soldiers to the
    Six-Day War, *Ruth Jaffe*, *M. D.* (*Ramat Gan*)   89

Another View, *Robert S. Wallerstein*, *M. D.*
    (*San Francisco*)   103

Cultural Patterns of Aggression, *Pinchas Noy*, *M. D.*   111
    (*Jerusalem*)

Another View, *Arnold Rogow*, *Ph. D.* (*New York*)   125

Notes on the Motivations for War, *Samuel Atkin*, *M. D.*   135
    (*New York*)

Another View, *Eliezer Ilan, (Jerusalem)*   169

Notes on Some Psychic Motives for War,
    Erich Gumbel, M. D. (Jerusalem)   173

Another View, *Louis Linn, M. D. (New York)*   183

Motives for Peace, *Jacob A. Arlow, M. D. (New York)*   193

Another View, *H. Z. Winnik, M. D. (Jerusalem)*   205

Some Aspects of Children's Aggressive Behavior During
    States of Illness and Recovery, *Albert J. Solnit, M. D.*
    (New Haven)   211

Another View, *Naomi Gluecksohn-Weiss (Jerusalem)*   229

Outlook: An American View, *Mortimer Ostow, M. D.*   233
    (New York)

Outlook: An Israeli View, *Rafael Moses, M. D. (Jerusalem)*   243

Preface

Since 1963, a number of American and Israeli psychoanalysts have been working together to promote teaching, practice and research in psychoanalysis in Israel. Their joint activities had hitherto been limited to exchanging visits and attending scientific meetings on an individual basis. There has also been an exchange of clinical and research papers, mostly through publication in the *Israel Annals of Psychiatry and Related Disciplines*. The working relation was formalized by the device of extending to the Americans corresponding membership in the Israel Psychoanalytic Society.

With the passage of time and an increasing closeness in colleagual relations both the Israelis and the Americans have pressed for a collaborative project. A combined meeting devoted to elucidating a subject of common interest seemed reasonable, and a psycho-analytic review of the subject of war, suggested to us by Dr. Louis Linn, generated a good deal of interest. I proposed that we turn to Freud's letter to Einstein, published under the title, "Why War?" as a point of departure.

At first the Israelis demurred, feeling that their views about war were suspect because they themselves are involved in one. Yet it is difficult to imagine anyone who is not involved in this problem. There is no one who is indifferent to war. One can make a case that to be a citizen of a nation which is struggling to extricate itself from a war for which there is little popular support and which poses no immediate threat to that nation, is to be in the same biased position as the citizen of a nation which must fight for its survival. In fact, the latter may be more closely in touch with historic

9

reality than the former. Certainly the heat of recent controversies in American psychoanalytic societies about whether the societies should take public positions on military and political issues demonstrates that in these matters many American psycho-analysts cannot avoid emotional involvement. I persisted with my suggestion, therefore, hoping that our discussions might develop contrasts based upon our respective points of departure, contrasts which in themselves would inform us about the subject of our interest, "Why War?". I hoped that participants would suspend the normal convention that prevails at scientific meetings of addressing oneself only to the subject matter presented, and ignoring those aspects of personality and attitude that are incidentally betrayed. I hoped instead that participants would look consciously for biases, for fixed attitudes in ourselves and in each other, so that by discussing them we might learn more about what it means to be at war and what it means to be at peace.

In retrospect now I find that the degree of objectivity achieved was impressive. Many of the participants were exposed to real stresses of war, actual and potential, recent and threatening. Knowing that the real experience of these stresses must exert at least some degree of bias, each of the speakers strove to overcome this and also to avoid the associated trap of leaning over too far backwards. The reader will be able to judge the degree to which the speakers were each able to cope with his own prejudices and to make a generally valid contribution. The reader will doubtless be impressed too by the earnestness and honesty of each participant and the attempt to be helpful, which created a tone most of us felt was unique for scientific conferences. It is this special combination of earnestness, honesty, and helpfulness which com-mends this book to the reader, and which raises the discussion to an unusually high level.

To make this book more coherent and keep its size reasonable, a good deal of editorial work was necessary. Some of the papers which pertained less directly to the topic were omitted. Fortu-nately most of them have been published elsewhere. Unfor-tunately, though, the discussion of these papers is lost. The floor discussion has also had to be omitted despite its unusually high quality and great interest, and despite the fact that it is in the floor discussion that the earnestness and seriousness were most clearly seen.

For this considerable editorial work, skillfully and generously done, we are indebted to Mrs. Martha Gillmor. What the reader has in his hands is less a transcript of the proceedings of the symposium than a book which has grown out of it. My colleagues, Dr. Heinrich Winnik, and Dr. Rafael Moses, carried the great burden of organizing the meeting and collecting and processing the papers and discussions. Both Dr. Peter Neubauer and Dr. Louis Linn reinforced my efforts in the United States, not only by their participation in the transactions but even more by their astute advice.

We expect that meetings of the Israel Psychoanalytic Society with its corresponding members will become regularly scheduled events, and we shall endeavor to make these meetings international psychoanalytic forums of major significance.

MORTIMER OSTOW

Introduction

H. Z. Winnik

In 1964, thirty years after the establishment of the Israel Psycho-analytic Society by M. Eitingon (1934), Dr. Mortimer Ostow suggested inaugurating a corresponding membership among our colleagues in the U. S. as an expression of the ties between the groups of the two countries, and in order to further the development of training and research facilities at our Psychoanalytic Institute. The suggestion was gladly accepted, especially because our geographic remoteness from the psychoanalytic centers of the Western World cut us off from sufficient communication.

At the suggestion of our American colleagues, "Why War?" the title of the letter-exchange between Einstein and Freud, was chosen as the theme of a conference to become this volume. I may be right in the assumption that one of the reasons for this choice was the long-term wars both countries are involved in and the resulting psychological problems which have to be faced.

War is the most destructive form of intergroup aggression — irrational for both the losers and the winners. It has been considered irrational for centuries, even when fought with so-called conventional arms. Its absurdity grew with the menacing potential of nuclear war.

The question "Why War?" was posed 38 years ago by Einstein "as the most insistent of all problems civilization has to face." That Einstein turned to Freud and not to any other expert for an answer to this question indicates that he was well aware of the role unconscious forces play in conflicts between groups and nations.

The question appears even more urgent and alarming today. It will presumably be posed as long as wars and humanity's inner protest against them exist. The question is based not only on reason but also on the deep longing for an age of peace, and on the rejection of the destructive form of human aggression. These feelings have found their expression in mythology, in visions, in ideologies; they still persist in the present day. Generally projected onto the past, as in the Saturnian age of Ovidius' Metamorphoses, or into the future as in the visions of our prophets, they have never been realized in the present.

We know that the contribution of the psychoanalytic theories to the prevention of war can be only very modest. The ideas proffered in analytic circles, as for instance, that heads of state and political leaders should agree to undergo psychoanalysis, or that all children should be analyzed (M. Klein) and other, similar ideas belong to the sphere of utopian theories and propositions so often encountered in this field.

But the germs of ideas may be planted in raising the question again, and psychoanalysis may have a contribution to make to an interdisciplinary investigation of a problem that concerns all mankind.

Aggression in Nations

*Shimon Peres**

The subject selected for this volume is a difficult one. But then one should remember the story of Voltaire, who said when a friend approached him and observed that life is very difficult, "Well, compared to what?"

All nations operate on the dual assumptions that each has both the right to equality and the right to be different. Every nation should be equal to other nations, in rights, in outlooks, in deciding upon and executing its own destiny, while maintaining differences of religion, customs, mores and so on. When these differences must be expressed in violence, we are at war. I am certainly not an authority on this subject. At most, I have been a client of it for a very long time. I will make some observations only as a client.

It is much easier to understand an individual, a person, than it is to understand a nation or any collective or group. Individuals are most obedient to law, to custom, to precedent. Nations are the makers of laws, of customs, and of philosophies. It is easier to understand an individual than a nation because you can meet an individual. You must imagine a nation. Since so many nations spent such an important part of their history at war, one must ask a basic question: Are there nations which are belligerent? Are there belligerent periods in the history of nations? Are there ages in the life of a nation which are characterized by a bellicose effort?

One cannot really answer this question, but I have speculated that there are nations which are belligerent now; there are nations which are pre-belligerent; and there are nations which are post-belligerent.

* Israel Minister of Transport and Communications.

What determines the state of belligerency in a nation may be the stage of its national development, its economic situation, its social standard. Belligerency may be a first stage in the creation of a state.

It is easier to create an army than to create a people. It is easier to develop a war machine than an industry. It is easier to run a nation by discipline than by compromise. It is not necessary to develop the whole of a people or the whole of a country in order to be at war at a successful level. The most modern sophisticated arms can be bought, the plain and basic discipline upon which an army is based can be taught, tangible and immediate prestige can be promised to all the people. But to create a nation, to create a people, to create a country, means facing many problems and many difficulties; creating so many organizations that the easier solution may seem to be in creating an army. Once a country has an army, it is half way to war. Especially if it has an army without the social institutions that create opposition and force second thoughts and insist upon alternatives. It is easier to create discipline than to create a system of checks and balances.

In addition to the structure of the nations, which has very much to do with the function of war, there are some more defined, more realistic reasons for its existence. Reasons but not logic. One example with which I am familiar, is the Israeli situation. The Arabs *do* believe that Israel is looking toward territorial expansion.

Once such a fear has been thoroughly internalized, events can strengthen it. Thus, when in the Six Day War, Israel did indeed conquer territories, the Arabs' fears were justified. This is the sort of vicious circle which is created by the initial fears, but does not explain how the initial fears originate and create belligerency.

While it is very hard to define the reasons for war, and the structures within nations that lead to war, one should never be fatalistic about it. One should never give up hope. One should never stop trying to reduce the terrible suspicion existing between societies. It takes as much courage to create peace as it does to create war, and it is *this* courage man must cultivate.

The Subjectivity of Israeli Psychoanalysts in Discussing War

Vicky Bental

When in the summer of 1968 Dr. Mortimer Ostow suggested as the basic theme of a conference, Freud's letter to Einstein, "Why War," his proposal was unanimously accepted by the members of the Israeli Psychoanalytic Society and we started exchanging views on this theme in order to draw up a provisional program.

Shortly afterward the Haifa Group of members met and the theme came up for discussion. Doubts were expressed as to whether, under the special circumstances of life in Israel, analysts would be able to deal with the theme in a sufficiently objective way at a time when we were still in reality at war. Almost daily, tragic events stir up emotions with their consequent subjective reactions. In such a special situation, could we be purely objective and our thinking abstract enough, no matter how hard we tried?

As Freud put it in "Thoughts on War and Death":

"Students of human nature and philosophers have long taught us that we are mistaken in regarding our intelligence as an independent force and in overlooking its dependence on emotional life. Our intellect, they teach us, can function reliably only when it is removed from influences of strong emotional impulses".

We brought our hesitations and second thoughts to the next meeting of our Society where, however, they were overruled. The majority opinion was that analysts should be able to discuss any theme in an objective scientific manner and to put personal emotions aside.

Following this decision, we actively participated in the preparations for the meeting from which this book resulted. But I was asked to describe the hesitancies of the Haifa group of the Psychoanalytic Society.

The Israelis are still at war with an enemy who vastly outnumbers us and who has again and again openly declared that his aim is to destroy our state and to annihilate its population. Most of our population believes that these threats were and are meant seriously.

We are reminded of Hitler's similarly open threats which were not taken seriously by the world at large and led in the end to the extermination of six million Jews and to catastrophic results for the whole world. We feel that the enemy around us is reckless not only with regard to us but, if need be, also toward his own people. As we see it we therefore have no other choice than to defend ourselves in order to prevent yet another holocaust. As a result, our aggressive impulses are aroused to ward off the aggression of the enemy and to fight for our survival. We have to mobilize our aggressive drives in the service of the life-instincts, and by warding off the enemy's aggression we are forced to destroy and to kill.

As Freud wrote in his famous letter to Einstein:

"The organism preserves its own life, so to say, by destroying an extraneous one."

We have to direct our aggression outward, toward an object, in order not to turn it against ourselves in a self-destructive way. I want to mention in this connection that in the years since the Six-Day War, what many of us feel are self-destructive tenencies can be observed in certain circles in which, as I would put it, by identification with the enemy, aggression is directed inward, against ourselves. In these circles the ever-ready self-hatred and bitter self-criticism of the Jew finds its expression, a dangerous character trait that may lead to destruction. These, however, are minorities, whereas the broad masses of the people react with open aggression against the outer enemy.

In June 1967, when the first shots were fired from our side we were the aggressors; but we acted to forestall expected aggression from the other side. It was — we firmly believed — a question of life and death. We had to fight for our survival and to become heroes against our will. The sympathies of the Western world were with us and we did not feel alone. Those days in June 1967 were hard and difficult, fraught with extreme danger and fear for the loved ones — fighting for our existence in the front-line. But there was no hate; the drive for both survival and the achievement of peace prevailed.

Later in this volume the reactions and psychological state of the Israeli soldier, his attitude with regard to aggression and to being called a hero, will be described. It was a strange phenomenon: an army with fighting spirit, longing for peace. We were victorious in the war, we had to be, we could not afford it otherwise. We hoped that peace would follow, that the aggression and hate of our Arab neighbors would be transmuted into peaceful cooperation. This hope of ours has so far proved to have been illusory. It has been a bitter disappointment. And while continuing to have to be aggressive and to fight, we are still waiting for a sign from our Arab neighbors that they are prepared to come to terms with us toward real peace and mutual understanding without threatening war.

Originally, we felt that the sympathies of the free world were with us in the days of acute danger. But we have become aware since then of a gradual change of attitude toward us—a difficulty in understanding our demand for security, which we feel so necessary for the prevention of yet another war. This lack of understanding and sometimes even identification with our enemy, is frustrating and frightening to us. As everyone knows, frustration also arouses aggression, and this is just what is happening in our case. We have become doubtful about whether we can find a common language even with our American friends. A little episode may illustrate this: One of us accompanied an American guest on a tour to the Golan Heights (it might have been about 1967 or 1968) and showed him the Syrian fortifications, their artillery-positions and bunkers from which our settlements below had been shelled for years, in order to demonstrate the danger the people had lived in there. But the guide had the distinct feeling that the guest was scarcely interested or impressed and was thinking, "So what?" He did not understand. I am sure that not all visitors react in this manner, but we learn too from letters from friends abroad that their previous conviction that we were not the aggressors has been somewhat shattered, so that we now have to defend ourselves against this suspicion.

I quote from a reprint of a syndicated column by, as they call him, "The American Longshoreman-Philosopher," Eric Hoffer: "Israel is not allowed to act and react like any other nation. It is expected to be forbearing and long-suffering in the face of provocations no other country would dream of tolerating." In these circumstances, we react in an emotional, subjective way. Since the war, certain changes have taken place in us. The growing terrorism from beyond the borders and from within has caused many of us to become more aggressive against our own will. It is quite remarkable, however, that there have been very few cases of open aggression by the public in response to acts of terrorism committed by Arabs; the urge toward revenge is restrained by the ordinary man in the street. You do not find real hate among them but a deep mistrust and skepticism about the real intentions of our neighbors.

One may presume that all psychoanalysts are pacifists, with a deep wish and longing for peace. We are against war and destruction as such. But aggression in this country is growing in reaction to the unabating aggression of the Arabs and their supporters. There are, however, some groups trying to overcome this aggressive trend by formulating peace-programs. Unfortunately, peace-programs will be utopian and unrealistic, so long as there is no response from the other side.

It is understandable that anxiety has increased under these conditions. Fear and anxiety are warning-signals of danger — very real in our case — against which man has to protect himself. However, not much mention is made of this anxiety, either orally or by written word, perhaps too little. Instead, there is denial, repression, and transformation into aggression, to ward off fear, and sometimes this also leads to cynicism or dangerous fatalism.

But, in general, life continues its normal course, as if nothing special were happening. For the men at the frontiers this is a source of strength, and in their letters home and their phone calls from the

Canal-Zone they try to dispel the anxiety of their loved-ones at home.

But there is one exception: life in the threatened settlements along the borders. Their members live in tension and anxiety in reaction to the constant danger to which they are exposed. But they remain at their places. We as psychiatrists and analysts, try to help by providing prevention and treatment of anxiety responses. And a number of us visit the settlements in order to better acquaint ourselves with the problems of communities living under the constant stress of exposure to unpredictable attacks. The children sleep and often live in their shelters. There are little ones who have never known it otherwise. The children trust their shelters and ward off their anxiety in play, painting, and fantasy. They feel insecure when visiting the town and required to sleep in ordinary bedrooms.

The youth serving in the army have a strong identification with their homeland and master their anxiety by means of the common group experience. Here and there fear is expressed among the youngsters by cynical remarks about war and death, but it is rare for a boy to try to evade military service because of fear. One frequently encounters the opposite situation, in which youngsters, declared unfit for military service for health reasons— physical or psychological—suffer severe frustration. They almost universally have the desire to "belong" to and wish to serve in a fighting unit. Yet they are not militarists and when on leave they like to shed their uniforms and be civilians.

I have tried to give a general picture of how we live, without claiming that it is comprehensive. I have tried to make understandable our hesitations and questions about ourselves: are we able to evaluate things in an unimpaired scientific way under the prevailing circumstances which provoke such subjective reactions as to what is right or wrong and which compel us to be aggressive and sometimes even cruel when we fear for the lives of beloved ones fighting for our survival at the frontlines? Are we not forced to become subjective, deeply involved in the situation? We have to defend ourselves against the accusation of being the aggressors when we know that we are fighting for our right to live here, in this country, which is, or has become, our home-land. We feel that our cause is a just one, though the other side may feel the same.

Freud wrote in his letter to Einstein: "... every war is not open to condemnation to an equal degree; so long as there exist countries and nations that are prepared for the ruthless destruction of others —those others must be armed for war." Since we belong to these "others," we see no alternative but to fight.

Finally, remember the subjectivity of Freud himself, in his "Thoughts on War and Death," written at the beginning of World War One, when he strongly and in a very emotional way identified himself with the German cause:

"We live in hope that the pages of an impartial history will prove that that nation, in whose language we write and for whose victory our dear ones are fighting, has been precisely the one which least transgressed the laws of civilization. But at such a time who dares to set himself up as a judge in his own cause?"

He himself had later on to revise bitterly his opinion about the great "civilized nation." But at the time he wrote he felt emotionally identified and involved. History proved him to have been wrong.

We do not know how history will regard our war in time to come. We are living this history and are prone to subjective sentiments and emotions which may distort any attempt to unimpaired scientific approach.

Another View

Edith Buxbaum

Dr. Bental has made a point about subjectivity. She quotes Freud who says "Who can be judge in his own cause?" This seems self-evident. The law does not allow a judge to sit in a matter in which he is involved. Superior Court judges have been disqualified on that basis in the U. S. The analyst is particularly sensitive in that matter; we do not treat friends or members in our own family, if we can possibly help it. Several attempts have been made by different analysts to analyze several members of the same family: husband and wife, or a parent and a child. I have tried it too. I was tempted because I thought it would be interesting and helpful to know the other partner in a conflictive relationship. In all these cases I found that I was partial to one of the two patients, however much I tried to be objective. The failure may have been my fault. I consider myself an average analyst and I think that the majority of analysts, being average, would make similar mistakes.

Another instance which points to the same problem is anthropology. Anthropologists can observe and examine cultures other than their own, but when they attempt to analyze the culture of which they are a part themselves, they lose their objectivity, and value judgments creep in which have no place there.

This analysis of this war situation falls into all three categories: there is a conflict in which the Israeli analyst is involved and therefore cannot judge. He is involved personally through his family, friends, and himself, therefore he cannot objectively analyze. He is part of that particular country, people, and situation, and therefore his observation is skewed.

We, the outsiders, are not sufficiently outsiders to serve in this role either. We are not objective observers but friends involved through personal relations, common past, guilt feelings and common anxieties.

Freud considered a defensive war justifiable. There are two mechanisms of defense which are at the disposal of all living beings, man and animal alike: flight and fight. If flight is made impossible, the only road left is fight. Both are used in the service of the life instinct, even though both may ultimately lead to death. Freud says: "There is nothing instinctual in us which responds to a belief in death. This may even be the secret of heroism." The heroic fight may well be based upon the denial of death for oneself — while witnessing the death of others contradicts this denial.

Israel's heroic fight is doubly so because the holocaust is not forgotten and every single death is known to many. The anomie of the big countries, the large populations, does not exist here. Everybody, however great the denial of death, is faced with the death of a beloved one, of a part of himself.

The idea of self-defense on the other hand offers an irrefutable rationalization for giving way to the instinct of aggression, which is of an elementary nature, "similar in all men, and which aims at the satisfaction of certain primal needs." It is used in the service of the life instinct, for the preservation of one's own life and for the destruction of one's enemies. The instinct of aggression has this dual role which makes it the greatest helper and greatest danger for all living beings.

Aggression can be used constructively and destructively against the outside and against oneself. This universal aspect of aggression, its destructive potential, is what we must consider in a discussion of war, be it the Arab–Israeli war, or any others. George Wald, professor of biology, Nobel Laureate in physiology and medicine, says: "War itself is an atrocity, by now become too dangerous for us to tolerate any longer." Too dangerous for us all because our poison gases, our napalm, biological, chemical and atomic weapons have become the broomstick–water–carriers over which we may lose control any minute. They are like the hypertrophied antlers, teeth or beaks, or tusks of animals which are at one time superb means of defense and attack, and at another time become unmanageable accessories which trap their owners in swamps and trees and make them unable to fend for themselves. The idea of the survival of the fittest does not work for us any more.

Today's victors are tomorrow's victims. "Would we not confess that in our civilized attitude towards death we are once again living psychologically beyond our means — and should we not rather turn back and recognize the truth? *Si vis vitam, para mortem,*" says Freud. Face your death if you want to live.

Vicissitudes of Aggression Viewed Developmentally.

Peter B. Neubauer

It may at first appear as if this paper does not belong to a symposium on the Psychological Bases of War. For here we will refer to aggressive strivings which seem to safeguard normal function, that is, they achieve a significant appropriate balance with libidinal drive expressions as both come under ego dominance. Moreover, the developmental point of view stresses those variables which contribute to the processes of unfolding of psychic function and structure formation and thus we may gain understanding of the aggressive drive at its best rather than the component which determines destructive behavior.

But as usual in psychoanalysis, a full view is necessary to determine the conditions which influence the change from the normal to the abnormal, the progression from regression and those which constitute "critical periods" with high vulnerabilities. It is in this sense that I shall attempt to bring into the discussion some of the developmental considerations.

To discuss the complexity of the aggressive vicissitudes in connection with the developmental process would reach beyond the limits of this presentation, for there is no aspect of psychic life in which the aggressive component does not take part. Furthermore, we have an outline of libidinal phase organization, but we do not have a similar outline for the development of aggression. This may have been determined by the history of psychoanalytic theory formation; it may also have been determined by the special attributes of the aggressive drive itself.

In the context of the theme of aggression and war, any discussion must attempt to lead to an understanding of the relation of the aggressive drive to self-preservation and to factors of group psychology. The object and aim of the aggressive drive must be differentiated from those aggressive expressions that have become modified by the ego for purposes of adaptation. When the task of self-preservation and preservation of the species was ascribed to the ego under the influence of the reality principle, a new understanding of the aggressive forces was possible. The destructive aim of the drive could be separated from the aggressive strivings serving mastery, control and survival. A developmental approach to this issue, therefore, could address itself to those factors that contribute to the transformation from the aggressive destructive strivings to ego function under the dominance of the reality principle. What are the external environmental forces that foster this transformation? What are the conflicts, the points of fixation and regression, that interfere with it? Could we learn how to assist the development in such a way as to achieve de-aggressivization and the emergence of neutralization of the aggressive drive?

When one attempts to understand the psychic functions that contribute to either war or peace, it is clear that many variables of the "psychology of groups" come into play. The idealization of the leader, the revival of oedipal and pre-oedipal conflicts, the diminution of reality testing, the regressive pull in situations of danger, the dissolution of the individual ego as it submerges into the group ego — all these are known variables. If we are again to follow this from a developmental point of view, we must raise questions about the child's relationship to parental figures, hero worship, the need for dependent relationships, group formation among siblings, the degree to which separation-individuation was achieved, and so forth.

Drive vicissitudes during prelatency impress us by the seriousness and intensity of the impact of the aggressive strivings, particularly those aspects connected with phase organization — that is, those more closely connected to the drives and their biological root. I do not speak here about development in terms of the broader emergence of all psychological functions, but of those components connected with libidinal and aggressive phases and their sequences. In the oral phase, we observe pleasure-seeking strivings for gratification and the cathexis with the object. On the aggressive side, we find the attack on the object with the wish to incorporate, simultaneous with the fear of being destroyed and in turn incorporated. Here we find the cannibalistic conditions. The measures of ego modulation — of mastery — are slowly evolving. In the anal phase, the sphincter controls serve libidinal purposes — to please the object, to bring gifts to him, and to endow anal products with narcissistic values. The aggressive component is expressed in the defiance against the imposed training, or the withholding, with anal-sadistic impulses, directed against the object or the self. In the phallic-oedipal phase, we recognize identification, strivings toward the objects — mother and father — at the same time as we find fears of losing the integrity of the body, of being castrated, as well as the fight for magic omnipotence for total control over others. The severity of this struggle continues into the oedipal period, in which the tie to the parent of the opposite sex, from a viewpoint of the drive, can only lead to the total elimination of the parent of the same sex, with the resulting fear of being punished and destroyed.

To sketch early phase development in these broad terms is justified only if it serves to remind us of the extraordinary struggle of the drives, in which polarization of impulses forever signals extreme danger. We are aware from our clinical work how neurotic and other pathological conflicts are based on these developmental conditions, and how strong the tendency is to link external dangers to these conflicts; how easy it is for man to return to conditions of polarization and to formulations in which modulations are eliminated and therefore the alternatives of survival or destruction appear so closely linked.

I will not pursue the development of libidinal phase sequences, but will instead select some developmental conditions that are based on ego development that in turn affect drive balance and distribution: (1) stranger reaction; (2) positions of negativism; (3) the primal scene experience.

Stranger reaction

In the second month of life the child, as yet not separated from the object, with little differentiation between outside and inside stimuli, is able to respond to the human face with a smile. This early pleasurable experience is an indication of the strength of the libidinal striving. But during this period object discrimination does not occur and the smiling response can be elicited under normal circumstances by any friendly person. It is quite some time later — around the seventh month — that the child develops the capacity to differentiate the known from the unknown object, so that recognition of the stranger can take place. This built-in maturational and developmental time-table is based on many complex factors. Often enough, one can observe that some children can differentiate objects much earlier, as well as respond differently to male or female objects. What may be significant here is the fact that recognition of the stranger evokes a negative response in the infant. We may observe either the turning-away from the unknown object, or an increased clinging to the known object; signs of danger reactions as expressed in crying, or as stranger anxiety that at times can be quite intense. Since this reaction is part of the general developmental experience, and a sign of appropriate developmental progression, we cannot assume that this response to the recognition of the stranger is connected with negative experiences of the past. It is not because the infant has learned to distrust the stranger that he turns to the primary object. Up until that time the child turned to any person who approached him in a friendly manner. Thus, we may assume that this stranger reaction serves a specific developmental purpose. While one wishes to avoid a teleological formulation, it is difficult to avoid the speculation that it may serve the reinforcement of the tie to the mother after differentiation has occurred, and may serve to increase the cathexis to a primary object for imitation and identification. It may be a phylogenetic expression that at this stage the outside non-protective world carries with it a by now built-in danger condition. There is the tendency, then, for the alien to evoke anticipation of danger, and therefore the aggressive strivings turn against the unknown. This milestone occurs prior to the child's next maturational step, namely to walk and thereby leave the primary object.

The overt reaction to strangers disappears soon. The internal alertness to the "non-familiar" continues. Reality testing is connected with the possibility of anticipating responses, of postponing gratification because one secures a more appropriate later achievement. When this is challenged by differentiation between the known and the strange object, then the unknown inevitably results in varying degrees of ego alertness and stranger reactions.

Surely, later stages of development may endow the unknown with expectations based on magic wish fulfillment; may serve to avoid the incestuous danger — family-romance — and stimulate excitement.

It may be fruitful to examine the early stranger reaction in terms of its relationship to ego maturational forces and to the drive distribution. Does it occur as a result of the emergence of a new ego capacity, related to perception, cognition, and sensory-motor organization serving self-preservation? Or is it based more on drive factors — that is, on the increased cathexis of the primary object? The earlier, more non-selective attachment to mothering is changed to mother, and at this stage any intervention is connected with a fear of "loss of the object." Whether one decides on any one of these propositions, or whether one assumes an interaction between both of these factors, what remains significant is the mobilization of libidinal connecting strivings and the aggressive response to eliminate and disconnect in order to further the developmental process.

Closeness to the object is a requirement, furthermore, for achievement of identification — to imitate first and then to become what and who the object is. This is later extended to the family, and then to the group and subculture. Implied is the exclusion of the "others" who do not belong. This is necessary to maintain identity and to avoid the dangerous identity defusion.

Thus we find here a reinforcement of the tie to the family and a turning away from the extra-familial. One may argue whether this stranger reaction at this age is an expression of aggressive components. There are alternate ways of explaining it. What is important to us is its anlage for what may become later endowed with aggressive, eliminating wishes against the alien. There are many conditions which foster the stranger anxiety and intensify its influence on further development.

Positions of Negativism

The second condition that may be useful to explore are the "negative positions" during development. These, too, are part of the normal development process, and they facilitate differentiation and a higher form of psychic organization. We can observe them during the anal phase of development and then again, in modified form, during early adolescence.

At the time when the child learns to control his body functions, to adapt to schedules, to recognize place and timing, he turns against the primary object with the phase-characteristic "no!" This is also the period of increased motility and "functionlust" that makes it possible for him to move away from the object. In Mahler's term, separation-individuation takes place. Apparently, in this stage, there is an increased mobilization of aggressive strivings expressed through motility and in the object relations. From the point of view of the drive, the attack is against the object who imposes controls. Anal-sadistic impulses are then counteracted by compulsive orderliness or cleanliness, ritual formation, or the opposite forms of behavior. From the ego's point of view, a distance between object and self has to evolve; *self-control is achieved by defying the controlling influence of the object.* This step is achieved, and individuation occurs, in disagreement and non-conformity. The stranger reaction seems to reinforce the attachment to the object by turning against the outsider; now in the negative position, the turning against the primary object facilitates the detachment from the object to gain separation and individuation and, later, a new level of relationship and psychic organization. The earlier balance between libido and aggression seems to have changed. One may propose the hypothesis that during this anal phase the aggressive drive becomes more activated, threatening defusion between the drives. Without pursuing the most important consequences of the aggressive vicissitudes during the negative phase, we want to stress its effect on ego function: we see increased exploration, curiosity, and the establishment of the I and the self.

Here we see the influence of the aggressive drive on developmental organization — namely, the change in object interaction with ensuing body mastery and spatial exploration.

The revival of the negative position during early adolescence has been explored and discussed in numerous ways. During the emergence of the secondary identity, or individuation, the adolescent turns against the parents to widen his identity and to evolve "his" values. He identifies with individuals outside of the family, and later with new ideas; he moves to extra-familial groups. Again, this is done by detachment from the influence of the parents, by attacking their values, by "creating a generation gap," as they share this position with other adolescents. This step serves the untying of the sexual attachment to the parents, the avoidance of the incestuous wishes, to free the adolescent for extra-familial bonds.

It is not necessary to review here the complex interplay of this struggle, as drive, ego and superego strive for reorganization and higher structure formation; as fusion, defusion and refusion permit a clearer view of libidinal and aggressive drive interaction. What is noteworthy is the recognition that the aggressive strivings are essential for this process; that to disconnect from the object is part of the developmental requirement. This cannot be explained by the mechanism of displacement of libidinal attachment, or by the choice of object of the libidinal drive, without recognizing the role of the aggressive drive component in this process.

This reference to the aggressive component for the evolvement of individuation and identity formation has often been used as a model for many group processes. Not only has youth been understood in these terms, but the emergence of nationalism and the struggle of minorities against outside patterns of control as well.

Primal Scene Experience

The child views the primal scene as being aggressive in nature. This constitutes a significant difference between the child and the adult, and deserves more attention than it has received so far. As one follows A. Freud's proposal to establish lines of development — the steps from dependency to independence, from play to work, and so forth — one wishes to add to it an outline of the sequences that lead the child from experiencing or fantasying the sexual act as aggressive, to the stage where he sees it as primarily libidinal and accompanied by feelings of closeness, tenderness and mutual consideration. This change occurs very slowly and only succeeds during adolescence.

We have not explored these steps enough developmentally, in spite of the long interest in the vicissitudes of libidinal organization and sexual conflicts. From infancy the child experiences libidinal pleasures connected with erotogenic zones. He knows of body pleasures stimulated by the object or by autoerotic activities. Still, the primal scene is for him an interaction of the aggressor and victim, of violation and submission.

It may be that during the phallic phase, when sex differentiation occurs and castration fear emerges, the child's own sexual strivings become inhibited by his fear of retaliation and later by his rivalry for possession with consequent fears of punishment and guilt. The later oedipal struggle endows the sexual act with a strong aggressive component that contributes to the development and consolidation of the superego. It is obvious that controls against the libidinal forces have to be great. Here again we see the aggressive drive coming to the aid of further development, inhibiting the libidinal object choice. Out of the destructive feelings against the object of the same sex and the fear of retaliation, emerges the incest taboo. Thus the child hears and sees what he projects onto the primal scene — his own conflicts. It seems that only during puberty, when increasing libidinal forces stimulate the search for a new object, tenderness and affection enter the relationship and increase the tie. Extra-familial friendship has been practiced during latency; the emerging capacity for sharing, rather than rivalry, takes part in the new sexual feelings.

The libidinal aspects are oriented to body pleasure and body stimulation, but until adolescence they are not integrated with affectionate object interaction. There is, then, this long period of development until sexuality is connected and integrated with affection. In the sexual act, the appropriate fusion of libidinal and aggressive forces emerges late, and only when the turning to an extra-familial object is possible — when the oedipal conflict is resolved. Many factors contribute to this development. The social equivalent of the primal scene — namely, the degree of observable affectionate interaction between the parents — may assist the child's capacity to become affectionate. Cultural components that either permit or inhibit the expression of sexual or erotic feelings, will play a role. There are numerous societal examples that connote sexuality with aggressive factors, as most vernacular references to the sexual act indicate. Furthermore, it would be important to follow libidinal strivings as they are transformed by the ego to serve self-preservation and the preservation of the species in sexual function; and similarly, to follow the participation of the aggressive drive as it serves the same aim in man's fight for survival when in danger.

The primal scene experience depends on the age of the child and the degree and form of exposure, and the degree of reality or fantasy. In the early years sensory modalities, perceptual impressions, will play a significant role. The exposure to the naked body, with the ensuing castration fear or penis envy are well explored. What is important here, is the length through development which is required to free man from his early impressions of the sexual act as being strongly aggressive in nature; how curiosity and pleasurable impulses and body sensations are linked with impulses of aggression against others.

I have sketched these developmental events — the stranger reaction, the negative positions and the primal scene experience — by referring only to a few conditions. These are actually complex interacting, psychic factors that need to be examined from all metapsychological points of view.

Short references may suffice to open further exploration and to show the various aspects of aggression in the developmental process. All three events share certain characteristics:

1. Built in to the epigenetic plan is an aggressive factor that is tied to the biological-maturational sequence.

2. The aggressive strivings serve both the destructive aim and the necessary developmental progression toward identity, mastery and self-preservation.

3. The turning against the object, the stranger, and the family indicates a complex interplay between attachment and detachment of child and object. Out of this, individuation and the self emerge.

4. The early history of the child reveals his simultaneous need for protection and mastery, with a concomitant fear of losing

the object, of losing the love of the object, and of castration. A secure love relationship emerges only during the adolescent struggle.

5. Psychoanalytic experience shows how frequently we find: fixation of, and regression to, earlier experiences, with defusion of drives to conflicts not resolved; the propensity to repeat these conflicts when the ego is not fully able to restrain the drive influences and to follow the reality principle. Thus psychic polarization may occur, since the mediating synthesizing function of the ego is not sufficiently strong. Either/or formulations become evident in conditions of danger: to survive or to perish; to be active or passive. The enemy is magically endowed with strength or destructive intentions, or one may endow oneself with the magic power to destroy unless the danger is assessed by an ego that has maintained control over drive and undue superego influences.

The answer to one of the questions about war and peace lies, therefore, in the relationship between external danger and internal response. How, and under what circumstances, can the ego assert its influence? Under what conditions do the regressive forces and earlier developmental vulnerabilities link up to support the resurgence of aggression?

Our understanding of how identity processes in the individual and the group are facilitated by both the libidinal force and by aggressive strivings against external influences should make primary or secondary prevention, or early therapeutic intervention, possible so that developmental fixations are avoided. The developmental model indicates that only after a secure identity is achieved can new levels of integration with the outside world be established. During the period of identity formation, repressive or punitive action will prolong this struggle and may lead to violence. We may see this in the attitude of the mother to the training phase of the child, as well as in the parents' reaction to adolescent defiance. This example may have relevance for group functions, national identity formation, or the understanding of subcultures, such as the black-white relationship.

These references to some aspects of the developmental process need fuller exploration of the many variables that must be taken into account in order to do justice to our understanding of the multiple determinants of psychic function. They are expressed, therefore, only to remind us of the developmental dimensions of aggression and to stimulate application of this understanding to a variety of social situations and conditions.

Moreover, the developmental conditions discussed can serve as an illustration of how ego maturational forces in turn affect drive distribution. Such observations do not minimize the influence of the drives on ego development, but they emphasize the mutual influences between libidinal phase and ego development. This gains additional significance when we examine it from a genetic point of view. We know of the many factors in the earlier history that co-determine phase specific conflicts and vulnerabilities. The overlapping of phases or the co-existence of conflicts from various phases — that is, of the influence of earlier conflicts on phase organization — can be differentiated more clearly when we can describe such phase-specific events. The stranger reaction and the negative positions are obviously not organized in terms of phases, but are essential features in a given phase that co-determine conflicts and their solution. These differentiations may be helpful for prevention and reconstruction.

As we follow the role of the aggressive drive in the cathexis, decathexis and recathexis of objects, we are reminded of Freud's suggestion that ego strength vis-à-vis one area may contribute a weakness in another. The child's turning against the stranger in the anal phase may contribute to increased vulnerability while he develops more dependency for need satisfaction; his turning against the object in this phase, may give him more independence. This raises questions of definitions of ego strength; should it be conceptualized as the capacity to fuse drives or, as these examples indicate, should it be seen as a condition permitting a flexible rearrangement between libido-aggression in accordance with the developmental demands and the environmental situation.

The dominance of the aggressive drive in the primal scene experience must be connected with narcissism to follow Freud's proposal that "narcissism is the universal original condition, out of which object-love develops." The repression of drive expression occurs during latency, and with it we find important friendships evolving. Assisted by the increased libidinal demands during puberty, a recathexis of the opposite sex occurs during early adolescence.

These back and forth movements between the cathexis of the objects and self, between libido and aggression, between narcissistic and object cathexis, facilitate higher developmental organization. These are factors that may highlight some points for the understanding of aggression and its vicissitudes.

Another View

Dov R. Aleksandrowicz

Neubauer's main thesis is that aggressive behavior has an adaptive* function and that this adaptive function is phase-specific, that is, the different forms of infantile aggression can be related to the special developmental needs of that phase.

I would go even further than that: As a rule, we consider destructive, undifferentiated aggression as something "basic," primary, while modified or "modulated" aggression is considered to be a derivative, mainly a result of external, educative influence, or of fusion with libido. I suggest that we reverse the propositions: Let us say that modulated, adaptive aggression is "mature," while destructive, indiscriminate aggression is "immature" because it is not biologically useful.

We may draw an analogy with libido: here, too, narcissistic libido comes first in the developmental sequence, and yet it is the mature, object libido that is the paradigm of sex, not the infantile form. Yet infantile, narcissistic libido has its functions. What then is the function of undifferentiated, indiscriminate aggression?

It can be explained in two ways:

1. Even the relatively crude, infantile aggression can serve an adaptive function specific to that early phase of development, as Neubauer aptly demonstrates.

2. The fact that aggression is undifferentiated during early

* "Adaptive" in this context means "biologically useful," both in the sense of adjusting to the environment and that of facilitating intra-psychic balance.

39

development makes it more malleable to influences that will shape it into patterns suitable for the individual and his culture.

This is a teleological explanation but it is my firm opinion that teleological explanations are essential for a biological approach to psychology. The teleology is only apparent, since it means that we explain the behavior of an organism in terms of adaptation and evolution.

I have no argument with Neubauer's main thesis, but I would like to make a few marginal statements, both with regard to some data and with regard to some premises. Let us start with the data: I am not entirely certain that the "stranger reaction" or "seven months' anxiety" is, indeed, an expression of aggression. It is an avoidance reaction, often accompanied by signs of distress, which we may *interpret* as anxiety. It is rarely, if ever, accompanied by motor reactions such as kicking or hitting. Thus, we should distinguish *two* types of negative reactions: withdrawal or attack. Can withdrawal and aggression justifiably be equated?

This brings us to the problem of premises. Neubauer, like most psychoanalysts, assumes the existence of an aggressive drive. But is there really such a thing? Obviously, aggressive drive, or aggression, is not a *thing*, but a concept, a model. Some scientists prefer to use the word "aggressive" only as an adjective; e. g., aggressive behavior, or aggressive feelings (rage). They reject the concept of "aggression" as an elementary force. We are not bound to agree with this, but we had better keep it in mind. If we assume that there is, indeed, a common denominator to all the different forms of aggressive behavior, then we are compelled to describe aggression in terms that can apply to all living organisms, from invertebrates to man. One way to find such a common denominator is by approaching the problem of aggression from the point of view of adaptation and survival value.

Yet the supposedly "infantile," indiscriminate aggression can be seen in the adult organism as well. Is it adaptive? Like other regressive phenomena, it can prove useful when the normal adaptive mechanisms fail. For instance, a trapped animal may injure itself by thrashing wildly in the cage — but it may also escape.

My last point is peripheral to Neubauer's paper but pertinent to the main concern of this book. Neubauer seems to be assuming that war is a sort of social disease, a malfunction of the adaptive mechanisms. In my opinion that is not quite so; at least it was not so in the past. War is morally repulsive to us and it presents a real danger to civilization, but if we want to study it objectively we are obliged to look at history. Until quite recently war had been a highly successful adaptive mechanism, with great survival value and considerable selective pressure. Only since the technological advances of the industrial revolution has the destructive potential of war begun to outweigh any of its possible benefits. Like other adaptive mechanisms that have outlived their usefulness, it has become a danger to the survival of the species it had served so well.

We should keep that point in mind when we attempt to eliminate warfare. If I am right in assuming that the specific behavior pattern we call warfare, i.e., flocking together in order to create strong identification bonds and divert aggression to strangers, is indeed an ancient adaptive mechanism, then its eradication will prove a very difficult task.

Woman's Role in Aggression

"Men have brought their powers of subduing the forces of nature to such a pitch that using them they could now very easily exterminate one another to the last man. . . . It may be expected that the other of the two "heavenly forces," eternal Eros, will put forth his strength so as to maintain himself alongside of his equally immortal adversary."

S. Freud
Civilization and Its Discontents, 1930

Lizzi Rosenberger

In thinking about women's role in aggression a question, as naive as it is unanswerable, springs to mind: why did women never make an organized effort to prevent war? Why have they never felt the urge — or the love — to protect the children they had borne?

To put the question this way, however, implies the acceptance of two hypotheses: first, that there is an exclusive relationship between mother and child, and second, that the social framework of society of which each individual is a part can be overlooked.

But the question concerns the realm of the conscious emotions and wishes of the individual, omitting the unconscious motivations of war and aggression in human society.

Woman's consent to war as an extreme expression of group aggression must, then, be examined in the context of the developmental processes that contribute to the formation of her personality and of her position in the human society of the present.

For an analyst, the approach to an investigation of aggression is necessarily limited by his specific training and by exploration of material gained from neurotic individuals. Although one can apply some conclusions drawn from this material to the normal, generalizations would be invalid. The only possible approach to the original question would, I think, involve the examination of woman's role in society in relation to man's; to examine the conditions governing the formation of woman's personality in the nuclear society; i. e., in the family, with emphasis on the vicissitudes of her aggressive drives.

First we must recognize that life in modern technocratic society has increased the amount of overtly expressed aggression and hostility. With his advanced technological and scientific achievement modern man has built up a narcissistic, inflated personality. He must divide attachments between human beings and the results of his invention and creation, the machine. In this struggle his fellow men seem to be losing.

Inherent in the worship of the machine is dread and horror of its power and destructiveness. At one time, in the distant past, worship was connected with sacrifice to appease the wrath of the deity and to ensure his protection. What will modern man sacrifice: his libidinal investment in his machine love-objects or his libidinal investment in his fellow men?

We must grant that technology is man's brain-child, the creation of pure intellect. What is woman's position and attitude in the evolution of this kind of society and what is her role in a man-governed society?

Woman's attitude to the organized expression of aggression such as war, and her participation in it, appears to be passive consent and endurance. However, as we look back over history, we encounter outbursts of aggression and of brutalities committed by casual groups of women in the wake of wars, revolutions, or social upheavals; but never for the sake of a socially sanctioned cause. Such outbursts occur on grounds of strong emotional motivation, provoking frenzied outbursts of uncontrolled group destructiveness.

Only once in the history of mankind are we told of organized warfare by women. The women were the Amazons, who lived and fought in remote ages of human culture. Their existence has been inferred from archaeological finds such as art objects in tombs, from monuments, from religion, myth, and legend and from remnants of social and legal institutions — rather than actually established by historical record and documentation.

The historian Johann Jakob Bachofen devoted most of his life and efforts to research into ancient times. His basic training was in jurisprudence, archaeology, and the philology of ancient languages. The object of his research was the formation of human society. In his writings he focuses on the crucial influence the relationship between the two sexes had on the formation of human society. Bachofen was an extraordinary man. He lived and wrote before Freud; yet his way of thinking and his approach to the material discovered in scientific research is unmistakably analytic. Like the great poets, he was able to grasp the "unconscious" motivations behind the facts and, like the analyst who reconstructs the individual's hidden past, he conceived the developmental phases and the dialectic dynamics behind the structured formations of human society.

In primitive society turning points in the relationship between the sexes are marked by social crises and turmoil. They are reflected in the projection onto god-images, related by myth, and expressed in the strong rivalry in the hierarchic order of Gods and Heroes. Out of their desperate struggle for primacy, we may infer the bloody events in the reality of terrestial life.

In his great controversial work *Das Mutterrecht* (*Maternal Right*) published in 1861, Bachofen comes to the conclusion that the phenomenon of the Amazons and their wars should be understood as a reaction against man's degrading and abuse of woman. He describes a pre-dawn phase of social life, which he called "Hetaerism" as a gynaecocracy, a primitive way of life run in accordance with the laws of nature. Fertility and reproduction are its supreme law, eroticism and unbridled sexuality its foremost expression. Aphrodite, goddess of sex-love, and Bacchus, the wine-god, are its representatives in religion and myth. The social structure seems eminently peaceful.

Procreation and the importance of the womb in this primitive gynaecocracy reduce the male to the role of a means used to achieve the prime goal. But, perhaps with the introduction of the primitive plow, man's physical superiority brought about a gradual change in roles, with men finally achieving ascendancy through strength and then using women for sexual pleasure. The structure of the gynaecocratic exogamic society that followed the Amazonic aggression against man and its subsequent suppression is different from the archaic one. Again, this change can be gathered from religious rites and from myth. Whereas Bacchus, the God of Wine, who symbolizes the ecstasy of lust, was a primary object of worship in the early gynaecocracy, Demeter and Dionysos were worshipped in the later gynaecocracy. Demeter is the stern guardian of married life; Dionysos symbolizes love on a higher, more spiritual plane.

The struggle for supremacy between these god images was extensive, indicating the interminable competition between the sexes over a long period of slow development in human civilization and culture all around the Mediterranean basin.

In the new gynaecocracy, too, motherhood is the central axis of life. In those dark ages, maternal love, bestowing loving care on another being beyond herself, is the first step to civilization. The child's love for his mother is natural and material. His love for his father indicates a much higher step of development: it is a spiritual love. It is the result of accepting man as father in the human family, in the maternal society, yet without knowledge of his biological role in procreation.

After having fought Dionysos intensely, woman accepts him and worships him as her preferred god. The rites of Dionysos performed in the springtime are a vivid expression of woman's "ambivalent" acceptance of both the higher values represented by Dionysos and of her own altered role in society. The final establishment of the Paternal Right indicates a new and decisive change in the relationship between the sexes, a change that asserted itself slowly, against prolonged resistance, over a lengthy period of time.

The rising image of the awe-inspiring, aggressive father-god Zeus, finally victorious, is enthroned. As the embodiment of the supreme paternal principle, he rules the hierarchy of gods. But to impose the final supremacy of paternity, he has to go to the extreme of denying woman her womanhood. In the image of the goddess

Athena, who sprang out of her father's brain and was not born by a womb, Zeus assumes the role of both creator and reproducer.

Both consent to and revenge against this denial of womanhood is expressed by the stern goddess' own image: she is depicted wearing her symbol: the Medusa's Head which according to Freup ("The Meaning of the Medusa's Head"), is "the frightened and frightening symbol of the castrated and castrating female genital".

These extremely sketchy outlines of the changes in the relationship between man and woman in primitive society suggest tremendous upheavals in the structure of society as well as in the personality structure of both sexes. If one may apply the understanding and insight gained by psychoanalytic theory and practice to this structure, the changes in woman's social position versus man's seem to have had a decisive structuring influence on her personality.

First there was the undifferentiated state, where natural right governed life and procreation was the foremost social function. The myths seem to suggest that male and female were less differentiated.

Sexual activity was not yet connected biologically with procreation. The womb and earth were worshipped in the images of the Great Mother Goddesses of fertility. Only the female progeny were of importance. Property was inherited through the daughters long after paternal right had been established. The throne also went to the daughter, as in Egypt for instance where, until historic times, marriages between brother and sister were quite usual. The brother appears as the queen's consort. In monuments and drawings, he is often depicted as sitting in his queen-wife-sister's lap.

The perfect harmony of woman's life with her natural needs, the socially acknowledged and enhanced importance of motherhood accorded her a superior role in society. Connected with the forces of fertility and death, with the phases of the waning moon, she was endowed with wisdom and healing powers. The riddle of life and death was given into her hand. Part of the veneration and awe inspired by the god image was transferred to her. Woman's position was one of mystical power, even when man's physical and spiritual superiority claimed and achieved social supremacy. Recent research in anthropology confirms that in some primitive societies woman's position is still similar in present times.

In this primitive stage, the social functions of man and woman were clearly distinguished. There were neither competition nor strong emotional links between them. Maternal love was the highest expression of interpersonal relationship.

The first change came about when man claimed his right as father in the exogamic gynaecocracy. The primal symbiotic exclusiveness between mother and child was disturbed by rivalry for the child's love between mother and father, rivalry between mother and child for the father's love, and rivalry between the siblings. Hostility was aroused.

The importance of female progeny was first overshadowed by the father's emphasis on having sons; gradually the importance of daughters vanished. The worship of Dionysos by woman provides an insight into the changes brought about in her personality. Dionysos, like Osiris, is both lover and son. Once a year he is torn to pieces by worshipping women, then desperately mourned. His resurrection is feted in wild sexual orgies, symbolizing denial of his murder and rebirth through love. Does this not appear to be an expression of ambivalence, of love-hatred for the son-lover, acted out in symbolic ritual? Woman seems to be different now from the primitive, passive being of nature-bound animalistic times.

The victory of the father principle was made possible by woman's acceptance of it through partial identification and submissiveness. Yet the image of the goddess Athena, with her symbolic Medusa's Head, expresses not only man's fear of woman but also woman's rejection of sexuality and her hostility to man.

Are these not the well-known concepts of penis-envy and castration fear, expressed by horror of the female genital? Thus Freud's basic concepts of the influence of the awareness of physiological sex differences on the child's psychosexual development in paternal man-oriented society are found in phylogenesis.

"The insight into the female child's pre-oedipal past comes as a surprise comparable, in a quite different sphere, to the disclosure of the discovery of the Minoan-Mycenean culture behind Greek civilization." (Freud : *On Female Sexuality*).

Male domination must be understood as a secondary formation, the product of the child's revolt against the primal mother, bequeathed to adulthood and culture by the castration complex (Brown).

Following Freud's explanations of the development of woman's sexuality in his paper "On Female Sexuality," some moments of decisive importance for the development of her personality are stressed:

1. the strong pre-oedipal tie to the mother;
2. the discovery of the male sexual organ (castration complex);
3. the change of object choice — i. e., the positive oedipal conflict.

In comparison with the development of the male child, the little girl's task of achieving genital sexuality is more complicated. In order to reach this goal she has to change from the homosexual to the heterosexual love object, from the pre-oedipal mother to the oedipal father. The basic bi-sexual disposition in humans endows the child with active and passive trends which are expressed through childhood and latency, indiscriminately by boys and girls alike. To achieve femininity, the girl has to forego a part of her activity and augment passivity instead.

The painful process of abandoning the mother for the father-object cannot be accomplished without ascribing guilt to the mother and deprecating her. Educational interference and/or the birth of a sibling easily lead to accusations by the daughter that the mother lacks love for her. Depreciation follows the girl's discovery of her mother's feminine body. She blames the mother for having borne her without a penis; when she finally accepts this fact, she is left with a lasting feeling of inferiority. Thus the little girl turns to her father out of hatred for her mother, but in most cases the libidinal attachment is not entirely withdrawn from the mother. The passive trends may stay invested in the mother-object. They are of oral-receptive and oral-sadistic origin.

Her turning to the father-object is achieved mostly on the basis of the clitoric, i. e., phallic-active, trends. Aggressiveness in the service of libidinal drives is turned against the mother object, at first freely expressed but later repressed together with a lesser or greater amount of activity.

With the acceptance of the lack of a penis and her own inferiority, the girl accepts the male's superiority, but not without resistance.

Thus two important characteristic traits of woman's personality, hysteria and aggressiveness, can be traced to these developmental stages. The outcome of the female "castration complex" can, according to Freud, be threefold:

1. negation of sexuality and renunciation of phallic activity, i. e., of masculinity;

2. stubborn stress of masculinity and unwavering hope of finally obtaining a penis (masculinity complex);

3. normal femininity with formation of the feminine oedipal complex.

Whereas the boy's solution of the oedipal conflict saves him from the castration danger, the girl is driven into the positive oedipal situation because of her acceptance of castration. This mutual relation between the oedipus complex and the castration complex decisively stamps woman's image as a social being. The male's victory over the castration complex results in narcissistic over-estimation of his sex organ and accordingly, in depreciation of woman. The girl's acceptance of "castration" results in a feeling of inferiority and at the same time, in overestimation of the male.

If we accept these premises, it is obvious that aggressiveness linked with libidinal drives arises very early in the development of the female personality, and plays a paramount role in it. Aggressiveness towards the pre-oedipal mother is basically the ambivalent component of the child's love for her. It is carried regressively to the oral-sadistic fixation point and repressed out of guilt feelings. Its contents can be expressed in neurosis in the form of paranoid fears, centered around oral-incorporative fantasies which also exist in male neurotics who have not succeeded in solving their libidinal ties with the preoedipal mother. Aggressiveness is also part of the girl's positive oedipal love for the father, but it is actively carried by the penis-envy which opens up several ways of solution, as mentioned above.

The institution of the monogamic paternal family is the pattern of western culture as it has developed out of primitive, uncivilized social structures based on natural law and the matriarchate.

Structured social life and culture are the result of sublimation. In the process of developing civilization, mental changes have occurred through transposition of the instinctual aims and restrictions of the instinctual drives. As man's intellectual faculties developed, he increasingly mastered his drives and his aggressiveness became increasingly internalized.

However, the female child's aggressiveness resulting from her disappointment in the frustrating penis-less mother cannot be internalized. It is reactivated in later life in relation to new objects. It interferes with the relationship to the heterosexual object and renews the childhood struggle against the pre-oedipal mother in the struggle against the husband in adulthood.

Aggressiveness against the "superior" male, owner of the desired and envied male organ, can be internalized through identification. Social life is based on social feelings which are aim-inhibited sexual drives (Freud), or neutralized drive energy (Hartmann), the outcome of the solution of the oedipal conflict and the castration danger. Identification replaces the possessive claims of object love.

Through identification, the individual carries on the social and cultural values of his society. The family in its varying structure ensures the continuation of these values by bringing up its children in patterns of education that correspond to the prevailing culture. It is in her role as mother that woman plays a decisive role beyond the restricted frame of the family unit as a member of human society.

Motherhood is certainly the deepest fulfillment of womanhood. The function of child-bearing, though biologically and socially of basic importance, is also influenced by the changes in the roles between the two sexes.

According to Otto Rank's remarkable investigation into the meaning of myth (*The myth of the birth of the hero*) and Frazer's

material in *The Golden Bough*, child-birth is considered one of
the greatest and most dangerous mysteries primitive man is faced
with — as is the small child in our culture. The oral fable of the
stork emphasizes the mother's role while belittling the role of the
father, who is not even mentioned. The legends of the heroes
dating back to a time when paternal supremacy was first struggling
against maternal supremacy, stress the profound ties between
mother and child, but also the uncertainty of man's position as
father. Man considers the child as his potential enemy and wishes
to destroy him. The mother saves her child-son by symbolically
exposing him — enclosed in a box — in water. In this way, heroes,
like Moses, have been saved from their father's wrath. The hero's
later rebellion against authority finds its justification in his father's
initial enmity.

But there are other legends and tales in which the mother's role
appears in an entirely new light. She initiates, or acquiesces in,
her new-born child's death or exposure. There is of course always
a mother-substitute, often in the form of the totemistic animal
that nurses and brings up the child, as in the legend of Romulus
and Remus.

In tales of a later date, the new-born child is a girl who is taken
away from her parents at puberty and is anxiously held in seclusion
by a "bad-mother" image. The abduction is predicted soon after
birth, which comes many years after the parents' marriage and,
although the danger is known, it is "forgotten" and no precaution
is taken to prevent the abduction.

The mother's ambivalent feelings for her child are quite obvious
in this material. In both types, it is the danger of incest that has
to be warded off by eliminating the son or the daughter from the
parents' life. But it is the mother's consent to the elimination
which is stressed.

In our times we recognize the content of these tales in the adolescent's "family-romance," in the fantasies and dreams of our neurotic patients. Hatred and fear of the pre-oedipal mother are not
entirely of the child's own making; in the dreams and fantasies
of pregnant patients we discover ambivalent feelings toward the
child. Here is the grain of reality in the child's avalanche of imagin-
ed and fantasied complaints and accusations against his mother

which are elaborated much later in the "family-romance." Women who are ambivalent towards their children carry this ambivalence over from their relationship with their own mothers. It is a new edition of the old unresolved conflict that prevented identification with the feminine role. The healthy, non-neurotic woman is able to enjoy motherhood and to establish a positive relationship with her children, or at least with some of them.

In discussing the importance of changes in the relationship between the sexes and the influence of these changes on personality structure, issues of importance in present times have to be taken into consideration. Some hundred years ago, when the first woman's revolution against man in modern times began — the fight for what has come to be called "Emancipation" — the roles of the sexes were neatly divided. Woman's place was in the home — the world was man's playground. The "double" standard of sexual morality gave a man sexual freedom denied to woman. The great writers of the epoch, such as de Maupassant, Stendhal, Strindberg, Ibsen, Thomas Mann, etc., have described the emotional suffering and emotional and moral deprivation of western woman in their times.

The revolutionary movement for woman's emancipation has achieved for women the privileges of participation in higher education and public services, has removed discrimination in professional work and has won for them full civil rights.

But at the core this movement has failed. It has failed because it sought to achieve emancipation of woman as a man, not as a woman. In an extreme protest against the degradation of woman's personality by man, it claimed freedom from the innermost female functions, expressing complete identification with man.

Nevertheless, it has once again brought about a change in the relationship between the sexes, a new turning point. In the social structure of society, a parallel change was achieved soon after the introduction of democracy and the trends to socialism. In Israel, for example, the emancipation of women represented by the "pioneer women" was one of the finest and strongest forces in the building of the new socialist society in the kibbutzim, with true equality for all of its members — men, women, and children alike.

These changes have affected man's personality no less than woman's. He has been protesting against the de-feminization of woman that emancipation sought to achieve, but also against the penetration by women into areas of life that he used to consider his exclusive preserve. At first he deprecated women's abilities; but he gradually came round to acknowledging her skill, talents, and performance and was forced to change his attitude toward her.

The First World War brought about radical political and social upheavals in the social structure of the European countries and their economic conditions. War and revolution shook the established patriarchical order whose emblems were the monarch and the church — for the state, the equivalents of the father figure in the family. Unable to provide adequately for his family's economic security, man had to forego a great deal of his prestige and masculine aggression. Woman's new economic and social position gave her greater independence, and man had to appraise her personality in a new light and to approach her differently.

In this situation woman's psychologically justified and socially enhanced passivity and pronounced dependency were no longer adequate to her new tasks and standing. While man had to forego part of his activity, woman now had to abandon part of her passivity.

Due to the basically bi-sexual nature of humans, activity and passivity are present in every personality in variable quantities. With the enhancement of greater activity woman is able to express more aggression, especially against obstacles in the way of her social and professional ambitions. Yet the factors that hamper her in her social achievements are connected with her functions as a wife and a mother.

Man, on the contrary, is allowed to display more passivity and less responsibility without arousing social disapproval. He plays a greater part in the care and raising of the children and undertakes many tasks in the family formerly regarded as exclusively feminine. With increasing frequency we encounter families in which the wife holds the authority while the father assumes the role of friend and helper to his children and sometimes also of protector against the wife's aggressive impulses.

Consequently the family structure can no longer be described as exclusively patriarchic. With moral and economic responsibility equally divided, the axis of the family is twofold, paternal and maternal at the same time, with the emphasis varying between the two.

Given that personality structure is, roughly speaking, an outcome of the oedipus conflict (and castration complex) and the introjects of identifications and sublimations, it follows that harmony between husband and wife, and their attitude to their children, depend in essence on their pre-oedipal past. The aggressiveness linked to the early libidinal drives resists internalization and cannot be sublimated but has to be re-enacted with new love objects.

Woman's altered position in a changed society has enhanced her activity. Identification with father and brother-images are often the driving motives for a professional career in which she has to use assertive aggressiveness in competition with men and women alike. Intellectual development enables her to sublimate part of her sexual drives and participate in social groups on grounds of aim-inhibited social feelings. All these achievements enable her to participate fully in cultural and social life as an equal to man.

In sexual life, increased activity in woman and passivity in man are often serious obstacles to the achievement of genital sexual gratification culminating in orgasm.

As analysts, we are faced with a large number of individuals suffering from frigidity and disturbances in potency. Divorce is on the increase. But we must not conclude that these changes in role automatically produce the neurotic disturbances and the marital breakdowns we encounter.

We also have to consider another factor which is decisive in the marital relationship: the human relationship, the basic non-sexual relationship that is the lasting tie between married people even after sexual fascination has vanished. For it seems that this basic non-sexual, (aim-inhibited) relationship is also generally lacking, or diminishing, in human relationships.

In his basic papers, Freud stresses over and over again the importance of the linking of sexual aim-directed and aim-inhibited drives directed to the same object in adult object-choice. If these drives are split, a full and satisfying relationship can never be achieved. Such a split is the outcome of fixation on the oedipal object which in adulthood is still repressed as the incestual object, or on the pre-oedipal mother. Thus sexuality is prevented from reaching maturity.

Woman's greater activity may play a decisive part in her role as mother to her son in the very years which are so fateful for the child's development. The usual sexual overestimation characteristic of a mother's love for her son combined with masculine activity are likely to create a strong pre-oedipal tie of dependency and intimidation which may prevent the development of the positive oedipal love for her, if the father's personality is not very strong and masculine, and may result in a negative oedipus complex and identification with the mother instead who is then felt as the phallic, castrating mother. In such a mother's relationship with her daughter, her active personality may evoke strong resistance and aggressiveness which, repressed out of guilt, may cause passive submissiveness and dependency or lasting hatred which will prevent identification with the female role.

Woman's active role in social life — so long as it remains an identification with the man — is to the detriment of the functions of child-bearing and raising which demand passivity and which are in many respects dependent on social consent. As the maternal functions interfere with her professional and social functions, they arouse conflicts connected with an increase in aggressive and ambivalent feelings toward the foetus and later the child, feelings and conflicts which often appear in analytic session with mothers and children.

The changed roles of the two sexes influence the structure of the family. The changes are continually repeated through the child's identification processes with the parent-images and through the mother, whose image seems to be "stronger" and more central to the child, out of his own dependency on his pre-oedipal mother.

> "Whatever has the effect of promoting the development of culture works against war."
> (Freud: Letter)

In the highly developed civilization of present times, men and women alike have achieved a high degree of sublimation of sexual drives, which means contributing to culture. And yet, as if to contradict this evident fact, we are confronted with widespread and indiscriminate actions of aggression and destruction, with wars in which sadistic cruelty predominates.

The means of destruction and cruelty are man's own creation. Technology is man's brain-child. It is based on pure intellect without investment of libido. The invention of technical devices so powerful as to threaten the very existence of its inventor must immensely increase man's omnipotence, but at the same time augments his fear of destruction — a fear which can be mastered, or lessened, only by inventing still more powerful machines of destruction.

But the threat of the Golem is immense. "Pure intelligence is in principle madness, a product of dying or at least of becoming mentally insensitive," says Ferenczi explaining sublimation as the ego-syntonic way of disposing of libido.

The two basic forces in man, libido and aggressiveness, have to be allied in order to preserve life. If sublimation achieves its goal in creating culture, it is still libido, but diverted from sexual aims to socially approved ones.

Technology does not promote culture. It seems to serve the purposes of destruction as a result of naked aggressiveness in man in his need for self-preservation against the threat of annihilation that he has brought upon himself. At this point a disastrous dissolution between libido and aggressiveness seems to have happened — but where are the libidinal forces invested? Can it be possible that sexual dissatisfaction as a result of the changes in the interrelation between the two sexes drives man to seek gratification and self-assertion in ever-growing prowess in a realm where his superiority is still unchallenged by women? We cannot know yet.

The changes in the family framework and the increased sexual freedom point to a process which is described by Freud over and over again — an ever-growing disparity between sexual drives and aim-inhibited drives.

As outlined before, the stigmata of the immature personality unable to forego immediate gratification, but also unable to

achieve sublimation, are naked aggressiveness and lack of em pathy.
To inflict suffering on his fellow-man is the expression of a very
early stage of development — the anal-sadistic stage to which man
seems to have regressed. But will this continue in the changing
relationship between male and female seen in the youth of many
western countries?

Woman's role in aggression cannot be grasped except in the
context of the relations between man and woman. At present,
women are unable to prevent war because they have neither the
force nor the power as an organized body to do so.

In man-governed and man-oriented society, woman will, according to the laws of her psycho-sexual development, identify with
man and with his aims in order to be able to assert herself in this
society and also to satisfy her narcissistic needs.

The changes brought about by her emancipation as a human
being offer her the possibility of contributing in two ways to
"strengthening the heavenly force of Eros so as to maintain himself
alongside his equally immortal adversary, death:" in her love for
her child, the love which once, in the remote dark ages of humanity
was the first step to civilisation, and in see kingtrue sublimation
rather than identification.

Another View

Judith S. Kestenberg

Rosenberger's thoughts are so rich in content and so full of ideas and questions that it is difficult to do justice to them.

Rosenberger considers woman's love and care of children as the cradle of culture that can counteract aggression. She feels that man's brain-child, technology, based as it is on pure intellect, detracts from man's libidinous attachments to people and promotes narcissistic omnipotence. She asks: "Why have women never, in the entire history of mankind, made an organized effort to prevent war?" If I understand this correctly, she is confident that women can work more effectively for peace when they achieve emancipation and liberation from oppression. She worries, however, that man's love of technology may outweigh woman's object-related efforts for peace by perpetuating the sacrifice of human children for the greater glory of machine-children.

Rosenberger hopes, as did Freud, to find a parallel between the development of culture and individual development of aggression. She traces woman's changing role in society from the first to the second gynecocracy and through phases of man's domination of women.

I was gratified to see that the hypothesis of two feminine phases in the evolution of woman's role in society corresponds to my classification of developmental phases, which postulates two separate phases of femininity early in life. The first can be observed after the passing of pregenital dominance, roughly between the ages of two to four. This time is characterized by a desire to create a baby, a daughter created in the mother's and the child's image, At the end of this phase the girl becomes very angry at her mother for not letting her have a child. There develops an intense "Child-Envy" and a vindictive desire to destroy children, not only siblings but all babies that are not the toddler's own. We see here a great similarity to the time of the not-so-peacefull great Asiatic Goddess Artemis, who destroyed babies during deliveries or demanded their sacrifice after birth. In this she resembled Adam's first wife, Lilith, who, after losing her own self-created demon-babies, became the dreaded demon-killer of other women's children. In contrast, Hera, representing a later period, watched over marriage and the successful delivery of children. Her wrath was turned against the rivals with whom Zeus betrayed her. She, as Eve before her, created the nuclear family.

The second phase in evolution, from which the Oedipal family emerged, corresponds to the phallic-oedipal phase in individual development. In contrast to the pre-oedipal girl, the oedipal girl is first and foremost concerned with the wooing of her father, which is associated with the killing of the Oedipal rival. The three-year old wanted a daughter and, in her disappointment, ended up wanting to kill children because she had none; the Oedipal girl wants a penis-baby, a boy, to be given to her by her father. She may, out of guilt, feel that she must sacrifice her ill-begotten child for fear that her mother (the feminine superego) will punish her for her oedipal sins. At the same time, the sacrifice of the male child, given by the father, may also gratify the wish to castrate and kill the male. It has been said that woman accedes to man's wish to kill his young son, his Oedipal rival, because she feels oppressed and must obey her master. Rosenberger points out that woman herself has destructive wishes of her own toward her children. It is those she must conquer and sublimate before she can effectively counteract man's aggression toward his sons. This is by no means an easy task, as it involves a complex interrelationship between the mother and not only her husband, but also her older daughters and sons and the newborn baby.

In many primate groups, as in homo sapiens, mothers and babies are put in the safe, nuclear part of the group while female adolescents hover around them to learn maternal behavior from their mothers. The young males are instructed by their elders to stand watch at the periphery of the group to guard territorial rights against strange invaders. Among certain primates (in captivity), when a strange intruder does come, he may be killed by the dominant male or the dominant female. On the other hand, when the invader succeeds in killing the patriarch, he proceeds to kill all males and all infants while the numerous females of the group watch without rebellion. The conquering hero becomes the new patriarch; he copulates with the females and originates a new generation of infants. Even in advanced human cultures, strangers who invade foreign territories sometimes utter the same threat the primates carry out; namely, that men and children be killed and the women raped. Stranger anxiety is partially inborn and partially cultivated by the need to teach the child to beware of hostile strangers. One of the first signs of human socialization is stranger anxiety. In group formation in latency, we encounter a concerted effort to exclude strangers and plot against them. No doubt, attacking strangers divert aggression from oedipal objects to outsiders. However, there is also a realistic aspect to our distrust of strangers. Mrs. Golda Meir said, I believe, that peace will come when the enemy loves his own children more than he desires to kill ours. As long as there are strangers in our real world who perpetuate the pre-oedipal wish to kill other people's children, we must protect ourselves. Yet, we must beware that, in doing so we do not give in to masochistic wishes to kill our own or to gnawing feelings of guilt which stem from a hatred, derived from infantile, archaic pregenital wishes.

Rosenberger is right in saying that there is great hope in motherliness being able to conquer hatred and war. We see such a trend in the early feminine phase which I originally called the phase of maternal preoccupation. The three-year-old *transforms*, with the aid of her mother, much of her remaining pregenital *aggression* into *motherliness*. Oral biting, oral envy, and cannibalistic desires to eat children are transformed into feeding patterns. Cruel anal messiness, aggression and lust for power are transformed into cleansing, healing, and altruistic surrender to the needs of infants. Urethral wishes to burn and drown are transformed into soothing and washing activities. Under the impact of early genital wishes, the young child becomes motherly. Yet, we are not quite rid of feminine aggression. Wanting to have a baby inside, typical of the first feminine (inner-genital) phase of development, must be counterbalanced by wanting to let go of the baby in delivery. Nurturing the baby in a symbiotic relationship must be counterbalanced by a need to separate from the child. The three-year-old mother, inseparable from her baby doll, suddenly drops it, loses it, or maltreats it. Unfortunately, even in adult mothers, letting the child go is frequently associated with a feeling of deprivation which leads to regression. A revival of hatred of the depriving mother becomes associated with regressive, pregenital wishes to destroy the inside and the babies who come from there. This in turn may lead to intense penis envy and to wishes to castrate the young male. Projecting her aggression upon males, woman may shift the blame for her injury from her mother to her father and from the father to the stranger who will, she thinks, rape and truly castrate her by tearing her insides. The more she has preserved pregenital forms of aggression or regressed to them, the less she is capable of letting her child grow up without a crude desire to kill the deserter. The more fearful she is of being cruelly hurt herself, the more frightfully castrating and aggressive she becomes and the more must she seek oppression out of guilt. The more she is able to transform pregenital regression into motherliness, the more tender she becomes and the more accepting of her inside — her true femininity — and of her role as wife and mother.

While woman expends her sublimations in motherliness in all forms (not only motherhood), man expends his fatherliness and motherliness in technology. He may extend his phallic prowess in worshipping phallic machines as a woman can extend her inner genital prowess in worshipping fertility. However, once man and woman achieve adult genitality, the consummation of genital love helps them to accept inside and outside in such a way that pregenital forces recede. Motherliness is then used both for nurturing and letting go while technology is used for providing. In this manner, technology does promote culture (even war-time inventions are turned to the use of improved consumer-production once peace is achieved). The less aggression is generated between the sexes, the less aggression there is between parents and children. At the same time, there is less need for envying one's neighbor for his economic security, less need for seizing power and destroying, less need for drowning him in a sea of tears or shooting him down with secret weapons, and less need for machines, spouting the semen of destruction instead of procreation.

In Israel we have not yet recovered from the pregenital assault upon us and from our submission to the monumental regression of the holocaust. We are still in the throes of anxiety, depression, and guilt over our survival. Let us hope that we can liberate ourselves and our young from the increase in crude pregenital aggression that leads to cruelties of war and undoes the sublimations and reaction formations of gentle peacefulness. We hope that a future generation will be able to identify with a mother, gentle and loving and yet letting go rather than hateful and castrating. The answer to greater peacefulness in women may lie in a greater acceptance of woman's biological destiny, and with it a greater tolerance of differences between the sexes and between people altogether.

The Individual, the Group and War

Bryant Wedge

To those who hoped that psychoanalysis might point the way to the elimination of war as a human institution, Sigmund Freud's response to Einstein's query was a profound disappointment. For Freud saw ".... no likelihood of our being able to suppress humanity's aggressive tendencies." Over the thirty-five years since, we have certainly had ample cause to appreciate Freud's realism; war and intergroup violence have broken forth irrepressibly again and again while the forces and institutions for the suppression and avoidance of war have failed to gain sufficient strength to contain or control military aggression.

But Freud's outlook was not really pessimistic. If aggression is irrepressible, he wrote, "... what we may try is to divert it into a channel other than that of warfare." He stated that reason and cultural change, as well as fear, might bring this about, pointing out that profound psychic changes accompany cultural development. His letter to Einstein, in retrospect, was both hopeful and useful. It laid down the broad outlines for a strategy to eliminate war; recognizing the ineradicability of human aggressiveness and noting the profound influence of culture on the forms of aggression, the problem becomes one of assisting the development of "man's cultural disposition."

There, regrettably, psychoanalysis virtually ended its contributions except for a few speculative essays on the subject. I think that psychoanalysis, if it were to reduce its isolation from other sciences of human behavior and systematically apply itself to the issues in collaboration with those sciences, would have the capacity to contribute substantially to assisting the process of cultural change, to devise social inventions that can channel, control, and manage the aggressive drives of groups of men so as to eliminate organized violence.

Here, I can do no more than to outline a few of the main lines of discovery in the other sciences since Freud's broad essay and to suggest how psychoanalytic thought, *if systematically applied*, might contribute to evolving new means for channelling man's aggressiveness. I believe that it is the human responsibility of pacifists like Freud and Einstein — and of every psychoanalyst — to seek to apply their knowledge and wit to the construction of a world in which group violence against human persons is as *unattractive and un-needed* psychologically as war among nations is obsolete as a practical means of resolving disputes.

Levels of Behavioral Analysis

A fundamental issue in the analysis of behavior is the level of focus to which attention is directed. Psychoanalysis concerns itself largely with intrapsychic forces within the individual person as these are patterned by the internalization of his *intimate* history; second, psychoanalysis concerns itself with the expression of these forces in the behavior of the individual person. A political scientist, J. David Singer, has shown that consideration of behavior of the national systems requires scarcely any appreciation of these intrapsychic forces, while the level of analysis of the international system needs none at all. Yet, there is no doubt that the manner of operation of the national and international levels of human organization depends ultimately on the participation or at least the consent of the individual persons whose aggregated behavior constitutes organized action — including war. Might we not, then, consider how the person relates to these larger contexts, how the various levels of transaction may serve to integrate the demands of drive-expression with environmental possibilities in ways that are not too threatening to survival or to such lesser expressions of love as self-esteem.

Professors Karl Deutsch of Harvard and Dieter Senghaas of Frankfurt distinguish seven identifiable levels of behavioral analysis — each linked transactionally with the others but each involving behavioral forces and mechanisms peculiar to the organizational level. These are:

1. Individual traits (intrapsychic processes expressed behaviorally.)

2. Personality as a whole

3. Small group levels

4. Large interest groups (political parties, industrial organizations, mass media, bureaucracies, etc.)

5. The nation-state

6. Regional and international systems of organization (government relations including international bodies and non-governmental relations including trade and traffic patterns.)

7. Humanity as a whole (virtually hypothetical as a construct but, nevertheless, the level of the "processes" of civilization of which Freud spoke so hopefully, if mystically.)

Even with respect to the first two levels on which psychoanalysis focuses its principal attention, there are undoubtedly shortcomings in our formulation of the sources of personal aggressiveness and particularly of methods of training and management that would encourage the diversion of aggressive drives and affects from violent expression. Especially, we have neglected the analysis of "obedient aggression" which is fundamental to the conduct of war. It has been shown experimentally, for example, that subjects will frequently administer what they believe to be painful and even killing electric shocks to a screaming "victim" under the command of an experimenter.

For psychoanalysis to contribute fully to the analysis of the roots of personal violence it will be necessary to work together with experimentalists. Certainly there is nothing sacred about the practice of drawing knowledge *only* from patients on the couch; the methods of analytic reconstruction are equally applicable to associative materials from specific experience. We could learn and classify, for example, the kinds of experience which lead some persons to be more ready to be violent than others, what elements of "innate" or competitive aggression find outlet in specific violent acts, how defensive anxiety turns to willingness to harm others, and what kinds of frustrations promote aggression. More important, perhaps, we could learn how violence-inducing fear or frustration or obedience or competitiveness could be reduced by social circumstances and how social training could aid the ego toward finding non-violent means to relieve the aggressive impulse.

I will comment on the next three levels of analysis, those of the small groups, the large-interest group, and the national state as instances of group membership which, although there are decided differences between the levels with respect to unit behaviors, call forth broadly similar responses from the ego. Freud, of course, was fascinated by group psychology which he considered "the oldest human psychology" in his *Group Psychology and the Analysis of the Ego*. In that essay, Freud recognized the profound impact of group participation on the behavior of individuals; while he attributed this in part to the re-arousal of infantile family complexes and asserted the releasing-from-repression effects of group participation, he noted the role of multiple levels of group membership on the formation of personal aspirations and on the structure of the ego-ideal.

First, let me call attention to observations by social psychologists of the behavior of small groups in conflict and co-operation which I am certain would have fascinated Freud. Muzafer Sherif and others have shown that whenever small groups of persons are brought together in common and shared circumstances for a length of time, over a few days they invariably develop a distinctive identity, a decided social structure with patterned interaction and mechanisms for accomplishing tasks and a sense of pride and loyalty in belonging. All of these phenomena are considerably heightened when the groups are faced with tasks that require working together to attain a common end — whether it is eleven-year-olds fixing a camp site or psychoanalysts establishing training criteria.

The next range of observations is even more striking. If, when such a group has formed, it is brought into contact with other groups with which there is a possible conflict of interest, there follows a process of invidious comparison. One's own group is seen as superior in a variety of ways — cleaner, brighter, more honest, etc., while the other group(s) is/are seen as harboring undesirable traits and elements. Social distance is established betwen in-group and out-group members.

If such established groups are then brought into competition — for example, competing on a group basis for prizes, honor, or recognition — the invidious images become rapidly stereotyped. The structure of these stereotypes is remarkably constant among all sorts of experimental groups and remarkably consistent with the view held in such nationally-occurring groups as nations in conflict. I shall borrow from an analysis of such images in Ralph K. White's *Nobody Wanted War: Misperception in Vietnam and Other Wars* to describe the sorts of stereotypes that are found. These studies are psychoanalytically fascinating, especially since their observations are wholly empirical and innocent of contamination by psychoanalytic formulations but are remarkably consistent with the language and predictions of psychoanalytic psychology.

White lists six principal components of the images held by the people of nations in conflict — pointing out, incidentally the "mirror-image" character of the stereotypes as has been noted by Urie Bronfenbrenner in the views that Soviets and Americans held of one another. I will discuss the implications of these components.

1. *The diabolical enemy image:* Regularly, the out-group that is seen as threatening some goal or value of the reference group becomes perceived as personifying clever and amoral force bent on damaging one's own group as a principal purpose. It is supposed — and evidence can always be adduced in support of the supposition — that the "enemy" has no sense of decency or fairness, indeed, has a proclivity for sneaky and underhanded methods. Further, the enemy is diabolically clever and plays on the morality of the group as though this were a weakness.

A group of eleven-year-old boys in Sherif's famous Robber's Cave experiment, for example, supposed that the competing group would mess up their swimming place and, having decided this, concluded that there were more stones in the water than before.

I found that professional diplomats in the American Embassy after the Dominican Republic uprising of 1965 were convinced that Communist groups were plotting to create incidents that would require military suppression and, indeed, a number of accidental encounters were interpreted in terms of this theory; the young Dominican revolutionaries, in turn, developed identical images of American purposes and similar interpretations of accidental incidents. The psychoanalyst will recognize the familiar mechanism of projection in these views although, as I will discuss later, this is *normal* to members of groups in conflict rather than a pathological ego defense measure. The well-known reciprocal views of "expansionist, atheistic, subversive, totalitarian Communism" held by whole groups of otherwise sane men in the West and the image of "lackeys and running-dogs of capitalist imperialism bent on destroying Socialist development" held by otherwise mentally healthy people in the Communist States represent similar tendencies which vastly complicate examination of the actual nature of the competing groups.

2. *A virile self-image:* Groups in competition regularly develop a kind of anxious concern for their status and prestige manifested by the double symptoms of assertion of strength and fear of humiliation if there shoud be any retreat. Eleven-year-old boys bragged about their strength, skill, champions, and heroes *within* their groups, and chastised members who advocated retreat or peace-making gestures. The obsessive concern of United States leadership about the consequences for American "credibility" of any retreat from what have long been recognized as impractical objectives in Vietnam is another case in point; here, the disparities in real power between the parties in conflict make the threat so ludicrous that it requires extensive rationalizations to sustain.

3. Another component of misperception is the *"moral"* *self-image* and the correspondingly "immoral" enemy image.

A particularly common variant of the moral self-image is the "black-top image" of the competitor, at least in times of non-violent competition. The members of the competing group are good people who are misinformed and misled by an immoral leadership. Whether it is the "hidden ruling circles" that the

Soviet Union sees in the United States or the "totalitarian dictatorship" that Americans see in the Soviet Union, the sources of evil are localized especially in places that are difficult to identify as humane.

4. *Selective inattention* is a major dynamic of misperception that sustains these invidious group images. As conflict escalates, there is a striking tendency to perceive only those items which would sustain the enemy image and to be blind to evidence that would contradict such views. This tendency is so powerful as to bring much punishment to serious scholars of the enemy's society; in extreme cases even a nation's accredited ambassadors are disbelieved when they report a disposition toward reasonableness on the part of the opposing leadership. Robert North, at Stanford, has shown that this happened on nearly every side at the approach of the First World War. In short, woe to him who would oppose a stereotyped image of a competing group with evidence; he is certain to become a victim of the selective inattention that suppresses unpopular truths.

5. *Absence of empathy* is notable because a psychological function that normally enables men to make judgements about the intentions of others becomes seriously impaired. The capacity to view the world and oneself from the other's point of view, to put oneself empathetically in the other's shoes, normally allows one to anticipate the impact of one's own behavior. But, when groups come into conflict, the capacity is lost; it is assumed that others will see things as one does oneself. The United States Administrations, for example, have been saddened and amazed that their allies and even many of their own people have perceived the Vietnam action in terms of a large nation bullying smaller ones — in fact, official announcements after five years of persistent criticism on this point continue to emphasize America's strength and power in such a way as to actually promote the unwanted image in others' eyes.

It is of course, exceedingly difficult to hurt or kill someone who is identified as another human being, and identification is a large component in empathy. It is, therefore, an ego-protective mechanism to dehumanize persons defined as enemies which, as Jerome Frank has pointed out, is even easier in modern technical war than in previous military encounters. In any case, dehumanization of the enemy causes loss of empathy and, therefore of the capacity to judge the other side's response to one's actions. This is a principal cause of miscalculation in intergroup conflict.

The question for the psychoanalyst, then, is how can empathy be maintained in the face of group conflict? For it is certain that whatever reduces miscalculation and whatever sustains recognition of other persons' human qualities will reduce one's inclination to violent action or to the unwitting provocation of violence.

6. Finally, in White's listing of sources of misperception in conflicts, comes *military overconfidence*. He notes that, "It is paradoxical but true that exaggerated fear can be combined with military overconfidence."

Regularly, *before* athletic contests, Sherif's eleven-year-old subjects bragged about how they would "destroy" the other side. Regularly U. S. military leaders have miscalculated their effectiveness in Vietnam, including Secretary of Defense McNamara's famous estimate — made after full review of the most complete and detailed evidence — that the United States could begin to withdraw its forces in the Spring of 1966 with the military conflict under control. Today the statements of a Sadat or a Dayan bear ear-marks of a similar dynamic in the Middle East conflict.

There is evidence that military overconfidence is particularly likely among professional soldiers — although it may at times affect whole populations and leaderships — and this is almost always on the basis of technical calculations that ignore the human-response capacities of the enemy. As it happens, one of the tragic facts of international life is that military instrumentalities and military advice become especially prominent in times of international crisis, thus bringing to the foreground of decision-making precisely those persons who occupy roles that demand an occupational absence of human empathy.

Now, before remarking on how psychoanalytic study might illuminate these regularly occurring group phenomena, I will briefly describe how cooperation has been induced between competing groups. Two elements appear to be essential: the establishment of direct human contact between members of the groups and the discovery of common goals that require cooperation to achieve ends desired by each interacting group. Outside these factors, only exhaustion, defeat, or subordination seem to limit cycles of intergroup conflict interaction.

Sherif and others have shown that direct contact in noncompetitive circumstances — for example, the two groups of eleven-year-olds viewing films together — does not, by itself, markedly reduce intergroup hostility but that such contact allows the less violent expression of hostility. When, however, the necessity for cooperation to attain commonly desired "superordinate" goals is introduced, there is a rapid decrease in intergroup tension. For example, the eleven-year-olds found that *both* groups had to pull a rope to start the food truck and that both had to cooperate in eliminating a stoppage in the camp water supply. In such circumstances, the stereotyped images melt, and a variety of friendly interactions begin.

Between larger natural groups, I have found that tension can be materially reduced in applying this formula in ways modified by the fact that large natural groups are not subject to experimental manipulation. In the Dominican Republic, for instance, I undertook to reduce hostility between the grouping of revolutionary Dominican youths and the United States diplomatic mission. There, contact was established in steps, first by meeting personally with each group as a neutral outsider interested in scholarly issues, some time later introducing to both sides groups of distinguished international scholars concerned with university development. This paved the way for direct contact between leading members of the United States Embassy and the Dominican University Community with the general purpose of finding means to cooperate in university stabilization and development which, we had determined, was wanted by both sides.

The first direct meeting was arranged carefully; it took place at the home of the University Rector, and a number of neutral persons — the visiting scholars, the Papal Nuncio, a Bishop, and the Mexican Ambassador — were present as buffers between twenty leading persons from both groups. In this real-life experiment, the findings of the laboratory were astonishingly confirmed. Group members paired off with their counterparts and argued their respective cases with considerable vigor. By the end of an evening no minds had been changed nor had any opposing argument been accepted. *But*, the leaders of each group concluded that the other side was reasonable (if mistaken in its views), serious in purpose, and capable of cooperation. They then proceeded to joint planning and have worked together ever since.

Here, again, in a national setting as in the laboratory, tension reductions followed direct contact and a variety of superordinate goal definition. I consider this to be one model for contributing to a process of peace: contact by intercession followed by direct contact followed by joint planning for common goals — which I term partial superordinate goals, since the immediate aim is not a peace treaty or high-level settlement of outstanding problems but merely learning to work together on limited issues requiring cooperation. I believe that a series of such arrangements between groups in conflict, regardless of their scale, can inhibit the conflict cycle and reduce the disposition toward misperception, miscalculation, and violence.

Possible Psychoanalytic Contributions

I have chosen to summarize a range of validated observations that have been made in complete innocence of psychoanalytic models of psychological functioning and which still lack the sort of explanation which would permit intervention in intergroup conflict with the purpose of reducing hostility and violence. I consider that all the phenomena described are subject to psychoanalytic interpretation and that such interpretations can be refined and validated by direct and indirect examination of participants in both experimental and real-life circumstances. What I am proposing is that the community of psychoanalysts support and encourage some of its members in detailed and scientific work on the psychological dynamics of group behavior. This would require close collaboration with behavioral scientists using other methods *and* it would require that psychoanalysts both sanction and fund specific investigations relevant to understanding of the war problem. We might here recall that Freud would surely have pursued this subject further and that even the founder of psychoanalysis had to appeal to humanitarians for funds to carry on his work; those analysts who have benefited personally and professionally from this work might well repay their indebtedness by a more active role in extending their science.

Here, I shall only remark on the most general dynamic that appears to operate in the production of group behavior. This is what the psychoanalyst, Charles Pinderhughes of Boston, has described as "the resolution of ambivalence by (normal) group paranoia." Pinderhughes's investigations of racial feelings have led him to conclude that perceptions of one's own body and of physiological processes which are associated with unpleasant feelings are readily linked with images and representations of other significant persons and memories. These "normal" projective processes are particularly liable to activation by group involvement, especially since group members reinforce one another in their "delusional" interpretations which are, moreover, insulated from reality testing by the limitations of contact with members of the despised out-group.

In the setting of this meeting I cannot forbear to report an example of this dynamic in the Middle East. Ten years ago, during a visit to a Kibbutz, I observed a play-therapy setting in which one of the toys was a doll in Arab costume. When I asked the therapist how Israeli children treated this toy it was explained that they play-acted all their rejected impulses with the Arab doll, including theft, violence, and sex. The psychologist deplored this tendency, already evident at the age of 2 1/2 years, but soon afterwards the same psychologist warned me against visiting a certain Arab village: the inhabitants might well rob and possibly kill me as they were so hostile and unscrupulous. The psychologist asserted he would never go there himself without adequate protection. Needless to say, the Arab villagers proved to be warm hosts but were equally and even more overtly convinced of the evil purposes of their Jewish neighbors — and were so instructing *their* children.

It appears to me that this general dynamic is operative in all the phenomena that I have summarized. This does not imply psychological disorder but is a normal manifestation of group life: every human person constructs his own interpretation of reality in the context of his association with unique groups of others. It is, however, an extended task to trace the develop-

ment of each of the empirically observed items of group psychology
at the different levels of analysis: notice, for instance, the complete
inversion of psychological interpretation in the "black-top image"
of the enemy as contrasted with attribution of identity of structure (intrapsychically and socially) implied in the diabolical enemy
image.

Interventions aimed at the reduction and correction of intergroup delusions would surely be made more effective by the
development of an adequate formulation of the dynamics on which
the delusions depend. For example, my own interventions in the
Dominican conflict were materially assisted by recognition of
the Americans' overestimation of the presumed hostility of the
unruly revolutionaries and of the Dominicans' identification of
the Americans with tyrannical superego structures. What is needed
then, is the construction of psychoanalytically based formulations
of group psychology that are as elegant and confirmed as are the
interpretations of the development of the neuroses — and their
treatment.

Steps Toward War

We now come to the study of the specific manifestation of
human aggression in the institution of war. In the first place
contemporary war is an exclusive property of national state behavior; as Freud noted, the national state monopolizes the exercise
of killing violence against the human person, most particularly
those forms of organized deliberate and systematic killing of the
people of other national states. Second, the whole process of war is
highly institutionalized; a large variety of formal conditions must
be satisfied before the national state can successfully engage in
military violence. In these characteristics war is thoroughly unlike
all other forms of human aggression, mayhem, murder, riots and
civic uprising; here the ego and the superego join with the drives
in the aim of killing.

It is well to recall here that the contemporary national state is
a very recent development in the history of man, scarcely four
hundred years old in the judgment of Hans Kohn, a preeminent
historian of nationalism. And the war behavior of national states
is distinctly different from that of earlier forms of warfare — so

different as to be essentially discontinuous in social and psychological as well as political form with such anachronistic events as tribal conflict or the Greek and Roman imperial campaigns. Earlier, individual leaders, small elite groups, or large special interest groups could decide on and prosecute military campaigns as a matter of assumed prerogative, while national state warfare absolutely requires the sustained mobilization of the sentiments of the entire citizenry to the national purposes of war. The national state is truly a new level of analysis of human behavior, itself a product of the process of cultural learning and its global diffusion.

The institution of war is, of course, much older, as earlier forms were evolved and codified in the dim prehistory of the race. The national state has simply preempted the use of the institution and, in the process, substantially modified it. I emphasize this point because a vast amount of political scholarship has clarified these issues since Freud wrote and since any analysis of the institutions of contemporary war must necessarily be directed to the specific group level of behavior; it is exceedingly easy to confuse precedent from historic periods or from other levels of violent actions when, in fact, entirely distinctive psychological and political dynamics are involved.

When one focuses on the issues of contemporary war in these terms as a good deal of scholarship has been focused, it rapidly becomes apparent that a very large number of conditions must be satisfied for a national state to engage in overt war and that going to war is therefore a *process* involving distinctive stages or phases of escalation. While there are a number of formulations of the stages in the production of war, I will here only mention some of the steps as outlined by Senghass. He points out that within any national body some individuals must first be convinced of the virtues of engaging in war and must set about recruiting many others. Then, large interest groups must find the idea compatible with their purposes. These forces can engage the sanction of the dominant elite of the nation which, in turn influences the mass media toward mobilization of mass opinion. At this point the national political system and the specific regimes become involved and undertake the recruitment of the government organization and bureaucracy to war readiness. Only at this point do

national policies and strategies become involved and these must
be reconciled with the war purpose. Since adversary nations are
now certain to be responding to the growing threat posed by the
mobilizing nation, the necessity arises for crisis decision-making
which generally reverts to a small group within the regime. At
this point there is a real risk of the process getting out of control
both internally and externally and this leads to an escalation of
commitments. For example, even when Serbia had capitulated to
Austrian demands, there was no stopping the momentum of the
aroused war-making impulse that precipitated the First World
War. Finally, into this process enters the role of the wider environment, the actions and accidents that may restrain or encourage
the opening of military engagements.

As a case in point, we might notice national state behavior
at the tenth stage, that of crisis decision-making. As I have noted,
the decision process becomes localized in a small group of
leaders and advisors at this point and one can analyze the forces
at work in such a group. All the rules of small group behavior
certainly operate in a complex environment. For example, perceptual distortion in viewing the nature and intentions of the
enemy and even of the nation's own population is certain to
enter in, in accordance with some of the dynamics of group image
that I outlined. Then, there is the phenomenon of the "risky shift";
it has been experimentally demonstrated that group members
tend to reinforce one another toward risk-taking beyond the
degree that the individual members would have considered individually. Military over-confidence is a decided risk as President
Kennedy learned with the ill-fated Bay-of-Pigs misadventure and
President Johnson learned in relation to Vietnam.

Analysis at these critical stages in the production of war is well
advanced in the fields of political and psychological study but has
scarcely been touched psychoanalytically although there is a vast
range of material available for such study. What could be made, for
example, of the consequences of Stalin's image of "Mother Russia,
beaten down and dragged in the mud" and requiring the defense
of her sons as compared with President Johnson's "manly" image
of "bringing home the coon-skin to nail on the wall."

Here, of course, I have touched upon another critical question: that of distinctive national psychologies and their dynamic consequences. In the final analysis, it can be seen, the elimination of the war menace will require a case-by-case study of the psycho-political dynamics of specific peoples and groups in specific encounters.

At this point, however, we can already envision broad strategies for war-preventing action. At each level of analysis and at each stage of war production an adequate study of the psycho-political processes involved would lead to the formulation of interpretations which would indicate how man's aggressive energies could be diverted to other channels than war-making. It is very difficult for national states to be aroused to the point of war-participation. It ought to be relatively possible to intervene at various points in the process if serious citizen-scientists were to mobilize energies to that purpose. Personally, I have chosen to intercede at the levels of international and national governments for the most part and have invariably found a powerful preference for peaceful solutions *if* any practical way could be found.

A General Strategy for Peace

So far in this essay, I have only spoken of the first five levels of analysis, but the two broader discernible levels of organization of human systems are the locus of culture change from which Freud and all of us can find hope for the elimination of war.

Regional and international groupings and linkages, among both government and private participants, certainly serve to restrain the war-making impulse. When members of different nations establish and institutionalize programs of cooperation for any purpose, trade, scientific exchange, or cultural enrichment, these serve to act as third systems or inter-system systems that then exert influence on the respective governments and nations in order to maintain their own programs. Numerous such linkages between any set of nations have the effect of "tying down Gulliver," that is, of constraining gigantic forces with many small threads and connections.

While the psychological needs of such intergroup groupings have been studied quite largely in the sphere of the social ego, there are undoubtedly points in the history of each such development that involve such individual strain as to open the way for the eruption of infantile impulses; until psychoanalytic observation has been applied to such developments, it is impossible to guess what sources of static and breakdown spring from the operation of unconscious forces.

It is at the final level of analysis of mankind as a whole, that exceedingly profound changes can be discerned, however dimly. What can be observed on a world-wide scale is the failure of the established and traditional forms of authority relationship to contain or manage the energies and aspirations of subjects. This is true between governments and people — one hardly speaks any more of the ruler and the ruled — between institutions and members and between parent and child.

A psychoanalytically sophisticated political scientist, Manfred Halpern of Princeton University, has pointed out that the hierarchical authority relationship has passed through several stages from that of acceptance by mutual assumption, through various forms of physical repression, isolation and boundary establishment to avoid conflict, direct bartering and contest of power, to a new phase, that of mutual transformation between parties in relationship. This formulation accords with that of John Spiegel, perhaps the only psychoanalyst to have undertaken the systematic study of human violence, who also points out the failure of hierarchical or linear forms of social organization to meet contemporary demands for social change and advocates the strengthening of capacities for "collateralism" of relationship. Here, indeed, is a challenge to psychoanalytic psychology.

There is no doubt at all that profound changes in intrapsychic organization will accompany the sort of alteration in models of relationship between parent and child that must, perforce, accompany a sweeping reorganization of social authority processes. I personally believe that the influence of psychoanalysis in the lifting of social repression of sexuality in the West has contributed materially to what could be characterized as cultural change of revolutionary proportions. In any case, just as psychoanalysts have observed a striking shift in symptom manifestation from the neuroses of crude repression to those of character and relationship, I believe that we are now seeing a still further change in which studies of neurotic preoccupation and symptom formation will be centered around the relations of men to their societies. I have no question at all but that the central methods and statements of psychoanalysis will assume growing importance in the understanding of man; the question is, whether the community of psychoanalysts will apply those methods in changing circumstances or will insist on definitions of man based in part on kinds of authority relations that are being modified by culture change.

I believe that Freud was correct in observing that war is an outcome of the exercise of suppressive force but I think he was wrong in recommending the same model on a broader level — that is, the development of a global authority — as a prescription for eliminating war; indeed, it seems probable that the use of violence or threat of violence to enforce authority at any level is apt to produce violence at all levels. Rather, his observation that cultural change might eliminate war would seem more likely of realization in the downgrading of the authority principle in human organization and relationships. I think that this is taking place and that whatever helps us understand and recognize and accommodate to these changes will assist in avoiding that last disastrous spasm of a dying era in human relations that could end the whole human venture.

Psychoanalysis can study these new forms; we can assist in the recognition of their consequences and limitations, we can provide some guidance to the social change process based on an understanding of the intrapsychic requirements of the human species. With certainty, psychoanalytic study at each level of behavioral analysis during each major stage of the war-production process would illuminate the hidden psychological causes of war and contribute to developing practical steps to abort the process and to divert the aggressive energies of man to less self-destructive channels.

Few professions and sciences are in a position to contribute to the "superior class of independent thinkers" that Freud thought might guide mankind out of the suicidal habit of war; psychoanalysis is in that position and now, thiry-five years after Freud wrote, could enrich mankind and the profession itself by an active and systematic — Freud wrote "fervent" — participation in the peace process that is now as clearly recognizable as is the war cycle.

Another View

J. A. Schossberger

The interrelatedness of the group and the individual, especially in war times, points to some fundamental problems pertaining to the contemporary human condition. Their scientific treatment involves the social and behavioral sciences, including psychoanalysis, in interdisciplinary activities of information exchange, so that all can check each other's findings and statements.

From the viewpoint of psychoanalysts and of group researchers, one would wish to invoke the anthropological aspects of the human emergence in evolution. To my mind, their relevance is related to the role played by the establishment of cerebral hemispheric dominance, and to the psychodynamics of the latency period. Both illustrate the leap from the hominids to the human strain. Handedness and the definite assertion of cerebral hemispheric dominance become fully apparent only in late infancy. Some years ago, I came to think of the bi-phasic onset of sexual maturation, customarily viewed as a self-explanatory basic fact, as being in need of some clarification. A great amount of libidinal investment during latency, centers upon the intellectual and intellectualized activities required to integrate and coordinate the audio-vocal language channel with the visual-graphic verbal channel of expression and comprehension. This physiological fact deserves more attention than it usually receives. Especially for the psychoanalyst, the functional transformation brought about by handedness and its connection with the picturing graphic representational ability, with corresponding changes in the visual performance, contributes new aspects to the psychodynamics of the latency period; these, and the psychosexual libidinal equilibrium during latency point to the close relationship of cerebral hemisphere dominance to human intellection and specifically to its aggressive sources and roots. One might say that the aggressive component of the welded, fused libidinal-aggressive drive impulses becomes specifically engaged and finally bound in the primeval development of inhibiting the hominid killer hand and transforming it, in a slow process of gradual advance, by subordinating it to the delicate guidance and control required to steer the human writer hand.

These findings hold the promise of uncovering the ancient and, in evolution, very archaic roots of human aggression, and of outlining its transformation up to the intellectual unfolding of the thought process and language activities; these slow processes have finally produced the present day lexic-graphic channel. They seem as yet far from concluded, but we note that they have become externalized and reprojected into the environment as the objectified extensions of thought, the mass media, recording, computing and relay apparatus of today. These projections and extrajects of human intellection constitute a tremendous attainment of sublimation which grew out of, and goes back to, the originally internecine homicidal inclinations of the protohominid strains that lived around here only two million years ago. For comparison, the picturing arts started about twenty thousand years ago or so, and writing, as we all know, as recently as about five thousand years back. Plainly, we have barely started.

Let me now turn to my second outlook, toward a view of the nature of the social bond. It was vividly illuminated in Dr. Wedge's presentation of direct observations how differing groups could be induced to communicate and to become integrated by practically forcing upon them a common language. These dramatic examples show how communication processes operate as outward organizers, so to speak, created by actual contingencies like the shared sport and play goals in camp, or the need to gather provisions and to plan for supplies. A shared language emerges of necessity. It operates as an instrument of reality testing. One is reminded of C. S. Pierce's words, on truth, that "... the progress of investigation carries (the explorers) by a force outside of themselves, to one and the same conclusion. This activity of thought, by which we are carried, not where we wish, but to a foreordained goal, is like the operation of destiny. . ." The syntax of a compatible shared language, is as close as mankind in its search can get, at its respective epoch, to the true syntax of reality.

All this points to the nature of the social bond as the widest range of the common language current in that particular social group. And this brings me to a basic element of human commerce, usually taken for granted, hence scotomatized for scientific analysis, namely, the social adhesive generated by the diverse national currency systems. First let me recall my earlier study of expression and communication, and of the connection between the nonverbal communication by means of transient expressive configuration from which the more permanent stable shapes of pictorial representation derive. When these in turn become set by convention and endless repetition, a redundancy effect is achieved, leading to the ideational symbols of pictogram, ideogram and alphabet. Finally, after a definable number of inhibitory echelons, the numerical symbols appear on the stage of human intercourse. The term "deanimation processes" suggested itself for these progressively accruing inhibitory operations, that lead, starting from nonverbal expression, to the numeric and formal logic of mathematical and geometrical symbolism and calculus. But further to the spiritual aspect, the pragmatic side of quantification operates when its non-denotational, universally ambiguous meaning, or rather lack of it, transforms the money note into a symbolic operator of tremendous efficacy. Because of its ubiquitous prevalence, money deserves more scientific attention than it usually gets from psychoanalysts.

For a long time there was confusion about the notion of value in connection with money and currency. Because of their multiply ambiguous, excessively redundant denotative meaning, money notes mean something else of value, rather than having their own value, to be treasured as such. Moreover, by its restricted validity within a limited territorial range, a currency also symbolizes the reach of group coherence. In this way, currency systems have been invested with veritable totemic qualities. Money is felt not merely to symbolize anything at all, but actually to provide all things; it is also endowed with the power to deny. By lack of it, the very life of its users becomes degraded and in the end, denied. This circumstance — that the social bond employs, as its quantified token units, separate and separating national currencies — has become one of the sources of international irritation, a game if you will. The silent power of experts in the uses of holding and withholding large amounts of money, makes for subgroup and intergroup outlaw activities and other sources of ingroup and intergroup struggle and conflict.

Psychoanalytical investigations of the question interpreting the meaning of property and possessions bring to mind an essay, from a now vanished era, just before the second World War, by Fenichel, on "The Drive to Amass Wealth." More recently, Harley Shands in "Personality and the Preservation of the Self," showed how territoriality in herds and groups points to the role played by the territory in symbolizing the human self-image. These hints must suffice here to indicate some areas of psychosocial, group dynamic and psychoanalytical research directed at elucidating the destructively competitive hostile and warlike impulses operating within and between individuals and groups. We might find what it means, to people and groups and in the context of nations and states, that power, possessions, and potential wealth are all symbolized by money and land in the form of real estate, and this at a time in the development of mankind when real wealth and real power have shifted: artificial materials can be made to order, matter and energy can now be produced according to plan and in an order of preference. The old material bonds now seem due to recede into irrelevance when, in a re-evaluation of the free creations of human striving, human relationships may become supranational and extraterritorial, in a new global sense.

This brings me to a further point in Dr. Wedge's paper: the problem of social tension. In order to bring about their resolution, it could be advantageous to examine the polarities between which the phenomena of social tension come about. Concepts of tension in physics depend on the parameters of reference selected by the experimenter, as in the tension phenomena delimiting the poles between which thermal gradients or electric currents manifest themselves. It seems to me that we have pointers here for deriving the concepts of psychosocial tension from the degree of linguistic discrepancy that prevails between distinct social groupings. If two people mean to talk about the same things, but use different languages, we have the kind of situation in which the problem of social tension may become quantifiable.

If man is to avoid war, he must know more about the obedient aggressive attitude. The word soldier relates to the word "sold," in German *Soeldner*, originally the mercenary soldier, a person paid for and bought with money. To this day, then, the effective power of men over men is wielded by buying them. The refusal to let oneself be bought exemplifies, through history, a spirit of heroic sacrifice. This freedom, comprising the freedom from war for individuals and groups, seems within reach today, if only those who manage these social forces acknowledge their responsible power for making peace come about.

Psychoanalytic Implications of Reactions of Israeli Soldiers to the Six-Day War

Ruth Jaffe

After the end of the war, Israelis thought it to be an isolated event. Only in retrospect did we come to realize that it was in fact only the beginning of an extended period of hostilities, the end of which cannot yet be foreseen. Continuing fighting in a war, which is not a full-scale war, goes on. Our young generation serves in the army for years as regulars or reservists, the latter ones leading double lives, both as civilians and soldiers, alternating their activities between peaceful family life, working or studying, and serving in their military unit, far from home and in constant danger.

The Six-Day War seems to be unique in modern warfare, due to its short duration and to the fact that it was fought against an enemy who was stronger in many respects. The time was too short for the accumulation and emergence of those byproducts of war which develop over long periods and which slowly change the mental climate and the attitudes of the individual soldiers who comprise an army. These byproducts, such as boredom, longing for home, exhaustion, disgust, hatred and others, lead to a sense of growing frustration and have their impact on fighting morale over the span of time.

In comparison to those long-lasting wars, this war was almost like an experimental situation, a war in a nutshell, so to speak. It should enable us, therefore, to deduce from the description of its soldiers and their attitude some prominent features of the army and the prevailing spirit in it.

I relied for this endeavor on informal talks with healthy soldiers, on my own observations as an involved citizen of our nation,
and to an important degree on a book called *Siach Lochamim*,
which means "Talks between Fighters." This book contains the
proceedings of small group discussions between soldiers, young
reservists from the different kibbutz-movements, after their return
home from the war. Many such discussions were tape-recorded and
parts of them selected for publication. My paper does not rely upon
serial investigations or scientifically examined facts, which have
yet to emerge. Nor does it deal with psychopathological phenomena
because mental breakdowns were nearly nonexistent in that
period of time.

The main topics with which I shall deal here, are the role which
the libidinal and aggressive drives played in this war, the accompanying affects, and the emotional and intellectual impact which
the war had on the soldiers during the first months after their
return home.

I should like to stress that the paper deals mainly with the
soldiers of battle units, which, in a modern army, do not comprise
more than 10 to 15 per cent. But small as this percentage was,
the soldiers of the battle units displayed all the features I am about
to discuss.

The motivation for the war was physical as well as spiritual self-
preservation in the strictest meaning of the word. Physical self-
preservation included family, home, and country, since all of
them could be reached in the span of a day's drive, at most, geogra-
phical and spatial distance being so small here. Spiritual self-
preservation meant the preservation of the country as a sovereign
nation. Being a tiny country, surrounded by the sea and hostile
neighbors who wanted to drive us into that sea, we felt the threat to
be very real. Since the hostile armies were much larger than ours,
the enemies' soldiers good fighters in individual confrontation,
their technical equipment modern and much more plentiful,
our chances, seen from without, were indeed questionable enough.
But this was not a war in which you could win or be defeated. The
alternatives were victory or annihilation.

Although the war is spoken of as the Six-Day War, for most of
the battle units it lasted not more than two to three days, due to

the movement of the war from one front to the next, each front mainly with its own units. The fighting began in the Sinai, continued in Jordan, and ended with the Syrians.

Standards for morale and good fighting were usually set by those men who served in the higher ranks of battle units and as volunteers in commando units, which were committed to specialized dangerous tasks. This group of young men consisted mainly of high-school graduates and members of kibbutzim. For years they were trained and prepared for arduous and prolonged functioning.

Military training begins at the age of eighteen years. Each soldier is assigned to a unit, with which he usually remains during his regular service and later in the years of his reserve duty. The unit was distinguished by its *"esprit de corps,"* especially by the feeling of brotherhood (*achvat lochamim*) between its members. The social difference between the officer and his men was usually underplayed, a fact that made for easy contact and confidence. Although the previously mentioned book *Siach Lochamim* describes only the experiences of kibbutz members, we learn from it how seriously the officers, themselves only a few years older than their men, took their responsibility toward them. They were regarded as good parents. They led the way in battle, providing the example of what to do and how, and presented a living image of a strong father. In addition, they made it their concern to know the whereabouts of everyone in their unit, they were considerate and made life as bearable as possible, were the providers of physical comfort, encouraged and praised, thus fulfilling the role of a good mother as well.

Typically, battle units became forged into real groups, with strong libidinal ties between its members and their leader, which provided support for everyone. In such an atmosphere of brotherhood and parental leadership, the individual soldier felt sheltered, could master his fear and function well. Since the individual superego was replaced by a collective one, he also could shut out a good deal of the traumatogenic events around him: the seeing of wounded and dead, the destruction, and the necessity to kill. The loss of group support in instances, for example, when a single soldier became isolated from his unit in the heat of battle, explains the panic he might then experience. Another rather frequent situation of loss of group support was found when the soldier, back home after the war, was left with his war experiences by himself.

In addition to the security provided by group cohesiveness, mutual responsibility and care, the soldier had another assurance. There were standing orders to spare the blood of the Israeli soldiers as far as possible, and not to expose him to avoidable dangers. He knew he would not be deserted in any circumstances. He, in turn, went to any length to rescue the wounded and to recover the fallen, often with complete disregard for his own life. Here the instinct for self-preservation seems to have given way to the need for collective survival.

Details of this group spirit are stressed here so much, because the general lack of it helps us to understand some aspects of the catastrophe of the Jewish Holocaust in Europe. Although the Jewry of Europe had not been deprived of leadership, this was a religious and communal leadership, not political, nor was it prepared for military operations. The Ghetto was not a unit, and certainly not a group, the libidinal ties there having been confined chiefly to the family. Yet because of these very ties, only few Jews dared to leave their families and join partisan groups or rise against the enemy. The conception of collective survival was not developed, because it had not been imperative until then. Pogroms had not been of very large dimensions and not extended over long time periods, and everyone was expected to save himself according to his own devices. In the concentration camps, moreover, conditions were such that the vital amount of libido and aggression had diminished to such a degree that many perished; the remaining ones being left with no more strength than was necessary for bare survival. It was the framework and organization for fight which was so conspicuously absent in Europe. But as soon as such a framework and a common spirit became available to the survivors of the Holocaust, as was seen in the War of Liberation in Israel, many of them became good soldiers. Similar considerations hold true for Oriental Jews, who were persecuted in Arab countries, although to a lesser degree, and who became good soldiers in Israel also.

Returning to the Six-Day War, another important factor was the nation's admiration for and pride in its army and in the deeds of its soldiers. This, in turn, increased their self and group narcissism and strengthened their self-confidence and fighting ability still more. The conviction that they were the best, and, at the same time, the most humane army of the world, added still further to their narcissism.

Another factor making for high fighting morale is actually never stated explicitly. It refers to the fact, mentioned earlier, that Oriental Jews also served in battle units. They were mixed in the units with the Israeli born, where they shared in the group spirit and in fighting. As equals, their inferiority feeling diminished markedly. Hidden abilities came to the fore, and with their impulsiveness and recklessness, they made their special contribution in fighting tasks. In fact, the army is, up to now, the major vehicle in the nation for the integration of immigrants from numerous countries, and it gave another dimension to the libidinal ties between the soldiers.

The latter fact is linked with another which may be the most decisive for the outcome of the war. It relates to the fact of the emergence of the Jewish State as a sovereign nation, still so young after a millenium of persecution in the *Golah* (Diaspora). Most of our young soldiers are of the first generation born in Israel. For the first time, Jews are no longer living as communities in a guest land, often a hostile one, but as a national group in its own country. Therefore the Israeli soldier does not perceive his military service as a peripheral and time-limited duty, but as an integral part of his life as an Israeli. It is part of his self-conception. Politics aside, it is the army that defends this new image of the citizens. The spiritual force of this image is indeed great and all-pervasive, and is shared by all ethnic groups of the nation. It can be said that the army represents today the most visible and vital part of the self-realization of the new-born Israeli nation.

The curious fact is that the army and its soldiers, and especially those of the battle units, were certain even before the beginning of fighting that they would win the war. It is true that the individual soldier, a tiny part of a great whole, regresses emotionally as well as in regard to important ego functions to earlier developmental stages. He relinquishes his personal superego and replaces it by the collective one. He acts on command only and renounces his personal judgment. He denies the degree of danger. But all this holds true for any soldier in any army of the world, and cannot explain the almost unrealistic certainty of victory. It is my speculation that this certainty lay in the basic trust which came from the libidinal attachments, the heightened narcissism and intact body-image which made him feel ready and fit for fight. We may also wonder if this basic trust perhaps revived regressive magic omnipotent attitudes. The soldiers themselves, as far as they could retrospectively think of an explanation, described themselves as having had a mystic feeling about their role in the war and its eventual outcome, and this feeling was in no way connected with religiousness or traditionalism.

We have dealt so far with the libidinal aspects of fighting. The soldiers themselves hardly speak of them—they seem to them self-evident.

Concerning the role of aggression, the attitude of our army toward it was one of wholesale denial. In such a representative book as *Siach Lochamim*, the terms aggression and aggressiveness are peculiarly absent. The negation of aggressive intent was similarly reflected in the attitude of the population at large. This attitude might be justified only if aggression is defined as unprovoked hostility. The necessity of war was forced upon us, and everybody felt that there was no choice but to fight for self-preservation and to destroy the enemies' instruments of war and their armies. But this, of course, could not be accomplished without aggressive action. However, the aggressiveness of our army was not a spontaneous one. It was evoked as a reaction and had survival as its goal, the threat of annihilation being all too familiar and real.

Aggression as the disposition to fight includes physical and mental preparedness. Aggression was experienced subjectively by many as a sensation of tension, anger, or covert rage, without being recognized specifically as aggression. This sensation, which began with the mobilization of the army, characterized the whole period of fighting and continued for a while thereafter. It always appeared with an admixture of fear, which depended upon the degree of anticipated danger. Aggressiveness did not, at the beginning, refer to a special target, the goal being merely a generalized wish for the destruction of the enemy. With the beginning of fighting, special targets were set. If the task was accomplished in the proscribed manner, the tenseness diminished, and a sense of satisfaction appeared. Obviously, a partial discharge of aggression, as well as of libido, had taken place, the latter as a consequence of the pride in having done a good job. Accompanying fear diminished also. The forms of aggression varied, ranging from those which were ego-controlled to more primitive and brutal ones. The difference has to be explained partly on the basis of the kind of fighting which took place, which was different in each sector of the front. It also depended on the pre-war personality of the soldier and his former traumatic experiences which had sensitized him to dangerous stimuli, lowered his threshold to them, and facilitated more indiscriminate forms of aggressive discharge.

Let us first look at the Sinai front, where the battle against the Egyptians was fought, with a large force of our army concentrated there. In this sector, the army was highly mechanized, and, although there was a certain amount of hand-to-hand fighting, the main destructiveness did not involve firing at individuals. "You do not see the crew in the tank you set aflame," and "When dropping bombs from an airplane, you do not see the people on whom they land." Therefore there were comparatively few conscious affects involved. The most important objective seems to have been the wish to do a good job. This was part of good fighting, but it had a special, more professional, connotation as well. The assigned task should be executed in the best possible way, according to plan, exactly, neatly, and quickly, with the smallest possible number of casualties. It also implied the wish to put to test all that had been learned during the long years of training. In all those parts of the front where modern war equipment was used or where special, dangerous tasks had to be accomplished, this feeling of doing a good job prevailed. The quality of the performance, with its ensuing satisfaction, seemed to have been more important than the ultimate destruction involved thereby, which appeared to have become more of a byproduct to them. Neat, ego-controlled, destructive aggressiveness, executed in teams, and accompanied by no more than realistically justified fear, seemed to have been the only really necessary components of warfare in this sector of the front.

This changed, however, at the moment when a comrade was killed or wounded. Then the fighting attitude became emotional. The falling of a comrade aroused hate against the enemy and the impulse to take revenge. If the comrade was killed in a cowardly way fury took over, and there emerged a drive for revenge by a more indiscriminate form of killing. Then even transgressions of war conventions might take place.

On the Jordanian and Syrian fronts, aggressiveness was heavily loaded with affects from the very beginning. The combat in Jordan took place against a well-trained army, the Arab Legion, as well as against civilians trained in hand-to-hand fighting and the use of knives. Their officially issued threats to annihilate the Jewish population in the event that they got the upper hand aroused strong fear and hatred. Modern mechanized warfare was almost impossible there, especially in the Old City of Jerusalem. And the house-to-house, roof-to-roof fighting was often really brutal. In the twisted streets the units were broken up, and a soldier might find himself suddenly alone, face to face with an armed enemy, without a possibility of escape for either of them. Deprived of the support of his unit, this often cruel fighting for sheer survival might arouse feelings of panic and terror in the soldier, resulting in mounting aggressiveness and brutality, which he felt bursting out from deep inside himself, impulses of which he had been hitherto unaware. This kind of experience might leave deep residues in those who were exposed to it, and made them hate the enemy and themselves alike.

Against the Syrians, there was open, long-standing hatred. For years, secure in their heavy bunkers on the Golan Heights, they had shelled from above the Jewish settlements in the Hulah Plain. The fight at this front, short as it was, was again different and most difficult, being a mixture of technical warfare and hand-to-hand fighting. In order to destroy the Syrian defense line and conquer their bunkers the soldiers had to climb steep mountains, constantly exposed to enemy shelling, with no opportunity to take cover. In addition to being extremely dangerous, the climb was physically exhausting in itself. Fear and hatred were great, but the units were not split up, thus at least providing mutual support.

As these details demonstrate, it is difficult to separate aggression as such from accompanying affects, like fear, hatred, and vengefulness. To a certain degree fear was always present during actual fighting (although frequently not consciously experienced), but much more so in all those instances when the soldier was exposed to the enemy without being allowed or able to engage in fight or to move into a safe position. Fear was often especially strong in those men who had grown up in Arab countries and been discriminated against and persecuted there. They were less sure of quick victory. This was especially true of the non-fighting units, whereas those in battle units were better able to conquer fear.

Fear signaled danger and helped the soldier to stay as alert as possible, and to sustain his activity until the danger had passed, thereby augmenting his aggressiveness. Excessive fear, however, impaired reality-testing and led to more indiscriminate forms of aggressiveness and to brutalization. Conversely, absence of fear was dangerous to self-preservation. It made the soldier less observant and even careless. Quite a few examples became known, in which soldiers, excited by victory and moved by pity, began to feel generous toward the vanquished enemy and forgot caution, only to be taken unawares and attacked by him. It was often such incidents that aroused hatred and the impulse for revenge in the soldiers.

Affects such as hatred and vengefulness generally did not add to the fitness for fight. When aroused, they, too, augmented aggressiveness, but would lead to the same kind of indiscriminate fighting and destructiveness as did excessive fear. Hatred appears as the counterpart of fear. The greater the fear, the greater the hatred. This equation presupposes that the enemy is felt as an equal or superior opponent. Seen in this light, it was interesting to observe the reaction of our soldiers after the anticlimax of the so quickly won victory. There were some who stated later that they had felt the victory to have come too easily, and there was a slight regret that the war had not been more of a real contest. This was true for those who were convinced from the very beginning that they would be victorious. Since they had not felt great fear, neither did they feel hate, and after the victory they were inclined to experience a sense of superiority toward the vanquished.

But those who had felt great fear and, correspondingly, hate toward the enemy before the victory, became contemptuous afterwards. Pity, and even more so feelings of superiority and contempt may be more detrimental than hatred, because (1) they deprive the enemy of his honor and thus stimulate him to seek revenge; (2) they create a distorted self-image of invincibility which may well lead to carelessness and impaired reality testing, and therefore they may become, over time, as dangerous to self-preservation as the lack of fear.

Therefore it may be said that affects like hatred and its derivatives, vengefulness and excessive fear, tended to impair those ego functions which are imperative to self-preservation, and they were liable to liberate aggressive drives to such a degree that the ego could no longer control them. It is ego-controlled aggression which makes for maximum efficiency at minimum cost during the fighting, and for humaneness after it.

I have not yet referred to the fact that our young soldiers, many of whom had been brought up as pacifists in spite of their military training, had had to kill and to see numerous dead and maimed, and extensive destruction. Often the first sight of a dead body, either Israeli or enemy, came as a shock to them. This frequently happened simultaneously with the necessity to fire their own first shot. But they got used to it very quickly. They seemed, however, to have been in an unusual mental state, which is difficult to evaluate without psychiatric examination. Seen from without, their ego functions seem to have been restricted to the necessities of fighting, whereby feelings and thoughts not related to fighting were shut out as far as possible. There are self-descriptions of their behavior having become automatic and their feeling blunted or blocked. Some described states which sound like derealization. To them, it all seemed like a motion picture, and shooting was like aiming at and knocking down dolls. Others had the feeling as if a kind of curtain came down, so as to shield them from seeing what went on around them. These defenses protected the mental apparatus against too strong stimuli, which would otherwise have impaired their ability to fight.

As mentioned earlier, the aggressive tension did not stop with the fighting. In retrospect, it seems that the joy of victory, as far as the soldiers of the battle units were concerned, found adequate expression only in Jerusalem at the Wailing Wall. Here, the tenseness gave way to feelings of festivity and mystic entry into history. At the other fronts the channelling of tension did not succeed, in spite of elaborate military celebrations. The fighters could not open up to joy. In those soldiers whose fears and hatred had been excessive and who had become increasingly aggressive, the anti-climax after the fighting was sharp. In some cases it brought about a momentary breakdown of inhibitions, resulting in blind, senseless destruction of enemy property.

After their return home, many soldiers, mainly those of battle units, did not immediately revert to their usual state of mind. They were uncommunicative and looked depressed. They had parted with their units and returned home alone. Their tension had not yet disappeared, and they still felt as if "in a dream." It had all happened so quickly, that they had not had time to absorb their experiences. Many of them felt that they had gone for the purpose of defending themselves and their country, and suddenly they found themselves to be the conquerors of foreign territory. The resulting confusion was aggravated by their ideology, which did not covet land, but sought for peaceful coexistence with the neighboring Arabs. There was mourning about fallen comrades and anxious uncertainty about those whose fate was not yet known. Since they were now deprived of the emotional support of their unit, they were thrown back upon their individual defenses. The self-confrontation with the fact that they had destroyed and killed, and the discovery of their primitive bestial impulses which they had not suspected in themselves could become traumatic. They had become disillusioned with their self-image and ego-ideal, and this added new dimensions to their mourning. They felt estranged not only from their former self, but from their home as well. Since they had had so many unfamiliar experiences they felt that they had lost the common language with their own people. This added to their inability to speak about themselves. They were called the "silent generation." The group discussions, quoted in the book *Siach Lochamin* were organized by the kibbutzim mainly to help their soldiers to open up and speak about themselves and their experiences. It may be speculated, furthermore, that massively evoked aggression, which could not be rechannelled quickly enough, turned against the self as depressive affect. It seems that the individual soldier could not defend himself immediately against the onslaught of his war experiences. His usual defense mechanisms failing him in the face of them, he underwent a transient period of mourning and depression. But since he was at the same time still in a mild dream-like state, he did not experience them too acutely. The different forms of isolation of affect seem to have diminished or disappeared after a period of time. Generally, the soldiers were spared lasting pathological symptoms, and after a time of working through of their experiences and/or with the fact that they were regarded by the nation as the saviors of their country, they eventually achieved a new equilibrium. Joy and pride could be felt only then.

It seems strange that aggression, conceived of as an instinctual drive which is, as such, spontaneous, and plays such an important role in everyday life, should have lacked this quality of spontaneity in the soldiers who fought in this war. Instead, a very strong motivation, that of self-preservation, was needed in order to evoke and mobilize aggressiveness in the individual soldier. Aggression here appeared more as a defensive reaction than as a genuine drive, although it could be triggered off and become autonomous under excessive stress.

To digress slightly, we observe that, in contradistinction to the individual who knows to what extent he can safely expose himself to danger, military headquarters and governments all over the world are apparently less sure. They often plan their destructive designs with complete disregard for the right of the individual to live. This factor makes for more ruthlessness. Man is more aggressive in fantasy than in action. His most brutal actions as an individual are limited by his physical strength as well as by reality testing; but his fantasy is not. In planned aggression, based on fantasy, reality testing is more complex and less reliable. Besides, planned war is impersonal. The planning is done far away from the actual battle and destruction. Furthermore, not only aggression enters into the design. Other components apart from drives and affects go into it, among them conflict-free ego functions. Use is made of new discoveries in science, and their appli-

cation for more efficient war techniques produces more sophisticated forms of aggression, without the individual designer as a
person necessarily being more aggressive than average.

Here the vital question arises, whether man's drives and ego-
structures are sufficiently integrated for him to grasp the full
meaning of interhuman mass destruction.Perhaps the destruction
can be understood rationally but not emotionally. The annihilation
of six million Jews is beyond our ability to comprehend and remains
abstract, while a report in the morning's news of a young soldier
killed yesterday, is felt as a personal sorrow. While man's affective
and instinctual endowment has not basically changed, his intellectual tools have developed markedly, so that he himself now invents
the machinery for his destruction. It seems as if there is something
lacking in man, a specific structure or mechanism which would
enable him to comprehend fully, and to act accordingly, or stop.
It is perhaps this gap between his intellectual tools and an all
inclusive reality testing together with adequate emotional realization of the effect of his designs, which is responsible for the inability
of mankind to stop war. It seems to me therefore, that our question
today is not only "Why War?" but also "What Could Stop War?",
the longing for peace apparently not being sufficient.

If the Six Day War had been a long one instead, and one between more or less equal opponents, there would be no need to
speak about it. What made it remarkable and calls for an answer was the unequalness of the war conditions on the two sides
and its short duration. One obvious answer would be found in
the fact that our nation resembles modern western nations in
technical knowledge and inventiveness; we were able to make
the best of our modest technical equipment, in contrast to the
Arabs, who could not use theirs efficiently enough. Yet the decisive factor remains the fighting spirit, as described before.

The Israeli soldiers prided themselves not only on not being
aggressive, but also on their army being the most humane one in
the world. The general belief that ours is a humane army refers to
the behavior of the soldiers toward their comrades, who supported
each other to the maxium extent possible, and toward the enemy,
as well.

In spite of occasional transgressions, it may be said that our army behaved like any other in the civilized world. But even in such armies there is cruelty and often disregard for the individual soldier, and there are differences in adherence to international conventions. When the enemy is regarded as being of more or less equal social and cultural status, the enemy behaves according to these conventions. But at the same time, he is more brutal toward those whom he sees as being inferior. The Nazi German army, for example, showed the full range, from their rather decent treatment of the vanquished French, to their brutality toward the Poles and Russians, reaching the ultimate in bestial behavior toward the Jews.

In general the Israeli army did not behave toward the Arabs with brutality, in spite of the fact that it regarded them as culturally inferior. We did not treat them as we expected them to treat us, had the outcome been reversed. It is in the light of this comparison, that our claim to humaneness has to be understood.

Conclusion: It was my aim to deduce from the feelings and attitudes of our soldiers in the Six Day War some prominent features of the army and the prevailing spirit in it. The following factors were found to be of importance: the need for self-preservation, the mutual libidinal ties in the army, the identification of the soldier with the nation and its ideals, an intact body-image, and ego-controlled aggression with the necessary admixture of reality oriented fear. No other drives and affects seemed essential, hate and vengefulness, in particular, being superfluous and harmful.

Finally, we should remember, that the war was not a war of conquest, but of defense. We were fighting mainly for ourselves and less against others. The love for our people was the decisive factor and not hatred against the enemy. That is why the libidinal aspects of fighting were stressed so much in this paper.

Another View

Robert S. Wallerstein

It is difficult for an American to discuss appropriately the observations of an Israeli colleague upon the *normal* psychology of the Israeli soldier, upon whom rests the awesome burden of preserving the integrity of the nation and the very life of all its inhabitants under circumstances that can only be called abnormal in the extreme, circumstances that we all fervently pray can some day, in the lifetimes of at least some of us, normalize. For a psychoanalyst, this difficulty is compounded, in that psychoanalysis has out of its general humanistic identification avoided intensive study of the mental world of the soldier, perhaps to avoid the inevitable implication of sanction of the military activity as a permissible role for modern and civilized man.

Freud himself had little to say on the subject. Out of the anguish of the first World War, he wrote his double essay, "Thoughts for the Times on War and Death," in 1915, in which he first discussed some of the psychological bases on which nations and individuals are enabled to fight wars, and the bases on which individuals can willingly contemplate and condone the death and destruction of which war consists, and then in the second part discussed some of the universals in man's attitude toward death, or more precisely, the bases on which they stand convinced in their unconscious (at least part of it) of their own immortality and thus can more readily allow themselves to risk death in their waging of war. But Freud specifically disclaimed (in his essay, "On Transience," published in the next year, 1916) any knowledge of the psychology of the soldier. "It would be most, interesting, no doubt, to study the changes in the psychology of the combatants, but I know too little about it."

Freud's only other words on war per se were in the famous exchange of letters with Einstein in 1933, written in the long foreshadow of the coming of World War II. There, too, he focuses in a renewed and deepened, but essentially unchanged way from his World War I statement, on the meaning and the psychology of war; but again not the psychology of the soldier. He did in the period between the Wars, in *The Ego and the Id* (1923), deal again with the nature of the fear of death, and in *Inhibitions, Symptoms, and Anxiety* (1926), deal a little with some of the psychopathology of the soldier, the nature and the psychological explanation of the war neurosis, the latter a topic he had also addressed in the same vein in the immediate aftermath of World War I, in his *Introduction to 'Psychoanalysis and the War Neuroses'* (1919) and his *Memorandum on the Electrical Treatment of War Neurotics* (1920). And this last, the psychopathological reactions to the terrors of combat has indeed been a subject of continuing psychoanalytic attention through the days of World War II and ever since. One need only mention Grinker and Spiegel's *Men Under Stress*, and Douglas Bond's *The Love and Fear of Flying*, as two of the best known and most influential of such contributions; in fact, the tremendous flowering of interest in and the widespread and growing acceptance of the psychoanalytic viewpoint as the dominant psychiatric perspective in post-World War II America could be said to have largely resulted from the transplantation of European (Central European) psychoanalysis from the Hitler exodus, into America, and there meeting the receptive soil of the body of American psychiatry. From this came the willingness to understand and accept the usefulness of the psychoanalytic psychology of the unconscious in its application to the psychopathology seen in the stress of world war.

Nonetheless, I cite all this, not to indicate how much relevant psychoanalytic literature there is antecedent to the contribution I was asked to discuss —the mentality, that is the psychology, of the normal (i. e., the average, the usual) Israeli soldier — but to indicate rather how little there is. There are few guideposts for those brought up in America, like myself, coming from a country also engaged in war, but in a far away foreign war, a war that in its unpopularity and divisiveness has racked the fabric of the country more than at any other time since our own Civil War more than a hundred years ago. There are few guideposts that we can bring to a consideration of the issues Jaffe confronts us with, the psychology of the citizen-soldier of a popular army on whose high morale, indomitable courage, and great skill the survival of Everyman in Israel has depended, and who, at the same time, more than in any other nation in recorded history, is truly himself Everyman, simultaneously fighting soldier and peace-seeking citizen.

In her consideration of this problem, Jaffe follows the classical psychoanalytic instinct duality, discussing it from the perspective of both the libidinal and the aggressive aspects of fighting. In view of the special relationship of the people of Israel to their citizen-army, it is understandable and natural that it is the libidinal component of the mentality of the soldiers which Jaffe discusses first. And parenthetically, Jaffe reminds us that this almost shortest of wars on record, only six days, was for the individual soldier on any of the fronts even shorter than that, but two or three days; with the unstated but clear implication to us that some of the psychological stresses and responses, reflecting the adaptive adjustment to this overwhelmingly acute situation, totally decisive for the survival of the nation one way *or* the other, might well be modified in the more usual war situation of chronic and sustained danger, uncertainty, suffering and misery.

About this first, libidinal aspect of the soldier's psychology, what does Jaffe suggest? In a struggle where the alternatives were clearly victory or annihilation, Dr. Jaffe pridefully concludes that the army represented and fulfilled "the most visible and the most vital part of the self-realization of the new-born Israeli nation." To extrapolate a little theoretically from these observations, this fortunate psychic outcome can reflect a welding of the most advanced psychic functions with some of the most elemental and primitive. Jaffe comments on the one hand on the brotherhood and the parental leadership in each unit of the army, the group spirit that goes to forge "a collective ego and superego," the conception of collective survival, the pride that is fostered and developed in what is felt to be the best — and the most humane — army in the world, the incidental but very important benefits from the role of the army as the great leveler and homogenizer in a society created from among so many of the nations and so many of the languages of the world. All these rest largely on the highest level of secondary process capacity, neutralized and sublimated altruistic energies, At the same time Jaffe writes of the inextricably intermixed components of "self and group narcissism," of high confidence in victory, of basic trust (to use an Eriksonian phrase) with all the attitudes of revived infantile magic and omnipotence, all resting on the most important, most basic, and most archaic psychic positions through which one must successfully advance in earliest infancy, if one is to establish the bedrock for any and all successful future psychic development.

One can make the comparison here with a similar point made in a totally different situation, the psychoanalytic transference, by Leo Stone in his book on the Psychoanalytic Situation. In delineating the nature of the real relationship between analysand and analyst, on the stability of which the capacity to endure the vicissitudes of the transference depends, Stone made the point that this real relationship rested simultaneously on the highest level secondary process capacity to work together in effective collaboration toward a logical and rational shared and prized goal, combined with the most elemental capacity to share and trust, rooted in the most potent and archaic of infantile experiences, successfully surmounted. It is the capacity for this fusion of advanced and primitive functions that marks those who can best succeed at difficult tasks, and this Jaffe indicates characterized the so highly successful Israeli Army en masse, at least uniformly those to whose mental life she had access. At the same time we must not overdo psychic reality at the expense of a realistic appraisal of objective reality. The certainty of the Israeli army of its victory once the war itself became unavoidable — and the concomitant absence even of *plans* for military retreat — should not be laid only at the door of psychological integrity resting in the ultimate on infantile magic and omnipotence; it was also true that the Army knew itself to be then superior in fighting capacity and technological mastery to its foes, and could realistically expect victory.

When Jaffe turns to the aggressive instinct component of the soldier's experience in battle, she is, as we always are when dealing with the expression of the aggressive urge, on more difficult ground. It is a truism to state that war consists of killing, but it is perhaps not a truism to remind all of us that the problem of the handling of aggression is not necessarily equivalent to that of the meanings of killing, an equation that at times seems to be slipped into in this contribution. And further, in discussing the denial of aggression in the Israeli military activity (what she calls also the peculiar absence of the terms aggression and aggressiveness from the book *Siach Lochamim*), Jaffe says, "This attitude is justified, if aggression is defined as unprovoked hostility." Such a definition of aggression is of course a political-military definition, and clearly a politically self-serving definition, not at all a psychological definition and therefore misleading to our psychological purposes in this context. It is as if a need is felt at this point to accept a rationalized cover for the aggressive discharge (destructive discharge) which fuels fighting and war for all men, as witness the emphasis at several places in the paper on the expressed satisfaction in doing a technically good job as a major subjective experience of the fighting. For example, Jaffe states, "In all those parts of the front where modern war equipment was used or where special dangerous tasks had to be accomplished, this feeling of doing a good job prevailed. The quality of the performance, with its ensuing satisfaction, seemed to have become more important than the ultimate destruction involved thereby, which appeared to become more of a by-product for them." For individuals and for nations there is at times a need to see it that way, as part of the forging of a necessary self-image — and in this sense, Jaffe's is, too, a political paper, and in the very best sense of that word.

But to me, the psychologically more compelling and more provocative data that Jaffe presents center around the what-comes-after the cessation of the fighting. Jaffe reiterates that "the aggressive tension did not stop with the fighting" and then says, "It ended in an anticlimax, which appeared in several different forms" — which she then goes on to develop with considerable description of, among other variants, what she calls the post-war depression. "They had lost their common language with their people." These data I would like to examine from an additional and a little different vantage point. In one context, with the abrupt cessation of the fighting, the task done and victory achieved, it was anticlimax; but this is the rational context of war as indeed nothing but one of life's possible tasks, albeit a particularly unpleasant and dangerous one. And there are the many references in the paper, including those I have quoted, to just these task aspects of war and fighting. But obviously war and its wholesale killing is psychologically far more than work and efficiency. It is, like the Sorcerer's Apprentice of legend, a setting into motion of powerful and demonic forces in the minds of men, which once activated can make for irresistible and irrevocable psychological changes which up to now have been studied by us all too little. Different men handle these stresses differently. Some are stated to have trouble until forced by necessity "to fire their own first shot" — and then get used to it very quickly. Or alternatively (I again quote) "Some described (continued) states which are like derealization. . . like a motion picture. . .like shooting at and knocking over dolls." Some, hidden by distance and complex war technology, depersonalize the aggression and/or dehumanize its victims, "a kind of curtain came down so that they could not see what went on around them."

With such reactions, so understandable and so logical in adaptation to such circumstance, why should we expect the inner turmoil to shut off just with the "logical" goal achieved, and victory won. Each man has put his fund of aggressive and murderous potential in the service of that goal — and his upset at the point that he is now asked as suddenly to curb it can be seen not as the puzzling anticlimax to be explained, but as the inevitable post-climax in all its varying forms. Are some so upset because they have found to their horror that they enjoyed all the savagery of killing; are others upset because they abhor so much what they had felt forced by circumstance to do? For all, they had had the sanction of the group (in fact, the pressure of the group) to do things that, as individuals, the overwhelming majority would never have felt able to do. And in the group they had forged a secret bond of shared experiences, of fear and killing and group regression. In wending their way home alone, they were suddenly bereft of the support of the group and *mourning* its passing. This I would offer in supplement to Jaffe's perspective on the depressions so commonly seen among the returnees ". . .that the massively evoked aggressiveness which could not be rechannelled quickly enough, turned instead against the self as depressive affect. . . ." In much milder and more innocent form, we see the same phenomenon in everyday middle class life when teenagers home from a group trip or a camp experience have no thought but to maintain the group contact, call each other instantly upon arriving each at his own home and thus ward off the re-entry each into their own family, for they too have shared adventure in a closed group and "lost their common language with their people."

Two further interesting perspectives (and sets of speculations) derive from Jaffe's data. The first relates to the observation of the apparent exception to the sense of anticlimax, of depressive loss and mourning in those fighting units which ended up in Jerusalem at the Wailing Wall. Here it was stated, "the tension gave way to feelings of festivity and mystic entry into history." Here only could the fighters "open up to joy" but here too the caveat is added that "these feelings did not last long with the soldiers who were not religious." We can add speculatively that it takes an emotional experience as powerful as the recovery of the Wailing Wall and the fusion with 2,000 years of historical yearning, yearning that has been passed on from generation to generation, and now is in the re-establishment of the continuity of history transcended; maybe only an experience of re-established continuity so powerful and fulfilling can reverse and overcome (at least for those receptive to it) the discontinuity and the danger to identify created by the behaviors to which men are forced in war.

The second observation has to do with the time span. We are used (too used) to military campaigns of months and wars of years. We look for major changes and major psychological difficulties in our soldiers who live through the experiences, including all the phases so richly presented by Jaffe. We talk of the inevitable "re-entry shock" of our own soldiers suddenly returning from combat to civilian life. What we see in Jaffe's material is the telescoping of all these sequences into so brief a time span, yet suffering no loss in their individual intensity and clarity. It is a fascinating testament to that plasticity of man that gives us ultimate hope for our capacity for necessary change that can ultimately insure our collective survival.

Which brings me to Jaffe's last and most difficult question, the one on which Freud too foundered, the question of "What Can Stop War?" The famous United Nations quotation, "that war is made in the minds of men" — has as corollary to it of course that so must be the possibility for stopping it. Jaffe by implication holds up the example of the Israeli army as at least a (relative) voice for ultimate peace even in its behaviors during war. She says, "We did not treat them as we expected them to treat us, had the outcome been reversed. It is in the light of these comparisons that our claim to humaneness has to be understood." That the Israeli army (and people) did not treat the vanquished as they themselves would most certainly have been treated had the outcome been reversed is indeed an example of that plasticity, of that possibility for change, that perhaps gives promise that the proclivity for destructive aggression and fearful retaliation can indeed ultimately be broken — amongst all peoples.

Cultural Patterns of Aggression

Pinchas Noy

Man's existence and his survival were forever dependent upon his success in defending himself against his two cardinal enemies: nature and his fellow men. He had to master nature in order to secure his physical needs; and, against his fellow men who contrived to kill him and to rob his property, he had to gather enough strength to defend himself. Since most men were too weak to stand up alone against these foes, they consequently had to unite in groups to follow, as Freud (1933) said in "Why War?": "... the path which led by way of the fact that the superior strength of a single individual could be rivalled by the union of several weak ones, *"L'union fait la force."*

This necessity to unite into greater groups in which "... each individual must surrender his personal liberty to turn his strength to violent uses" (Freud, 1933) required the formulation of a system of laws and regulations that would enable the men of the group to live and act jointly, i.e. to develop a *culture.*

The task of any culture, once established, is to guarantee its very existence. This requires activity in two directions: first, accumulation of enough power to fight against nature and other groups of men threatening the culture, and second, the development of a system for transmitting the values of the culture from one generation to the next.

In order to fulfill these tasks, the culture must bind the basic human drives and utilize them for its own aims. The assumption is that the drive of aggression is used for the first task—that of accumulating and operating power; while the libido is used for the second task—the procreation of offspring and the transmission

111

of the culture's values through them. As will be shown, each of the two tasks is accomplished by the binding of one drive while using the second drive to fasten and secure the structures which operate in the dispensing of the aim-directed drives.

From this viewpoint, it appears superficial to state simply that culture represses or allows the acting out of a drive; for it consists of a more elaborate and complex system which binds, displaces, and channels the basic drives to utilize them for its own needs.

Modern psychoanalysis describes the ego as a structure compounded of systems of inhibitions, thresholds, channels, and regulations active in processing the basic drives in the service of reality. This concept may be broadened to culture, which will here be conceptualized as a complicated structure responsible for the processing of human drives in the service of human needs, the needs for continued existence and procreation.

When speaking about the needs of a culture, we have to realize that those needs vary from one culture to another, and that even within a given culture, they vary from one historical period to another. It thus means that there is no one general structure of culture, but rather a variety of structures, each in a dynamic state of continuous change and development

The aim of this paper is to examine the means by which drives, and particularly aggression, are processed by these cultural structures so that we may obtain an understanding of recent changes occuring in our own present time.

Let us first examine the structures that process *aggression*. This drive is the compelling force of all values united in the concept of *power*. The means for mastering nature in order to utilize it for the achievement of human affluence are included in such values as agricultural, industrial, or scientific power. The means for defending oneself against one's fellow men are included in the value of military power. Most elements of power are dependent upon the collective effort of men, and are therefore dependent on the means for channeling individual aggression into a general pool, available for the use of the group—which may be a military unit, a production group or any other sort of collective unit. A system for the accomplishment of such canalization has to be included within the structure of any culture.

Aggression, by its very nature, is an *individual drive* aroused by the stimulation of interpersonal tensions, such as frustration, envy, competition, etc. Persons who become objects of aggression are usually those closest to the subject and with whom the subject has developed some sort of emotional relationship. However, the persons most apt to become objects for aggression are exactly those toward whom any expression of aggression is prohibited by culture because they mostly belong to the same action group. The objects of aggression of a child are his parents and siblings; of a soldier, his officers and peers; and of a worker, his boss and co-workers.

The free acting out of such aggression may endanger the unity of the group, and must therefore be prohibited. But culture, however, cannot allow itself simply to use the mechanisms of repression and reaction formation in order to eliminate aggression, because it needs the same aggression for its own purposes. It needs it as a driving force for the combined enterprise of the group, to fight its common opponents and enemies. The trouble is that the larger the group, the more remote are the enemies to each individual, physically as well as emotionally. A peasant, for example, may hate his neighbor whose sheep always trespass on his property, but he has no reason whatsoever to hate an unseen enemy living beyond the mountains. Nevertheless, because of the possibility that some day he may find himself fighting this remote enemy and would need his neighbor alongside him, he must hate his far away foe and love his neighbor. To achieve this rechanneling of emotion, aggression must be displaced and projected against the common enemies of the group. In other words, aggression arising originally as a result of intergroup tensions must be redirected against extragroup objects. Such a shift is accomplished mainly by the actions of two mechanisms — *displacement and projection.*

According to Freud, the structure responsible for the processing of aggression is formed and maintained by the aid of the other drive—the libido. To quote from "Why War?" (1933): "... a community is held together by two things: the compelling force of violence and the emotional ties (identification is the technical name) between its members..." It means that the libido, the drive that determines identification, is required in order to enable the processing of aggression.

The whole structure is a dynamic one, since the equilibrium among its different parts varies according to the immediate needs of reality for the investment of aggression. In times of peace when no aggression is required against extragroup objects, the activity of displacement and projection is reduced, identification decreases and the expression of more intragroup aggression is allowable. The possible result may be a reactivation of various political, ethnic, religious, or inter-class struggles which were dormant within the group until then. However, when confronting the danger of an impending war, the element of intragroup identification is strengthened, intragroup struggles are terminated or deferred, and the mechanisms of displacement and projection are reinforced. A recruiting phase of aggression such as this occurs regularly within any nation that is preparing itself for war. We saw it recently in The People's Republic of China, where the nation was swept by a tremendous wave of identification with its leaders, as well as a wave of aggression against all existing or imaginary enemies. And we, here in this country, still remember the thousands of oppressed and miserable peasants and workers in the Arab countries surrounding us who crowded into the streets and screamed "*Jtbach el Jahud*" ("Slaughter the Jews"), when those countries were preparing themselves for the war against us. It was clear then that most of those people who screamed "Jew" never knew what "Jew" meant, what a Jew is, where his country is, or for what reasons he should be slaughtered. But, they all knew very well why they hated their miserable and poor lives, their exploiting effendis and their oppressive regime.

At present, a similar process is slowly occurring in our country where the people's will to continue to fight is being reinforced by the mechanism of projection expressed in the cultivation of the feeling that "the world is against us."

It is difficult to say that the dynamic cultural structure responsible for the processing of aggression always functions so neatly. In many instances it may disintegrate, and aggression, then acted out "wildly," may destroy the whole structure. This may happen when a massive outbreak of intragroup aggression occurs, such as in the case of a civil war. Examples of such "social pathology," like any psychopathology, can teach us a great deal about the normal functioning of the system.

It is known that there are no wars which are as cruel, as brutal, as sadistic, as devoid of any rules or restrictions as civil wars. Kasantzakis, in his book *Pappa Janaros*, describing the Greek Civil War, speaks sardonically about "the sweet pleasure of killing your brother." Many other writers and historians were also impressed and astonished by the enormous amount of aggression displayed during various civil wars.

This phenomenon can be explained according to the hypothesis presented above, which postulates that almost any extragroup aggression is only a displaced one, and like any displaced energy, it loses its intensity and impact along the long chain of displacement. Any expression gains in intensity the closer it comes to its origin, i.e., to the interpersonal situations arousing it. For example, nations may fight one another during a war, but despite having been involved in a most intense struggle, when peace is restored they may, in a relatively short time, "forget" their hatred and live in peace and harmony, as the countries of Western Europe do today. But a quarrel between two ethnic groups living together in the same country or town may not be forgotten for generations.

Let us try to apply this knowledge to our war: We are often overcome by a feeling of hopelessness with regard to any future prospects of peace, particularly when we see the hatred, resentment, and hostility directed by the Arabs against us. But we must remember, indeed, that these feelings are at most a result of displaced and projected aggression, and therefore, like any so-called "symptomatic" aggression, may be redirected against other objects, and hopefully perhaps even rechanneled into constructive and positive outlets.

To complete the picture, let us, after this somewhat exhaustive examination of the cultural structures responsible for ensuring man's physical existence, examine shortly what happens on the second front, that of culture's means for ensuring the transmission of its values from generation to generation.

The assumption that any function of procreation is under the dominance of the libido is taken for granted. But the process of sex and childbearing does not suffice to ensure the survival needs of a culture. A culture has no use for children unless they are educated to absorb and identify themselves with all the values of the given culture. Lidz (1963) shows that the main means for transmitting the values of a culture is the *family*, and if we examine the cultural structures that process and bind the libido, we will observe that all the mechanisms are directed so as to channel any outlet of sex into the institution of the family, while any expression outside this framework is inhibited.

Please allow me to digress a little and to approach another aspect of the topic, which although not directly related to the issue of aggression, has relevance. It is the specific importance of the family structure within the Jewish tradition. No nation or religion in the world has put so much emphasis on the preservation of the family institution as has the Jewish culture. The family was described above as the main means for ensuring the transmission of a culture's values from one generation to the next. But whereas for other nations it was the main means, for the Jewish people, for a very long time, it was the one and only means.

Other nations had other means beside the family to ensure the propagation and survival of their values; this included common land, towns, art, architecture etc. The Jews, on the other hand, were dispersed all over the world and shared no common land, economy or defense. All their national identity and sense of belonging depended exclusively on their faithfulness to their spiritual values; the survival capacity of the Jewish nation, was therefore entirely dependent upon their ability to transmit those values from one generation to the next. Since the cardinal means of transmitting this "*Jidishkeit*" was the family, the Jewish culture was forever anxious that no child should grow up outside the institution of the family. A child that was not educated to absorb the values of the Jewish culture was of no use to it and was therefore even dangerous. Illegitimate children, therefore, were condemned and banned from Jewish society unless adopted by a Jewish family or some surrogate institution. This was done as an act of survival, rejecting any element which might endanger the existence of the culture.

Turning to my main subject I must examine how the family structure is maintained in general. Here we will see the inverse of what was previously shown concerning the structures which process aggression. The family, which is the structure processing the libido in the service of culture, is held together and maintained with the aid of the second drive — aggression. Any attempt to break down the family unit or endanger its formation is confronted by the aggressive reaction of the surrounding society. In many cultures, up to our present time, the only instance where any expression of direct aggression, even murder, is allowable, is in defense of the so-called "purity of the family."

The structures for processing aggression and libido for the needs of culture, as described up to this point, were almost completely static for thousands of years, with slight variations from culture to culture. However, the development of industrial society and modern technology brought many changes in these structures.

The changes regarding aggression are related, as always, to the changes in the patterns of power operation. In pre-industrial society the operation of power was mostly dependent upon the collective effort of men. Military power was dependent on the number of soldiers who were willing to march together as a single unit. The military model in ancient times was the Greek Phalanx where the strength lay in the fact that thousands of soldiers were willing to fight as a single unit, and where each soldier was only a brick in the advancing living wall that overran the enemy.

The production of food and goods was also dependent mainly on the collective effort of the group. The methods of agriculture and production were simple and unchanged for generations, and all that they required of the workers was to follow simple instructions in order to perform the repetitious and automatic work.

What it meant was that, in the service of survival, that is of collecting and operating power, culture forced people to renounce their individuality and personal initiative, to reconcile themselves totally to the rules of their group. As a matter of fact, all cultures, philosophies, and religions of ancient times cultivated and safe-

guarded these values of reconciliation, constancy, and renunciation of individuality. At that time, any person who attempted
to rebel and who expressed some sort of original and novel idea
was condemned or executed because he presented a threat to the
existing cultural system.

The rapid development of industrial society marked by the
advances in science and technology required basic changes in
these static patterns. The discoveries of science and the progress of
technology called for people with specific talents and professional
abilities. The development of new industries required persons of
energetic ability and initiative. The military, now using more and
more sophisticated weapons and machinery, required soldiers who
possessed ability, skill, and initiative. All these new demands
resulted in a gradual change in the entire economic, social, and
educational systems in the direction of encouraging and cultivating
a greater degree of individuality, originality, and creativity.
These changes in culture also influenced the political and economic
systems which had to adapt themselves to the new requirements.
Most autocratic regimes in the Western world began to disappear
and gave way to the democratic and liberal systems which were
based on such values as personal and economic rights and the
freedom of the individual to strive toward his self-realization.

Concerning power and aggression, these changes resulted in the
division of the firm structure processing aggression. The accumulation and operation of power was no longer merely a group
effort, but gradually became an individual enterprise. Along with
it, all that characterizes power operations such as competition,
rivalry, envy and hatred, entered into the life of the group.
Aggression could no longer be sanctioned only as a group effort, it
now entered into an ever growing part of the interpersonal relations
within the group.

The system of culture's defense mechanisms responsible for the
processing of aggression also had to adapt itself to the changes
which were now imposed upon it by this new situation. The task
became a more complex one. On the one hand, it did not change:
the unity of the group still had to be secured and aggression still
had to be displaced and projected to be available for the group aims.
But, in addition, the "free play" among the various forces inside

the group had to be implemented, a process which required the investment of a considerable amount of aggression. The system, therefore, had to allow intragroup investment of aggression, but at the same time had to control this aggression so that it would not endanger the existence of the group and its ability to act against outer objects.

On a more concrete level, the problem is one of forming a group in which everyone would be allowed to use enough power to destroy his fellow neighbor economically, but never permitted to harm him physically; where one would be allowed to use every possible "trick" to knock his competitor out of business and even frighten him with his potential inability to provide for the needs of his wife and children, but yet not be permitted to touch that man's children in any way.

The problem became how to channel the *differential* investment of aggression, so that it would be reinforced in its free consumption in one sector, while inhibited in the adjacent sector. This task required strengthening of the whole system of interpersonal restraint in order to prevent any "leakage" of aggression into any of the prohibited channels. The results are evident throughout the industrial centers all over the world. Human relations have become more and more formal; courtesy and politeness among men have sometimes grown to a grotesque degree. Emotional and warm human relationships are sacrificed and loneliness and alienation fill the space which is devoid of all human interest. Representative of this condition is the life of the typical New Yorker whose inter-personal relations are dominated by the "Shma Israel" of the New York religion— "I don't want to get involved."

It appears that human groups can safeguard their interpersonal relationships from the acting out of uncontrolled aggression only at the cost of eliminating emotionality and spontaneity from these relationships. These elements are allowed expression only among very close friends and relatives, amongst whom no economic competition exists.

It would be an overstatement, though, to say that this system has really succeeded in differentiating permitted and prohibited aggression. Anyone familiar with the American economic system knows how much blatant aggression has penetrated the entire system so that many times profit is made with the aid of "muscle." And if one is repeatedly surprised by the fact that most Western countries could not eradicate so called "organized crime," one can only conclude that it cannot be abolished because it has become an integral part of the system.

The last decade has confronted us with many meaningful cultural changes, changes which will certainly influence our entire future way of living, including the patterns for the processing of human drives.

In another paper (Noy, 1970) I tried to show that the impending cultural changes which are presently expressed in what is called "the youth protest" are really the first signs of a far reaching revolution which will influence all our patterns of behavior, thinking and education.

From amongst all these changes mentioned in my other paper, those that are relevant to our present discussion, are the changes already taking place in the concept of *power*. Since power, as pointed out previously, is the main channel for the investment of aggression, we must expect a radical change in culture's structure for processing aggression as a result of these expected changes in the concept of power.

What are these changes?

The build-up of industrial and economic power in the Western world has reached a point near saturation, where the production potential is almost infinite and is limited only by the consumer's needs. When the state is reached when every nation possesses such unlimited industrial potential and will be able to provide far more than it will actually need, the industrial potential will no longer serve as a means for national strength.

As for military strength, the Big Powers of today have already accumulated enough power to destroy one another several times over within a few hours. Thus, for the first time in history, a situation has been created in which a nation's survival no longer depends on its potential power, but rather on its skill in knowing how *not to use* this power.

Even in the struggles where military might may still be an advantage, as in the many so-called "small wars" now taking place in the world, the operation of power no longer requires the investment of aggression. The soldier involved in battles in the past could not function without being motivated by aggression. He could not put a sword through the body of his enemy without feeling hate for him, or without enjoying the actual act of killing. Modern warfare, however, is, and will be more and more in the future, a technological struggle in which the soldiers of the opposing sides will not actually confront a real living enemy, but will only operate the technical instruments of war.

The skillful operation of these technical instruments requires a coolheaded, quick-thinking, and emotionally detached soldier. In a dogfight between two supersonic jets, for instance, when life and death depend upon the ability of the pilot to plan and decide his action within a fraction of a second, the one blinded by rage and hate would certainly to be the one to lose. Only the one able to act logically and unemotionally would be able to survive.

This rule is, more than in any other war, demonstrated in our own national war. Here, millions of people, motivated by hatred, fanaticism and hostility, tried, and continue to try to overrun and exterminate a small nation which is only looking for peace and the termination of the existing hostility — and they failed.

In accordance with this new state, everything connected with power has already begun and will continue to lose value, and this has already begun to influence the ideology of Western society. As always happens, in times of social and cultural upheaval, the young are the first to react to the changes since they are the most sensitive strata of society, with their intuition always open to sensing the new, even while it is still forming.

If we examine the spirit of the youth protest taking place today, we will see that they behave as though the time has come to do away with aggression as a means of solving problems between human groups. They talk about a new culture of "flowers" and "love" and despise any sort of desire or eagerness for power. It is also interesting to note that the main image of power in our culture, the "masculine ideal," has lost all meaning for them. For centuries, the man has been the incarnation of the Western world's aspiration for power: the tough, strong, courageous, clear-headed, and goal-oriented man, who constantly strove for the acquisition of power, whether by climbing in military rank, academic achievement, political influence or by amassing wealth. As they abandon this image of man, the young also reject the polarization between the image of the "strong man" and the "weak woman." Instead they have shifted toward a gradual approximation of the two images toward a middle line; and today we see long-haired men who wear jewelry and women who dress and act as freely as men.

It is unfortunate that we, as psychoanalysts, cannot share the optimistic hope that the time of aggression has passed. We must be a little more pessimistic, because we know that aggression as a basic drive, cannot be eroded, and certainly cannot be abolished by changing its social purposefulness.

On the contrary, we have good reason to worry about the new state, because what is really apt to happen is that all the traditional cultural channels for the processing and binding of aggression will become clogged, forcing its expression in other ways.

With the reduction of the value of power and the prospect of a future when man's survival will no longer be dependent upon the operation of power, the whole structure created by culture for the processing of aggression becomes useless. The first signs of the disintegration of this structure are already appearing at present. When we hear of the outbreaks of aggression now taking place all over the Western world, we are repeatedly impressed by the aimlessness of these expressions of violence, which seem to be acts of bare aggression, stripped of any sort of ideological cover. Such preliminary signs sometimes give rise to the anxiety that the breakdown of the old structures will lead to a new era, one of acting out uninhibited and chaotic aggression.

As psychoanalysts, although unable to be optimistic enough to believe that aggression can be eliminated, we nevertheless have no reason to go to the other extreme and anticipate times of chaotic aggression. We know that culture has, and will always have, its defense mechanisms to guarantee the channeling of aggression. We can also be sure that when one pattern of defense proves inadequate, a new pattern will take its place. The history of culture proves that culture as a dynamic system is always able to adapt itself to the changing needs of human existence.

The first signs of such a new pattern are already evident. Freud always stressed the fact that the main device for combating aggression is the libido, and now we are really confronting an enormous growth of everything related to sex and love. We sometimes wonder how the influence of hundreds of years of the repression of sex were cast off within several years, and how things prohibited and condemned by culture only yesterday are now open, acceptable and legal.

If we examine the contemporary youth's preoccupation with sex and love, we must note that it often seems to be a compulsive activity, as though they were trying to seduce themselves into believing that they *should have*, and be busy with, love and sex all the time. This compulsive preoccupation betrays, as any compulsive behavior does, the defensive elements included in the new era of so-called "sexual freedom."

But that is not the only explanation for the "sexual revolution" now taking place. This phenomenon has its causes in various social events, including the changing dynamics of the family, all issues which are beyond the scope of this paper. But beyond all these other causes, sex is used today as one of the main means of defense against the danger of an outbreak of aggression, which has been freed from its traditional structures.

What structure will evolve to permit culture to adapt in order to cope with its future needs is still unknown. Freud (1930) concluded his essay "Civilization and Its Discontents" with this statement: "The fateful question for the human species seems to me to be, whether and to what extent their cultural development will succeed in mastering the disturbance of their communal life by the human instinct of aggression and self-destruction" (p. 82). Today, as in the days when Freud wrote this statement, we can only conclude by repeating the question with which Freud finished that essay: "But who can foresee with what success and with what result?"

REFERENCES

1. Freud, S. (1930) *Civilization and Its Discontents*, London: The Hogarth Press, 1963.

2. Freud, S. (1933) "Why War?" in *Collected Papers*, Vol. V, pp. 273–287.

3. Lidz, T. *The Family and Human Adaptation*, New York: International Universities Press, 1963.

4. Noy, P. "The Youth Protest" and the "Age of Creativity" *J. Creative Behavior* 4: 223–233, 1970.

Another View

Arnold Rogow

With respect to Noy's paper, I have some questions of definition. It is not really clear to me what he means by the term "power." Social scientists have been wrestling with the word power for a long time, and cannot agree on what it means. And some have given up using it on the grounds that it is not definable. There are many varieties of power: economic power, political power, military power, and as you know there is even psychological power, as in the phrase to "psych out" someone, referring to a situation where one person has a clear psychological advantage. These kinds of power differ from each other. Power for General Motors is not the same as power for the Pentagon. The power of the United States is a very special kind of power.

I also want to raise the question: if power is so elementary and basic, why isn't it used in all cases, where the power side has the advantage? Why doesn't the United States destroy Cuba, for example, as many Americans would like to do? Obviously such questions of the limits of power, the extent to which power is used, when it is and when it is not, are very important, and these questions I find missing in Noy's paper. Of course, one cannot include everything. But I think these are important questions because he makes a good deal of the use of power and the importance of power as a motive in human affairs.

It also is not clear, at least to me, what Noy means by aggression. He states at one point, "Aggression is used to accumulate and operate power." I am not sure what that means. And he also says "Aggression is the compelling force of all values united in the concept of power." Again I am not sure what is meant by

"... united in the concept of power." Does this imply that there is an inherent power drive that organizes and channels aggression, that in some sense power is more basic than aggression in human motivation? Does it mean that power is more deeply rooted in the psyche than aggression? If so, this seems to me to be a dubious proposition, not only on psychoanalytic grounds but also in terms of social science.

Noy says aggression is aroused by such conditions as frustration, envy, and competition, But when Noy discusses the Arab-Israeli conflict, he seems to leave this rational approach, so to speak, and talk about hate as a factor in inducing aggression. He tends to talk as if the Arab attitude towards the Israelis is psychopathological and not really based on any of the things previously discussed: frustration, envy, and competition.

The point I wish to make is that there are many kinds of aggression, as there are many kinds of power. And there is always the question of degree. There is a big difference, it seems to me, between aggression in the invasion of another country, for instance, and aggression, let us say, in business. Surely no one intends to go back and forth between one and the other as if there were no basic difference. To use another example, we in the United States cannot agree on what constitutes aggression in our own relations and our relations with other countries. Presidents Nixon and Johnson have said that North Vietnam is the aggressor in Vietnam. President De Gaulle said that the United States was the aggressor power and indeed the most dangerous threat to world peace. How does one reconcile these two statements? Obviously you have to define what you mean by aggression to get anywhere. So much for problems of definition.

I have some reservations about the substantive side of Noy's paper. I may be wrong about this but it appears to me that Noy tends to accept two views about the origins of society which I think have been rejected or at least seriously questioned. One is Freud's view of the primal horde, as set forth in *Totem and Taboo*, which, by implication at least, Noy appears to accept to some degree. I thought that this assumption of Freud's had been rejected by all cultural anthropologists and most psychoanalysts. I am a little surprised, therefore, to find Freud quoted as an authority on the origin of society, since there are great doubts about the basis for his generalizations.

Further, Noy also seems to take the social contract theory, which we associate with John Locke and Thomas Hobbes, as the literal truth when he says that society originated when men emerged from a state of nature to organize some kind of government. This was intended as more of a metaphor, more as suggestive of the conditions of civilized life as viewed by Hobbes, Locke, and other social contract theorists. They did not intend to be taken literally, and indeed we have no evidence whatever that this is how society started. We do not know how it began.

The point that Locke and Hobbes were making is that unless there is a civil society, unless there is a social contract setting forth rights and obligations, nothing is secure. Nothing is protected. But that is a different point than Dr. Noy is making.

I also have some reservations about his notion that the most intense aggressive impulses are always felt toward those closest to the subject. Certainly there may be much aggression between parents and children and between siblings, who after all constiute the whole of a child's world for a long time. The only ones he can attack are his brothers and sisters and parents. So, too, there may be much aggression between employers and employees (but this may have a very real economic basis). But is the principal object of a soldier's aggression his officers and peers? That strikes me as rather strange. I do not think this is true of modern democratic armies. It might have been true of past armies, where the soldiers were beaten regularly by their officers, as in the days of Wellington. It is certainly not true of World War II, in my experience. I doubt if it is true of the Israeli army as it has been depicted here.

But in any event, it seems to me that the basic difficulty is Noy's assumption that aggression within the primary group is more or less natural, but that aggression outside of the primary group is a result of displacement and projection. No one can deny that the function of war propaganda is to promote such displacement and projection of private motives of all sorts onto a real or imaginary enemy. The function of this propaganda is to whip up hatred and so on.

But I think that the reverse of Noy's proposition is actually more true, namely, that there are strong cultural sanctions against intra-group aggression, against what happens in the family and society. To the extent that these sanctions work, aggression is under control within the family and within the community. *No such sanctions exist against aggression directed at outsiders.* If a group or individual is stigmatized as an outsider, it follows that the most intense aggression can be expressed and even condoned and re-warded. It follows for example, that there can be genocide, there can be terrible destruction and terrible death. This is precisely the experience of our own time.

Contrary to Noy's argument, it seems to me that civil wars are not the most destructive because they seldom end in the total annihilation of the other side. Perhaps in the old days such wars were terribly destructive because of death through infection of wounds. Nowadays total annihilation is a possibility when the other side is regarded not as a part of a society but as something inferior to it, something different from it, something outside of it altogether.

Indeed, when we look at past wars in any detail, we are struck by the fact that they were very different phenomena from modern warfare. The American Indians, for example, did not destroy each other's societies, although they would fight all day. But at the end of the day there would be twelve dead Indians or thereabouts. This suggests that perhaps, in an Indian society, there was a certain amount of ritual in the whooping and yelling and hollering and war dancing and so on which Westerners and the white man have always interpreted literally as ferocity.

In the American Civil War, I think the major cause of death was infections and diseases, not just wounds incurred on the battle-field itself. In any case, none of this compares with the slaughter of the six million Jews by the Nazis. That was not a civil war. Jews were not fighting the Nazis. Nor did the American Civil War compare with the slaughter of the Armenians by the Turks, or the deaths in two World Wars, or what, tragically, may still come about as the result of the intense racial violence in the United States today between whites and blacks. There are even some Americans who think the United States is moving towards another final solution with reference to black citizens.

Of course, the Arabs quarrel and fight among themselves but I am sure that their most intense hatred is aimed at the Jewish State which they wish to destroy. My point is that sanctions which operate in the primary group where they control and, to a certain extent, regulate hostility and aggression, are missing in the inter-group situation. And this it seems to me is the major problem of our time. We have no compunctions whatever about killing anyone deemed to be inferior, or evil or Communist or whatever. I can go further and say that *we reward the absence of sanctions*, we reward aggression in all sorts of subtle as well as visible ways. I am struck by two facts related to the social underwriting or lack of under-writing of superego functions that serve to limit aggression. On one hand, the United States Government finds it increasingly difficult to admit the claims of conscience. You perhaps know about the question of Conscientious Objection. Until recently, any one refusing to kill on the basis of nonreligious or ethical grounds was forced either to leave the country or to go to prison. Many of them are in jail.

When the Supreme Court finally ruled that a CO can object reasonably to the war on the grounds of ethical convictions, the head of the draft board then said that this is not as simple as it might appear. To qualify as a conscientious objector, a man would have to prove that he had been a CO for years, and that he objected to all wars, not just the one in Vietnam. He has to prove a long history of ethical, philosophical and moral beliefs before the draft board will accept his position. This is only one of many examples.

In general, the role of superego restriction in the United States has diminished in recent years. Perhaps it is true to say that we have become more and more what might be called an acting-out society, where more and more expression is permitted in the way of aggres-sion, in the way of violence, in the way of id impulses of all kinds. We have become a society which is tolerant of sexual permissive-ness in all of its forms, and at the same time we have become increasingly tolerant of violence in all sorts of areas. Even though I cannot prove it, I am tempted to suggest that Vietnam is leading to a new way of behavior for American soldiers. And it is in Vietnam that you find in extreme form certain tendencies I have been discussing. On one hand, a weakening of superego restrictions leading to the murder of women and children and the needless destruction of unarmed villages, and on the other hand, the increasing frequency of rape, which I think is a new problem in the American Army. These developments in Vietnam express in extreme form some clear-cut behavioral tendencies present on the home front.

It is probably true, as Noy comments, that in some societies internal violence increases when external violence decreases. But not always. And again, to return to the United States which I know best, the United States has become more violent during a war, more violent in terms of its internal politics, and I believe that the violence in American society would decrease rather than increase if the war were brought to an end. So something of the opposite of what Noy said is the rule may characterize the United States if and when the Vietnam war comes to an end, which of course is a big "if".

Much depends on what factors are involved in the rise and fall of aggression. Here I think Noy has some of his emphasis in the wrong place. I do not feel that all aggressive behavior on the campuses and in the cities is aimless, although some of it is, to be sure. Many of the angry students are responding to some very real problems: the depersonalization of the American University for example, its self-corruption with military contracts, its indulgence of professors who are over-paid and under-worked and who above all try to avoid teaching. The fact is that in many universities in America the thing to do is *not* to teach. The most prestigious professors teach nothing at all, or very little. The students are reacting to this in the one way they know how, in any effort to get attention from the university authorities who were indifferent to these problems for a very long time. Until recently, no one was more inaccessible in the United States, except perhaps the President of the country, than the President of the university.

The frustration of the black is a very real one. If what Noy means by violence is black violence, he does not spell out what groups he has in mind. I think it results from hopelessness and despair. And the blacks in America have a lot to feel hopeless and despairing about. I think their despair is going to get worse unless something is done about their condition. And I am not sure anything will be done.

Now of course some of the violence is due to the breakdown of superego controls, to regression to a kind of primary process behavior and to poor ego development. Let us grant this. But a great many of the students, it seems to me, have basically turned against aggression in a way that perhaps psychoanalysts find hard to accept. There are new patterns emerging in some of these kids which do not fit the Freudian model, do not fit what we consider to be the basic essentials of psychoanalytic theory in certain respects. I think some of these students are really committed deeply to peace, to *not* being aggressive, to *not* going to war. I do not think, for example that some of these kids will ever fight again except in pure self-defense. I think they will remain outside the formal structure of the "Garrison State." They will fight if someone attacks them. I do not think they will ever fight in a foreign war allegedly waged on behalf of peace, truth, beauty, justice.

But I agree that Noy rightly points out the central problem, which is how to direct aggressive impulses into peaceful channels, how to find, in the phrase of William James, a moral equivalent for war. No one has solved this problem and I think there is a very good reason why no one has solved this problem. I do not think it has been sufficiently touched on in this volume, quite apart from any Thanatos theory: *war is a very desirable state for certain nations. I might even say an essential state, and for certain individuals.* In the United States war has by far paid off much more handsomely than peace.

In the United States, war has generated much prosperity, especially during World War II. It is the single most important factor in ending the great depression of the 30's. It has raised living standards. It has generated wealth to a degree unprecedented. It has redistributed some of this wealth. Even the blacks have benefited because their incomes and job opportunities have increased. It has improved the general health of the nation. It has conferred innumerable benefits on that class of citizens known as veterans who thereafter are taken care of at a level which is well beyond the level most of them would have reached had there been no war. It has promoted innumerable careers, and given many men and women opportunities for careers they would never have had otherwise. And above all, it has given the nation a sense of purpose. What substitute can you find for this? The answer is: we have found none up to now. Perhaps the United States is in deep trouble because it has found nothing to take the place of a war which everyone can join in and agree to.

Now, the Vietnam war is not that kind of war. You can argue that the Vietnam war is a marginal war in terms of economic conditions but it is already clear that if the Vietnam war is terminated, sections of the United States are going to experience major economic trouble. Some sections, such as California where there is much industry, are already facing widespread unemployment and other general economic hardship. No one, in other words, has worked out an American solution to the problem of "war as the health of the state." This is the phrase of Randolph Bourne, used about 50 years ago, and it holds for the American state today. That is one reason, perhaps the main resaon, why Americans are so often at war. We have fought more wars since 1789 than any country in the world. I personally have little doubt whatever that when the Vietnam war ends, it will be followed by some other adventure somewhere else. Perhaps in the Middle East.

Perhaps the real reason for the troubles today, and one main reason why aggression is so widespread in human affairs, is that to some extent it works. It does something for nations as well as individuals, quite apart from satisfying a basic urge toward aggression in the human psyche.

It may be that the Vietnam war will change this historic relationship in the United States between war and the society at large. The Vietnam conflict is the first war in American history that has not worked on a large scale basis to promote cohesion and submerge domestic problems of importance; in fact, it has largely served opposite ends, no doubt partly because it cannot be won and has already set a record as the longest war in our history. There is every prospect of increasing violence as long as the war continues, and who knows in what directions at home and abroad this violence will tend? It would be very useful indeed for psychoanalysts and their organizations to direct some attention to this and related questions.

The major problem in this sphere may be the problem of finding ways to promote consensus within societies and between nations, and the development of sanctions which will discourage aggression toward outsiders as well as insiders. Put another way, the problem is how to encourage feeling that the ties which bind us are stronger than those that divide us, that we are not just Israelis and Arabs, or Vietcong and Americans, or whites and blacks, but fellow human beings with common hopes and aspirations. How to achieve this result may be the most pressing problem of our time.

Notes on the Motivations for War*

Samuel Atkin

Introduction

Thirty-five years ago Sigmund Freud, in dealing with the question, "Why War?" applied his dual instinct theory. How does that question present itself today to a psychoanalyst? And how does he go about answering it?

As analysts, our first inclination is to look for the instinctual sources of war. It is the study of man's aggressivity that immediately engages us, even though we know that there have been cultures in which war, as organized social activity, did not exist. Still, this particularly destructive variety of cultural expression persistently begs for an explanation in terms of drive theory, since we assume that the evolution of man's instinctual equipment goes very far back, and that the resultant psychic organization must have remained essentially unaltered since the dawn of human history.

We are at once challenged by the fact that war is a *social* institution, rather than a direct, individual expression of man's aggressive drives. Psychoanalysis so far offers no clear-cut idea of the innate psychological factors that enter into the social behavior involved in the institution of war. Although we know that ultimately the locus of social action is in the individual mind, there are many factors in the group process — which has its own laws, observable and definable by its own methods — that may lie out-

* I am indebted to my colleagues in the "Study Group on Aggression" (Psychoanalytic Research and Development Fund), in whose deliberations I have participated since January 1969.

side the realm of psychology. Whatever the psychological components that enter into war-making, we are dealing with a hybrid entity, which does not lend itself readily to comprehension. The phrase, "psychological motivations for war" thus remains, psychoanalytically speaking, a vague concept, Common sense says we should have an answer, but it is thus far inaccessible to our psychoanalytic formulations.

We must therefore attempt to split off from the larger problem of "war motivation" those internal, primarily emotional factors that must ultimately bear on the individual's relationship to war. These are the psychoanalytically observable *instinctual* components that enter into what I call "war readiness" — a term I have borrowed from Edward Glover, but which I use in a different sense.

I would define war readiness as that *state of mind*, partly conscious but largely unconscious, that is *genetically antecedent* to the social and psychological behavior involved in the war institution. Being purely psychological, it is to be differentiated from war preparedness, which is an integral function of the war institution. It is also to be differentiated from war mindedness, which is the psychological response to the demands of war preparedness.

The study of the *unconscious roots* of war readiness lies within our field, irrespective of the specific form and function of the war institution and of the stage in social evolution at which it makes its appearance. This same constellation of drives and motives may enter into many different forms of societal expression, of which — given other social conditions and other social determinants — war need not be the most characteristic.

Although the focus of our interest in this paper and in this volume is psychological, to comprehend the phenomenon of war requires, to begin with, an inquiry along the lines of political science. We must ask: (1) What is the form and structure of this social phenomenon? (2) How does the social institution of war fit into the functioning of the community organization as a whole? (3) How does this institution function in times of peace?

We can make two assumptions about man's social institutions. One is that man has been existing in a community with social institutions ever since that evolutional dawn that is lost in prehistory. The other is that the evolution of *any particular social institution* — the social institution of war is one example — can be very rapid and can also be of quite recent origin. This is an important distinction from the basically constant instinctual organization subsumed under war readiness.

Although there has probably always been some kind of war making in accordance with the cultural patterns of tribal societies, some of it would bear only the faintest resemblance to war as we now observe it. The prevalent view is that war is not a ubiquitous expression of man's inherent aggressivity, a universal human activity.[1]

The war institution as we now know it is a comparatively recent historical phenomenon, no older than man's recorded history. It began at that stage of civilization at which man emerged from tribal societies and proceeded to organize larger and ever more complex political units eventuating in the modern autonomous and sovereign states. It was in these latter that the war institution became a *constant* and *inevitable* factor!

Within the state, the official use of force and violence promoted peace and law, so that a relative peace prevailed among the individuals, as well as among the various social groups contained within it. But the sovereign state, in facing *outward* toward other sovereign states, dealt with them in terms of guarded, yet often unmitigated hostility, cold self-interest, and apprehensive vigilance. It established military organization to run a military machine and to plan war strategy, while a diplomatic corps conducted its "foreign affairs" — the understanding on all sides being that the alternative to the hostile suspense that was now called peace would be violent conflict — namely, war.

Let us reduce this state of affairs to a simple formulation. A political unit is made possible only by the fact that men are united in their community under law, as administered by the state, which has a monopoly on violence. Ordinarily not too great an amount of active violence has to be used by the state, since man by and large consents voluntarily to its demands. This is because: (a) the ties that bring men together into social entities are largely libidinal; and (b) man is a social animal, whose social functions are perhaps acquired by way of constitutional endowment, yet are certainly developed in the rearing process. Socialization promotes the displacement of libidinal forces onto social institutions. We find furthermore that the political unit — the nation, the autonomous and sovereign state — is invested with a "collective narcissism" (R. Waelder) of well-nigh megalomanic proportions: patriotism, a sense of national glory, and a readiness for boundless sacrifice and for war.

Toward the outsider, even where there is no hostility, there is, commonly, what may be even worse: an all but total narcissistic indifference. Under the sign of national narcissism, the evaluation of the outsider and his life is highly intolerant; it is liable to verge on the delusional, the paranoid. The sovereign state "on the other side" is, in that respect, the mirror image of this one. We witness here the clean split of emotional ambivalence, with all the libido as centripetal and all the hostility as centrifugal! I know of few clinical phenomena that demonstrate the fact of ambivalence more conclusively.

The Political Unit

The Bronze Age, with the introduction of an advanced technology, most notably the sword, and the evolution of the political unit (subsequently the sovereign state) ushered in the modern war institution. It is essential that we describe more fully that entity of which the war institution is an integral social function.

The political unit is defined by Aron[2] as "a political collectivity that is territorially organized"; it is consistent and *uniform* in its diplomatic-strategic behavior, irrespective of the organization of the political unit, however varied. "International relations are relations among political units, the latter covering the Greek city-states and the Roman and Egyptian empires as well as the European monarchies, the bourgeois republics or the peoples' democracies."[2] In the development of the state since the Renaissance, the "ideal political unit" is the nation where the community of culture[2] and military order meet and coincide to create the political unit, in which all individuals participate in citizenship and more recently, in universal suffrage. It is completely sovereign and totally independent of the 'external world'. This form is called ideal because "when each nation has fulfilled its vocation,

Peace would rule among the collective beings, free and therefore fraternal."

The political unit, or the nation, is composed of a great variety of groups, organized in correspondence with the multitude of human needs, individual and social. These groups are biological (the family), cultural (religions), economic, esthetic, and a host of other types. They may be either permanent and stable, or transient and evanescent. They may be cooperative or they may be conflictual and competitive.

In contrast to the situation in international relations, where there is a complete split in ambivalence, with all the erotic, libidinal components functioning within the group, and all the aggression, hostility, competitiveness and violent conflict directed outward, there are many social institutions in which both cooperation and competition are integral. For example, take labor and management. They cooperate in production, yet have conflicts of interests. Consequently they are essentially stable even though ambivalent.

In striking contrast to the overt aggressivity between political units, we ask, how is the peace of a political unit maintained? What of its intra-national life? Freud, in *Why War?* (1963 [1933] Standard Edition, XXII) states that the community must be maintained permanently, with authorities to see to it that the laws are respected and to superintend the execution of legal acts of violence. The recognition of a community of interests leads to the growth of emotional ties (identifications) between the members of a united group of people — communal feelings that are the true source of their strength. Freud also speaks of "ideals that give expression to important affinities between members." (p. 208). He then goes on to remind us that "the violent solutions of conflicts of interest are not avoided even inside a community. But necessity and common concerns bring such struggles to a swift conclusion with probability of a peaceful solution."

The War Institution[3]

Let us examine more closely the modern war institution. This organ of the national state may be backed by a military class as in a dictatorship, or by the whole citizenry as in a democratic nation, or by some variation of these. In essence, the war institution functions in the same manner and to the same ends irrespective of the political organization.

The two principal concepts of military strategy and of diplomatic conduct are, broadly generalized, offensive and defensive. But their political meaning is that of a political unit imposing its will on others and not letting the will of others be imposed on it; i. e., of safeguarding its autonomy, maintaining its own manner of life, resisting subordination of its internal laws, or of its external action to the desire of others.

Of central importance is the absolute and unqualified principle of *sovereignty* in the relationship between states. It is the master theme in strategic-diplomatic activity and foreign relations and the immediate reason for the threat or potential of war.[4] The wish for equality is transferred to this absolute condition.

The desire is for security *and* force, even when they are contradictory. *Power and glory* — the glory of the nation or the idea for which it stands is ever sought for. Other ideas — cultural, linguistic, religious, politico-philosophical — are featured, but they take a subordinate position to national sovereignty per se.[5]

Nations that are autonomous and sovereign "accept the plurality of centers of armed forces," and in international relations they assume "the plurality of autonomous centers of decision... with the implicit risk of war," since "each claims the right to take justice in its *own* hands and to be the sole arbiter of decision to fight or not to fight" (Aron).

The primary characteristic of diplomatic - strategic behavior is that it occurs "in the shadow of war and is therefore obliged to take the relation of forces into account" (R. Aron). This may be contrasted with economic behavior, which is based on *value* or *utility*. Economic motives, of course, figure in many wars, but Aron, like most political scientists, does not give them a Marxian priority.[6]

The political scientist T. H. Pear quotes Emery Peress and writes: "War takes place whenever social units of equal sovereignty come into conflict." He adds: "Few will disagree with the tenet that national sovereignty (as the main stumbling block to peace) is a very recent development and does not arise from original human

nature. Although civilized people have abandoned the idea that
their planet is the center of the world, they do so regard their country; and create an entirely false perspective. . . the primitive method
of observation. . . .is the only method admitted and used by [all the]
national governments. . .resulting in a hopelessly confused and grotesque picture of the world." "Every government constructs its
own mental pattern. . . built around its own centre. . . as the *real*
one". "The citizens of every country will be at all times convinced —
and rightly so — of the infallibility of their views. . . of the world
and history. . . and the objectivity of their conclusions." (p. 33)[7]

Psychoanalysis

As we have noted, war is a social institution in which the factor
of violence is *socially and politically* regulated. "War is not a
relation between man and man but between state and state, in
which individuals are enemies only occasionally, not as men. . .
but as soldiers. ." (Rousseau, *Contrat Social*). . . "individuals
have no motives for hating each other. . Violence is limited to the
clash of armies. . ." It is this gap between individual motivation
and social behavior that must have puzzled Freud when he said
that the *psychological* motivation for war was an obscure problem.[8]

The relationship between individual psychology and social action is constantly confronting us, yet the interfaces between these
modes still mystifies us. Freud, in his dual instinct theory — a
brilliant intellectual device, and sound metapsychologically —
assumed that the same forces (and mechanisms) as operated in
the individual generally held for the community as well.

Putting aside this problem in social psychology for the time
being, I shall confine my inquiry at this point to a consideration
of the individual's "war readiness." (I shall be restricting this
term to those emotional factors that operate in the individual,
and are psychoanalytically observable.) War readiness is the
psychological state of man in relation to the war institution —
both preparation for war and war activity — as he cooperates
with, conforms to, complies with, resists, ignores, despises, or
glories in it. War readiness is not to be confused with war mindedness, which is a mental state of compliance with war activity;
it is also a different dynamic concept from war motivation. It

is rather a psychological disposition or predisposition, attributable mainly to primitive psychological mechanisms that stem from a very early pregenital development. Superego psychology seems to figure very little in it. When we approach war motivation, on the other hand, we seem to be dealing with a higher level of psychic organization, either conscious or preconscious. Here superego elements do enter prominently.[9]

Before proceeding with the psychology of War Readiness, let us pause to examine the phenomenon of the drastic and absolute boundary line that is drawn between the two contrasting emotional attitudes: the emotions invested in the political unit sovereign state, and the attitude towards the outsider-sovereign state. Here is a clear-cut split in ambivalence. All the *libido* is directed toward the political unit and all the *aggressivity* against the foreign state — the stranger. What are the psychological factors that could conceivably account for such a striking state of affairs?

The degree to which psychoanalytic psychology — especially early developmental psychology fits the political facts here is noteworthy. Standing out most prominently is the fact of *ambivalence* — the existence of love-hate in relationship to objects, and the very possibility of its complete split, as manifested in the radical boundary described above. When this primitive psychological state manifests itself in psychopathology, it does so ordinarily in the form of a narcissistic neurosis. The extreme self-centeredness underlying adherence to particular interests and points of view — the self-glorification, self-righteousness and *absolute* conviction of right — all this corresponds to a narcissistic state. Toward the outsider, there is an apprehensive suspicion, a vigilant, suspenseful unfriendliness — and as noted above, in the absence of hostility, what is worse: a callous indifference. Taken together, this bears a striking resemblance to paranoia.

In its original diffused state, ambivalence is a prominent feature of narcissism. Freud describes the earliest state of narcissism as attributing all that is *pleasurable and benign* to oneself and projecting on to the external world all that is *disagreeable, uncomfortable, tension-producing,* and hostile. A narcissistic state that occurs even earlier than unpleasure is *indifference*. When it occurs later in life, Freud calls it "a special case of hate or dislike."

Freud also spoke of a narcissistic link with aggression, including destruction of the object.

Stone[10] has written about the extension of the narcissistic principle into human social organization, and its relation there to the problem of aggression. Glover writes of a projection, a psychic displacement that acts with great vigor in group relations — viz., an attempt to convert an *inner psychic* stimulus (an inner enemy) to an *outer reality* stimulus (an outer enemy).[2,4]

Within the political unit, man must learn to master the hate component of his ambivalent relationship with regard to other members of his own society. "Instinctual problems concerning love and hate can give rise to the most violent conflicts. One particular outcome of violent conflict is the loosening of destructive impulses — which in turn produces still further conflict, [necessitating] the inhibition of violence"[2,4] (p. 206)— and its displacement to group prerogative. "The power lost as a private individual is regained through the group. The repressed hostility lends itself to projection to the outsider." (p. 206). To this can be added the frustrations, the self-sacrifices and the renunciation of narcissistic gratifications that are required for his participation in social life. The role of unconscious homosexuality is closely tied to narcissism and ambivalence. The intensification of the homosexual libido in many group relations in the political unit, and certainly in the war institution, is suggestive. Glover also thought that a strong homosexual fixation reinforces narcissism and produces an accompanying "anxiety readiness." It is suggestive to think of anxiety readiness as a predisposition to war readiness.

In contemplating the displacement of libidinal ties from the family to the social group, one is struck by the part that *kinship* plays in the splitting-off of aggression for projection outwards. Stone[10] refers to the dialectical relationship between the immunities granted by kinship and the intense hostilities that are provoked early in life. Ambivalent homosexual feelings, having been worked through, make possible powerful feelings of fraternal love, as well as its sublimations. In group relations, there is bound to be a diffusion of instinct, with resulting tension and floating anxiety as well as aggressivity seeking an object. This latter is generally directed toward the outsider. Freud posits that hostility toward loved ones stems from ambivalence; aversion to strangers, from narcissism.

We must consider another important fact in modern civilization. In contrast to the conditions that prevail in the family group, most of the group relations in the large and complex political units are within groups ever more distant from the individual. In most economic, political, and cultural groups the relationships are impersonal and may verge on the abstract. The usefulness of the functions of these institutions and the benefits they confer give them stability. This may remain true even when these institutions may develop features objectionable to the individual. This increasing distance of the institution from the individual — particularly the increasing distance between individuals — removes these relationships from those libidinal and compensatory processes and the "immunities granted by kinship" prevailing between members at a closer distance, where sexual aims and aim-inhibited feelings are possible. We would expect an intensification of the aggressivity and ambivalence with the resultant pent up aggression seeking projection on the stranger.

Money-Kyrle[11] points out that, as a consequence of projection on to the outsider, reality testing becomes inoperative, while anal-sadistic fantasies have full play and are able to feed the flames of hate and alienation. Aside from these unconscious effects, the sheer effect of powerful aggression-laden emotions on perception and on judgment is demonstrable.[12]

To return to war readiness: Depending as it does on the early development of the mental apparatus, I would consider it a fairly constant and fixed state. On the other hand, the degree of tension may not only depend on the *internal*, psychological situation; it may be altered by the *external* situation, such as war preparation, war propaganda, or the imminence or outbreak of war.

We can conceive of a "flash point" — representing the culminating effect of those factors that precipitate war *readiness* into war *motivation* or war *mindedness*. This is a point at which the individual reacts, consciously or preconsciously in a variety of ways. One might be the precipitation of a war neurosis; another might be the arousal of traumatic feelings of helplessness about events in that strange world, outside the individual's private world, over which he has no control. A reaction of violent aggression may be the defense.

One "flash point" in the outbreak of war that Glover singles out is the situation in which the tension in the unconscious hostility between males is touched off by an unconscious homosexual regression within the group. This results from social permission to let loose the repressed anal-sadistic drives that have been connected with the sublimated homosexual bonds that had until then effectively reduced the rivalries between males. He asks, but does not answer, at what level of the regression the "flash point" occurs.

A reaction formation against this transition from war readiness to war mindedness may be peace mindedness — a state of mind that is closely related in its dynamics to war mindedness.

Let us not be misled by the extent to which so many essential manifestations of man's life resemble infantile mental states, and also enter into psychopathological formations. In the most mature expressions of object love, such as romantic love, parental love, religious experience, patriotism, creative experience, etc., we find the essential participation of narcissism and drives such as also enter into war readiness.

The characterization of the war institution as a "social psychosis" may very well be merely pejorative and scientifically unsound. The war institution may be regarded instead as a component of the political unit, which is a historic development of the social and cultural life of man, intrinsic in his humanity.

The war institution can thus be seen as a manifestation of the nation's will to survive and to maintain its character. The national self-consciousness and the self-esteem of the citizenry serve to integrate and strengthen the nation. There is much of value in the joy, pride and glory for its citizens who share in this sense of national destiny. The shining flame of glory, as a virtue and a goal, has only recently been dimmed, and then only among some of "us intelligentsia." In "Why War?" Freud wonders whether his and Einstein's pacifism is "constitutional intolerance, an idiosyncrasy," (p. 215) and thus presumably true of only a minority. (In the *New Introductory Lectures* he says: "As regards conscience God hanos de an uneven... piece of work; — a large majority [have been given an] amount scarcely worth mentioning.")

It is the defensive function of projection of aggression, of course, that makes possible the existence of the political unit. It is ego-syntonic and, in most instances, thoroughly acceptable to the individual's morality. For most, patriotism — the exaltation of the group — is a legitimate, acceptable, rationalized displacement of the individual's narcissism. The same legitimacy can be applied to the hate component of ambivalence, the most repressed and the most sacrificed to the civilizing group process.

Can we expect man to "live above his emotional income?" An uninformed emphasis on psychopathology may tend to explain man away instead of explaining him. The ambivalence of human nature is a fact; also man's pregenital instinctual needs must be served. Man needs ambivalent and ambiguous symbols because of his "ambivalence in thought and function."

Only a small portion of the human situation can be subsumed under what is rational, or even what can be described and defined in psychoanalytic terms and concepts. The emotional, irrational aspects of man's mental life reach into the most highly integrated psychic functions. Even in his symbolic functions, and particularly in his language function, the "emotive" category stands side by side with the symbolizing-categorizing faculty, the most prominent in secondary process thought.[13]

Since prognosis involves diagnostic concepts, it is interesting to consider some recommendations for the ending or amelioration of war:

Albert Einstein naively recommended that, to achieve peace, man must decrease as well as control his aggressive drives. I am afraid that this can be realized only by "mutation," — which was actually recommended by one desperate essayist as a cure for war.

The modern era can be described as the age of expanding communication between men in the civilized world — trade, navigation, empire, universal religions, as well as the written language and the printing press — culminating in the almost instantaneous and universal intercommunication of the last century. Some writers (Money-Kyrle[11], Alix Strachey[4], the GAP report[12]) have suggested that increased communication between isolated peoples will advance peace. Others have expressed the belief that international education and enlightenment will achieve it. And yet one recalls the sense of shock and disenchantment that was occasioned by the instantaneous falling apart of the cosmopolitan community of enlightened spirits, at the time of World War I — a collapse of which Freud wrote in "Thoughts on War and Death." (1915, SE XIV).

Some writers, like Franz Alexander,[14] saw as a solution the replacement of autocratic governments by democratic, popular ones, since "the people" are against war. Alas, the burden of evidence indicates that increases in democracy and civil liberties have had no such effect. One example, apart from the relatively recent civil wars — such as those in Russia, the United States, and Britain — are the Napoleonic wars of liberation. In the last century, 1820–1945, the era of the greatest political emancipation, there has been no decrease in the making of wars.

The most striking instance of false hope is the modern industrial state, which is a democracy with no discernible military class and no burning military ideals. It is ruled in its civic life and in its declared international relations by the same moral principles; as the result of advanced technology, there is no demarcation between the production of civil goods and military goods. And yet, with all this, there is no abatement in the war potential. The entire citizenry, without marked distinction from the diplomatic-strategic organization that is still in power, is identified with the state in war preparation and war making. In this system, "There is no damn thing you can do that can't be turned into war," — as Hannah Arendt (p. 25) puts it.[15]

The atomic age has introduced new angles and new horrors, but without altering the basic model. The strategy of atomic deterrence has only increased war preparation while adding a component of passive aggression in the nations that are opposing each other in the Cold War and sputtering conflagratory sparks. All the old attitudes there are still retained, with an increase in the moral dangers. The vastness of the potential has been responsible for the introduction of a numbed incomprehension and a general civic passivity — all the while people are cheering the astronauts and getting poised to throw weapons, this time from the moon. The basic model of "sovereign political unit against the outside world," with the concomitant split in ambivalence, and the constant war potential still remains.

In line with the hopes for peace, mentioned above, which were based on the belief that universal enlightenment and the "growth of civilization works against war," let us dwell for a moment upon Freud's utopian hopes for the rule of reason to end war. In *Why War?* (p. 213) he writes of an "ideal condition, a dictatorship of reason. Nothing else would unite men so completely and tenaciously, *even if there were no emotional ties between them.*" [Italics mine]. This concept of ideas without emotional cathexis having the power to determine human events goes contrary to Freud's crucial doctrine, which is revolutionary in its philosophic implications and basic to his psychoanalysis. In the *Interpretation of Dreams*, he says, "No influence can ever enable us to think without *purposive ideas.*" [Italics mine] (p. 528).[16]

Are we really dealing here with contradictions within scientific thought? No! It is a clash between a scientific thought and a philosophy of life, one bordering on faith. Every age has its own dominant world view. Freud lived in an age where 'enlightenment' (and the foremost place in it was given to "science") bore a messianic mission. H. Arendt, quoting Lessing, states, "education of mankind" would coincide with man's coming of age. She reminds us that Karl Marx said that knowledge would free man from the economic determinism he postulated — equivalent to Freud's lapse in his psychic determinism. Prior to 1890 Freud was strongly influenced in his *Weltanschauung* by Herbert Spencer and Marx, who predicted the withering away of the force of society against the individual, and with it presumably "the withering away of the state" (cf. Lenin, Engels, Marx). Individualism was the most prized spiritual flower of Freud's age, almost the official religion of the times.

It should be pointed out that much of contemporary writing on war contains similar utopian hopes and confidence in the final victory of man's reason over war — even when these conclusions fly in the face of the authors' main thesis.

I. F. Stone[17] expresses this faith in universalism in his plea against Jewish nationalism (Zionism), which he contemptuously calls a "Lilliputian Nationalism." He writes, "Universal values can only be the fruit of universal vision" and he recommends these to the Israelis and the Jews as well. "But wouldn't it be better were the Soviet Union to wipe out anti-Semitism" so the Jews would not long for a national homeland or the Israelis would not hold out a hand of welcome? These Utopian longings are presented as opinions in the realm of practical statesmanship and as statements of political science. They are recommended as practical solutions to desperately urgent human predicaments.

The opposite pole of the dilemma is expressed in Vladimir Jabotinsky's[18] plea for "A Jewish State Now," an address to the House of Lords in 1937 (long before the Holocaust). He describes the position of a people without a land, without a sovereign state, as a "state of permanent disaster," facing "an elemental calamity, a kind of social earthquake." Unless the Jews could "build up their own body social," they are faced with "xenophobia of life itself." This is contrasted to the usual and inevitable prejudices against minorities. I am reporting this not as political propaganda but as the statement of a concept of nationality held to be organically rooted in an unavoidable, almost biological, reality. Is it to these *necessities* that man reacts with his grand dreams of a universal society — of universal peace?

Let us consider further the effect of replacing the instinctual by the intellectual. ("Where Id was, Ego shall be.") It would seem that the balance is weighted *for*, rather than *against* war. It is true that reason means delay, control, reality-testing, so that fantasy has less sway. But decathecting the drives in the civilizing process works counter to sex and pleasure (*Civilization and its Discontents*). And the opposite effect to the one that was indicated above as being hoped for is one possible result of the degradation of objects to symbols; a man is "a category;" "enemy", "kill the enemy!"

Lest we leave all hope behind, an optimistic, long-term view may yet be derived from my line of argument. As we have seen, war is a product of a recent historical evolvement — the sovereign political unit. I have already referred in my introduction to *transient* social and political events (institutions). Unpredictable political alterations deriving from economic, technological, geo-economical or geo-political developments may yet serve to *break up the basic model.*

Psychoanalytic Social Psychology

In our investigation into the psychological motives for war, we have been unable to get very far beyond some insight into war readiness — that is, the individual's predisposition to war-(and peace)-mindedness and its variants.

Some crucial questions arise here: Does the individual contain within himself motives of a psychological order, hitherto unfamiliar to us, yet which find expression in social institutions? Society and culture being at one and the same time a historic continuum outside his person and at the same time somehow his own issue genetically, how is the individual *identified* with society and its institutions? In what way and to what degree is culture *internalized*? Has man a social psyche?[19] How does the individual implicitly and largely non-consciously participate in the social institution of war? (Here the unconscious would have to be something other than the repressed.)

What is there in psychoanalytic theory to help our inquiry and ultimate clarification? Freud's group psychology takes a long step toward the comprehension we seek. Based on individual psychology and explaining a social institution at the *interfaces* of the individual psyche and the group process, Freud's theory of group psychology was a breakthrough into *sociology*.[20] It should have opened up an era of psychoanalytic social psychology. It did not. One wonders why psychoanalysts have not followed Freud into this realm and elaborated his socio-psychological model, applying it to other social institutions.[21]

It is not that psychoanalysts have been unaware of this need. Glover, following Freud, says that "social psychology" starts in the eight-months old infant. Here, in the interaction between infant and mother (and others) is the *interface* in the communication process within which the culture is transmitted to the child.

According to Heinz Hartmann, the mother communicates and transmits the culture through an instance which he designates as the "social compliance" of the child. (This process is a less obscure and more easily understood psychological phenomenon than the more familiar "somatic compliance.") He says that "a given social structure selects and makes effective specific psychic tendencies and their expression in certain developmental trends. . . with an effect on the id, ego and superego and ultimately as. . an essential approach to [the] genetic development of object relations."[22]

Hartmann's idea that the "social situation" selects and affects specific psychic tendencies can be usefully reversed to the following proposition: that the psychic apparatus, in accordance with its individual and unique propensities and organization, responds selectively to the social situation or structure that impinges on it in the rearing process. Furthermore, the "social situation" is ordinarily complex and many-faceted. The selection of the stimuli, or the selective response to stimuli, is a developmental and structuring process and would result, within this social context, in a unique and highly individual or characteristic cultural personality. The response also involves the whole reactive and participating gamut of defenses; non-response, abandonment and flight to narcissism, negation, repression, regression, isolation, turning into the opposite, etc. The resulting socially determined character formation might well be the *anlage* of this individual's response to, relationship with, or identification with the social situations as encountered in the future. It would result in a great variety of attitudes toward any social institution or any other cultural entity. This would also be true of his response to society's demands on the individual in a particular social situation. (Compare the multiplicity of emotional attitudes expressed in the varieties of warmindedness with the preponderantly uniform acceptance of war as manifested in the overt social behavior.)

Let us examine this interface further. When we look more closely at Hartmann's highly abbreviated term, "the social situation," we glimpse a larger problem for our inquiry. We take cognizance of the fact that, in psychoanalytic study, we are ordinarily concerned with and aware of only a fragmentary datum, abstracted from what comprises the "social situation." We study sphincter control training, specifically, or feeding routines or cleanliness training or control of aggression; yet each instance is only *one portion of a cultural complex.* The sociological examination of this cultural constellation (that is, of this "social situation") along with the simultaneous and correlated application of psychoanalytic explication — a simultaneous and correlated sociological and psychoanalytic study of the interaction at the *interfaces* of the organism and society — would constitute the subject for study by psychoanalytic social psychology. This could be extended into the psychology of the *individual's* participation in *social* action.

But psychoanalytic theory has been applied mainly to the study of the family and has remained almost exclusively so preoccupied.[23] The methodology works best in studying intra–family relations as seen from the point of view of the individual. The family as a social group has thus far received relatively little attention, not to speak of the family as a component social group of the larger society.[24] This has led to a conceptual "illusion" (to use the term as a metaphor) — the illusion of the "individual" as somehow being someone with an existence apart from society. Society is thus viewed as an external and often alien and oppressive force.[25]

Freud reconstructs the drama of the primal horde, which puts man on the "path" to culture and civilization.[26] It is the union of peers of the primal horde, triumphing over the tyranny and violence of the father. Their union "now represented law in contrast to the violence of a single individual... [and now] right is the might of a community. It is still the same violence as to methods and purposes." In this theory the aggression (violence) of the individual is displaced onto the group, now newly integrated into a society by these primitive pre-human individuals, who, up to this point, it would seem, had been altogether asocial. The newly formed group — a society of individuals identified with each other — now becomes a civilized, law-governed community.

Sociology and Psychoanalysis (Interdisciplinary)

Let us return to the question of the psychological motivations for war. Thus far we have been looking at war unequivocally as a social institution. When participation in war is not foisted on the individual by external compulsion, his participation in it takes place within the context of group formation. According to Freud, group participation is entered into through the identification of peers with each other, and in their common relation to the command of the leader and the social idea he represents. Furthermore, the internalization of social ideas and their social sanctions brings about the individual's identification with the culture and its values (in this instance, with the war institution.).

In fact, J. R. Pitts[27] remarks that, with the introduction of the concept of the superego, Freud *moved away* from his early theory of constraint of the individual by an external culture or society to an imago of an "individual," who is *confronted* or *opposed* by society, and in any event, stands apart from it.

It is interesting to consider the possibility of another determinant of theory formation — this time a subjective and temperamental one, in relation to Freud's personality. He states that "Culture has an *otherness*, rather than an I-ness or a Me-ness,"... May this not be the *feeling of unreality*, the remoteness from reality that one encounters in many sensitive (and often neurotic) people? The subjective factor may of itself contribute to this exaggeration of the illusion of "individuality," accompanied as this image is by a convincing sense of concreteness and "reality." The subjective factor may be objectified in psychoanalytic theory.

To make more concrete the possibility of an interdisciplinary approach that would bring psychoanalysis closer to a psychoanalytic social psychology, I have chosen the behavioral sociology of George H. Mead.[28] Here we encounter formulations that are remarkably like Freud's in vital ways, yet which lead to a different conception — namely that "the essence of all human experience is social; hence perception and communication are social. The internalization of the 'other,' 'taking the role of the other,' is an intrinsic aspect of human thinking — the unit of the social system is not the 'individual' but the dyadic role expectation, which involves expectations from the self and the alter; this is the social 'me'" (Pitts). There is no "self," no mind, no thought *apart from the social process*, which develops within this social context.

This concept of man is predicated on basic psychological functions and processes postulated by Mead. It carried even further than psychoanalysis the implications of the psychological process of identification and internalization of objects. If it were to be synthesized with Mead's behavioral sociology, Freud's group psychology could be generalized and universalized, so that it could apply to the individual's relationship to and participation in many varieties of social groups.

The most important medium of social communication, or the reification of the social interchange, is language. There is no thought, or mind, or self, or "I" without language.[29] In this theory, man is encountered from the *first* as a social animal, equipped with language, mind and thought; he is virtually unthinkable apart from his social organization. We know practically nothing of the evolutionary transition to this social man.

The "other" in the dyadic relationship postulated by Mead is the keystone both of the individual psyche and of that social unit that is essentially the definition of the individual. Mead's "other" may be regarded as crossing the conceptual path of Freud's alienated "cultural-other." We have here a crossroad of two theories; far apart, yet close together.[30]

Let us again compare these two theories. The psychoanalytic group process consists of the identification by the egos of "peers," and of the relationship of the peer group to the ego ideal, as represented by the leader. In Mead, the internalization in the ego is of *social items* (through the medium of language) — items belonging unequivocally to the culture and to the group. Although not always specifically elaborated, identification between individuals is an inevitable result of both of the processes, presented by Mead and Freud.

Let us try to apply this sociological theory to the variegated relationship of the individual to the war institution. There is the difference encountered between conscious ideas and feelings and effective social roles. It may occur that the cultural items internalized and subsequently introduced into the social act may be only partial; but they have their extension and continuity in the larger cultural constellation and in its history. On the other hand, it may occur that the ego may identify itself with the national ideal (nationalism) on one level and at the same time react against militarism or war, a partial item on another level. The ego may remain unaware of a portion of the "whole" or may actually repress one part of the whole. The striking inconsistencies between the ideas people have about war and the actual roles they fulfill in war preparation and war activity may be explained along these lines.

We see how comprehensive is man's connection with his institutions. It seems more difficult and less productive to view the individual's relationship to his institutions (eg., the war institution) as simply being *compelled by external forces*. Rather, we anticipate that the social institution will prove to be *obligatory for the individual* to an extent that is much greater than a psychoanalyst might have expected.

Clinical Observations

We have seen how limited are the means that the psychological method appears to offer us to probe comprehensively into the psychological motives for war. Our device of separating off war-readiness — which we defined as the individual's predisposition for war activity, and which lends itself to the methods available to us as psychologists — is an inroad into the problem; but the specific question of psychological war motivation still evades our solution.

Let us tackle the problem another way: by observing the degree and manner of the individual's participation in his social institutions. The relationship of the individual to society's demands and expectations for the assumption of roles becomes conscious only when conflict and friction are generated. This occurs when these demands and expectations clash with more personal interests, or where there is a conflict between social roles. Various forms of nonconformity, particularly those that generate conflict or guilt, would then become conscious.

The drives would also become conscious when the social action feeds into a direct gratification of a sublimated instinctual wish. This might occur in connection with religious feeing, patriotism, neighborly sentiment, etc. Aggressiveness that raised the level of intrapsychic conflict, or which increased inter-personal conflicts, might also bring the social-instinctual drives into consciousness.

One would expect then that, ordinarily, compliance to social and cultural demands would find expression, in addition to consciously assumed social activity, in largely unconscious or non-conscious social drives largely acted out with little or no awareness. Where members share values, there is little need for awareness and the motives remain implicit and nonverbal. Where the motives reside in the superego, it is a superego shared with the like-minded members of the group.[31]

What, then, do we actually observe in the psychoanalytic situation?

Before applying the pragmatic test of examining the behavior of patients in the psychoanalytic situation, let us take a look at a "mature" person as he would be perceived at the present stage of clinical psychoanalytic theory. Our description would contain several seemingly paradoxical components: On the one hand, the "mature" man is concerned about his fellow man, is socially responsible, is sensitive to the concerns of the community and is capable of social involvement. Stated in psychoanalytic terms, his libido cathects objects freely and fully; he has a well-developed superego; and he has undergone a comprehensive internalization in his psychic development.

On the other hand, this very man seems in many essential ways to be quite independent of external social reality. He is capable of retaining the integrity of his character even when extreme changes take place in his cultural environment. In psychoanalytic terms, he is "autonomous," relatively "free" from the imperative to conform to social demands and able at times to remain "uninvolved" with society.

I will present some general impressions relating to our theme of a dozen patients in analysis,[32] most of whom have been in analysis for years. In the last six months I have listened to them with the "Why War?" inquiry in mind.

The most obvious "general" observation is that analytic patients *spend very little time talking about matters of social concern* or about impersonal environmental realities. Very little that is not immediately and intensely personal is communicated. Of course, this varies with patients. To a lesser degree it varies with the eventfulness of the times, although it is striking how little repercussion world shaking events have in the analytic hours.

What are we to make of these observations? Are the patients sensibly making the best of the psychotherapeutic situation? Is this a specific effect of the transference on the patients' communications? At first glance these observations seem to confirm the classical psychoanalytic view that the culture has an "otherness" in relation to the individual, in contrast to the "I-ness" which Freud speaks of.

Perhaps something may be learned by studying those patients who *do* talk and those who *do not* talk about the environment in general, and political events in particular, as to what characterizes each group.

In examining the group who talk almost exclusively about personal matters, we find here, to our surprise, the patients with the strongest egos, those with the highest development of a distinct and differentiated self, with rich object relations consonant with substantial internalization and identification, and with fully formed superegos. We have the paradox that the most mature and most socially engaged are the least articulate in the analytic situation about culture and society.

These same patients do talk on social themes where social values are idiosyncratic due to cultural differences between patient and analyst or when there is conflict or guilt about values, or where actual anxiety is present due to current conflicts.

Curiously, it is the asocial and the narcissistically neurotic who are more communicative in the analytic situation about impersonal reality and social concerns. I have found that a great deal of talk and preoccupation with the external environment is correlated with a poorly developed ego or severe pathology. The self is poorly differentiated; there is a defect in ego boundaries. The outside world is highly *personalized*. These patients have difficulty in differentiating less personal social roles from those roles pertaining to their family group membership. Notable is an impaired ability to play the multiplicity of roles inherent in the functioning of an adult. Social attitudes directed toward them are perceived by them as personal; in fact, they have difficulty perceiving the impersonal as such. In the very sick patients, nothing can be conceived of as differentiated from their personal needs — they "use" objects (Winnicott).[33] They consider themselves very "sensitive" and are readily offended or disappointed by the quite appropriate social behavior on the part of others if it does not conform to their private needs.

On closer examination of the sicker patients one finds a poor cathexis of environmental entities as well as of objects. Reality keeps slipping away and needs constantly to be recaptured, by dwelling on it, recalling and recapitulating it, and very actively reorganizing and re-establishing it. When reality is frustrating or threatening, it must be reconstituted *verbally*, so as to allay apprehension and anxiety. These delusion-like formations are usually transient, evanescent and are not organized into a larger gestalt: Denial, projection, intellectualization are readily called into use.

Anna Freud has pointed out that where the superego is poorly formed, objective anxiety is experienced in place of guilt. Usually an aggravated aggressive component increases either guilt or objective anxiety. Contrapunctally, where there is minimal development of civic sentiments (analagous to poor object relations) there is also an analagous uncritical relationship to society and authority, which makes for conformity and a poor differentiation of the self from the environment.

In conclusion: it came to me as a surprise that an objective examination of the communicative behavior of patients in psychoanalysis demonstrated that the more mature individuals, with good object relations concordant with comprehensive internalization, communicate least about social concerns and participation. They live out their social roles *implicitly* and mostly nonconsciously. They *do*, rather than talk.[34] They think (and speak) about their societal involvement only when frictions, conflicts, or problems arise.

One would infer, then, that in the process of internalization there is a restructuring and a synthesis of the social, cultural and moral ideas into the individual's ego. Hence they are not felt as something apart from the person and as belonging to the social realm. They are integrated with the more exquisitely personal and they are thus experienced. When the superego is highly developed, guilt is a *personal* datum, an *inner* fear or tension. The total effect, then, is that unwittingly, when the person is talking about himself, he is simultaneously communicating something about his society, which is part and parcel of his being.

In contrast to these patients are those who talk much about the external environment and on social and cultural themes. These are narcissistic patients whose development has by and large been arrested at the pregenital level and who suffer from narcissistic neurotic problems. Most significant for our reconstruction is their relative failure to *internalize* their environment, and to *synthesize* their socially determined drives with their more discretely personal ones, with a consequent blurring of the boundaries between what is perceived as the inner life and external reality. Those who spent the most time speaking of political events and problems were extremely insecure people, who had great difficulty mastering their aggressive drives.

Among this articulate group I found three different types:

A) Narcissistic patients with a poorly cathected reality world, who are constantly groping for an orientation to their environment. They personalize the environment and have a limited capacity to comprehend reality, as apart from frustration-gratification experience. They are also incapable of differentiating among social roles, even though they are usually able to function more or less adequately in a social role.[35]

B) Better endowed narcissistic patients with a stronger ego, who also falsify and tend to personalize their environment because of a large aggressive component and prominent projective defenses. They suffer to a lesser degree from the same defect as those described above, in assuming and differentiating social roles.

C) Otherwise relatively mature personalities (transference neuroses) whose superego functions are external to them, due to special circumstances of a social (institutional) character. Among these were two priests whose superego was structured and ritualized for them by the church. Consequently they experienced very weak religious sentiments and a paucity of self-conscious, affect-laden moral attitudes and ideas[36] that one would expect in people with a religious vocation. (Is there perhaps a corollary between this situation and the unconscious participation of the individual in the social institution of war, which rules his conduct in accordance with prescribed ritualized behavior?)

Conclusions

With the advent of the advanced technology of the Bronze Age leading to the emergence of the enlarged and increasingly complex political unit, the modern social institution of war was ushered in.

In "Why War?" Freud applied his dual instinct theory to explain *both* the social action of war-making by the community and the individual participation of its members. Thirty-five years later, his theory still illuminates brilliantly many essential formulations of the political scientist about the structure and operation of the war institution.

Freud's biological theory is so broad and general that the *categorical distinctions* between the sociological and psychological modes that are operative in war present no obstacles. It might even be suggested that Freud originated his dual instinct theory in order to be able to explain such destructive human activities as war. Yet that theory does not draw a clear psychological connection between man's aggressive instincts and the *social institutions* of war.

Psychoanalytic theory — with or without the dual instinct theory — does make comprehensible 'war readiness' — that is, the individual's predisposition to war. It has failed so far, however, to answer satisfactorily a host of specific questions about the individual's psychological participation in his social institutions in general, and in the war institution in particular. For example, we cannot account psychoanalytically for the phenomenon, documented by social anthropologists, that where war-making is obligatory to the culture, motivations for war are obligatory in the individual; and conversely, where war-making is not obligatory to the culture, motivations for war appear to be absent in the individual. Nor is there yet any proof that aggressiveness-combativeness in the individual induces war-making in the culture.[1] What is required is the building of a firm conceptual bridge between the sociological and the psychological — between man's culture and his instinctual drives.

Earlier I pointed out the transiency of social institutions and suggested that we might pin our hopes for peace on the possible transiency of the war institution, given certain unforeseeable conditions. This expectation would have to be tampered, however, by the degree to which the war institution does succeed in expressing directly the more fixed instinctual drives.

Some crucial questions arise here: How does the individual implicitly and largely nonconsciously participate in the social institution of war? Does the individual contain within himself motives of a psychological order, hitherto unfamiliar to us, that find expression in his social institutions? Society and culture being a historic continuum outside his person and at the same time his own issue genetically, how is the individual identified with society and its institutions? In what way and to what degree is culture internalized? Has man a social psyche?

Focusing on these questions, clinical evidence seems to indicate the internalization of the culture, and its synthesis in individual character formation. This developmental process seems to be correlated particularly with the capacity to form object relations of constancy, and, notably with the formation of the superego. It is also correlated with the capacity to assume roles, to differentiate between them, and to live them out appropriately.

What is there in psychoanalytic theory to help our inquiry? Freud, in his *Group Psychology and the Analysis of the Ego*, took a long step forward toward the comprehension we seek. Based on individual psychology and explaining social institutions (the church and the army) at the interfaces of the individual psyche and the group process, Freud's theory of group psychology was a breakthrough into *sociology*. It could have opened up an era of psychoanalytic social psychology. One wonders why it did not — why psychoanalysts failed to follow Freud into this realm, and eventually to elaborate and to expand his socio-psychological model, and to apply it to other social institutions.

We believe that a sociological-psychoanalytical study of the interaction at the interfaces of the organism and society is essential if we are to understand man both as the *creator* and the *creature* of his social institutions, the most destructive of which is war. Studies in early child development can be a fruitful source for investigating the socialization process at the interfaces of the individual and his culture.

A comparative, interdisciplinary approach to man's social essence, from the points of view of psychoanalysis and G. H. Mead's behavioral sociology was suggested to illustrate the possibility of broadening the scope of psychoanalytic theory as a social science into a psychoanalytic social psychology.

Some may ask whether dispassionate scientific inquiry into a political entity that is endangering our very survival at this very moment is not fiddling while Rome burns. Let us remind ourselves that in the tradition of psychoanalysis, we analysts equate knowledge and understanding with health and cure. Perhaps knowing and understanding ourselves and our adversaries may yet help to build a world of peace.

REFERENCES

1 Ruth Benedict, in *Patterns of Culture*," New York, Mentor Books, (1947) remarking that we are now in a state of perpetual warfare, nonetheless concluded, from the point of view of cultural anthropology, that warfare is not the expression of an "instinct of pugnacity." The cultural patterns of a community, as expressed in its institutions, determine the expression of the aggressive drive, so that this expression varies in different cultures from a highly individualistic (solo) war activity (among the Plains Indians, the warrior is superior) to warring as a more organized group activity, and to a pacifistic community, as among the Zuni. Benedict regards warring as an *asocial elaboration* of a cultural trait that traditionally runs *counter* to biological drives, a point of view elaborated by A. Kardiner in his studies of the Alor, etc. (This approach is close to that of adaptational psychopathology.)

Glover, in his *War, Peace, and Sadism*, London: Allen Unwin, 1947, in discussing Tribal War as a phase of biological adaptation, emphasizes the role in it of animism and the projection of primitive impulses. He dwells on the relative humaneness of war at that stage, with its rituals, its moral content and its expiations of guilt, and contrasts it with the relatively depersonalized aspects of modern war.

2 Aron, Raymond: *Peace and War*. Gordon City, N.Y.: Doubleday & Co. Inc. 1966.

3 *The Dictionary of Social Science* defines *war* as a uniquely human cultural phenomenon, a socially recognized "deadly quarrel" between sovereign states, to be differentiated from more general "Deadly Quarrels." Our basic definition of war undergoes little qualification as to types of wars listed, the most important being interstate, where political units recognize each other's existence and legitimacy; superstate; and imperial wars. When intragroup conflict attains the intensity of war, as in civil war, the parties in conflict usually organize into states and assume for themselves the prerogatives of sovereign states.

I am indebted to Raymond Aron for most of the content of this section.

4 This bald fact has entered the discussion of war and peace only recently. Psychiatric publications as recent as the GAP Report (1964) give faint recognition to the central role of sovereignty in determining international relations.

Among analysts, Glover characterizes the emphasis on the practicing of "sovereignty" as crucial to war motivation as "dangerous rationalization." "Behind these reality relations are onfantile interests and unconscious psychological factors to territorial aggrandizement." (Glover, above p. 87).Alix Strachey, (*The Unconscious Motives of War: A Psychoanalytic Contribution*. New York: IUP, Inc., 1957) recognizes the importance of the sovereignty factor; but only halfheartedly, since the cardinal realities of political organization and function are not seriously taken into account as a paramount reality. Both these analysts treat the state as a "regressive group formation" [sic] as presumptuous, bumbling, and dispensable, expendable—in short, a nuisance. EG recommends returning to the family as the sole social unit, an unlikely prospect, if not inherently impossible.

5 Nations with a multiple content of these values and cultural entities are in no way different in conduct from more homogeneous nations. "Sovereignty" is accepted as an absolute good by the preponderant majority of citizens of nations. To quote Aron: "The art of politics teaches men to live in peace within collectivities, while it teaches collectivities to live in either peace or war."

6 Aron finds no explanatory evidence for the evolution of modern war, either in reference to the social evolution of prehistoric man or in the evidence of evolutionary changes since modern war came on the scene. He finds the causes for here indicated as constant through historic time and quotes Richardson that wars have not increased from 1820-1945. However, Aron lists Quincy Wright's factors of Bellicosity as contributory, i.e., (a) habits of cruelty (as in

religion, sports, etc.). (b) aggressivity; (c) influence of military morality; (d) tendency to despotism and to centralization (p. 333).

[7] Pear, T. H., Editor: *Psychological Factors of Peace and War*. New York: The Philosophical Library, 1950.

[8] "Two men — the *diplomat* and the *soldier* ... no longer function as individual members but as *representatives* of the collectivities; the ambassador... *is* the political unit in whose name he speaks; the *soldier* on the battlefield *is* the political unit in whose name he kills his opposite number." — Aron, *Op. cit.* p. 112.

[9] One example of this is to be found in the study of the war neuroses which, according to Simmel, Abraham and Freud, are essentially transference neuroses.

[10] Leo Stone: Reflections on the Psychoanalytic Concept of Aggression, Psychoanalytic Quarterly, XL, 1971, pp. 195–224.

[11] Money-Kyrle, R., The meaning of sacrifice, Int. Phychoanal. Library, 1930.

[12] From the GAP Report No. 57, *Psychiatric Aspects of the Prevention of Nuclear War*, 1964.

[13] Atkin, Samuel: Psychoanalytic Considerations of Language and Thought. Psychoanalytic Quarterly, XXXVIII, 1969, pp. 549–582.

[14] Alexander, F.: *Our Age of Unreason. A Study of the Irrational Forces and Social Life*. Philadelphia & New York: J. P. Lippincott Co., 1942.

[15] Arendt, H.: *On Violence*, New York: Harcourt, Brace & Jovanovich, 1970.

[16] Freud, S. *The Interpretation of Dreams* (1900–1), S. E. IV, V.

[17] Stone, I. F.: Holy War. In: *The Israel Arab Reader*. Edited by Walter Laqueur, N.Y.: Bantam Books, 1968.

[18] Jabotinsky, V.: A Jewish State Now: Evidence Submitted to the Palestinian Royal Commission (1937). In: *The Israeli-Arab Reader*, Ibid.

[19] Glover says that the group psychology is a part of the individual's psyche. This may be a part of his Ego Nuclei theory. Op. cit.

[20] S. Freud dealt with the army and the church in his "Group Psychology and the Analysis of the Ego." (1921) S.E. XVII.

[21] Talcott Parsons, after criticizing individual psychologists as well as sociologists for making *ad hoc* extensions from their own theory to that of the others, demonstrates the feasibility of focusing the sociological and the psychoanalytic theories on the same problem by giving a sociological de-

scription of the average American family alongside a psychoanalytic theory of intra-family relationships to very good interpretative and explanatory ends. (Talcott Parsons, "Psychoanalysis and the Social Structure." Psychoanalytic Quarterly, XIX. 1950. p. 577)

22 Heinz Hartmann. "The Application of Psychoanalytic Concepts to Social Science." *Essays on Ego Psychology.* New York: IUP,1964, pp. 90-98.

23 This conceptual stricture — the exclusive preoccupation with the family, as though it were the sole social group — has simultaneously enriched psychoanalysis and limited it. The "family drama" model has been almost exclusively dominant in psychoanalytic investigations in the realm of the social sciences (except for Freud's formulation in *Group Psychology and the Analysis of the Ego*). This is true of Freud's hypothesis of the birth of civilization (in *Totem and Taboo*). Religion, as well as civilization, is conceived of as a neurosis arising out of emotional conflict in the family setting (*Future of an Illusion*).

24 Some analysts regard groups as "pathological formations,"(Alix Strachey, Glover). Glover calls war a "mental disorder of the group." (*War, Peace and Sadism*). Society is, in short, an external tyranny to which the individual is subject.

25 The writings of Marcuse and Fromm are likewise a call to man to free himself from the tyranny of society, thus implying the same kind of dichotomy between the individual and society, a dichotomy genetic as well as existential.

26 This primal horde theory, which is primarily based on the family drama — although paradoxically and circularly, it is supposed to give rise to the human family group and its drama as well — skips over the probability of man's development as a social being from a very much earlier evolutionary time. The origin and formation of man's basic social institutions is hidden from us!

27 Pitts, J.R. Personality and the Social System. In: *Theories of Society* Ed. by Talcott Parsons et al. Glencoe, Ill. The Free Press 1963 p. 685-716.

28 G. H. Mead. *Mind, Self and Society.* Chicago: The University of Chicago Press, 1962. (Actually his views were advanced in the first two decades of the 20th century.)

29 The relative neglect of the crucial significance of language in human psychology can be correlated with the underestimation of his social function. (See also S. Atkin, 13).

30 The meeting of these two theories serves to extend and enlarge each other's conception of man. Each scientific theory complements the other. However, as powrful as Freud is in clinical phenomenological data, so weak is Mead in this respect. Although Mead recognizes Freud's concept of the superego (called the "censor" in the '20s) he never arrives at the recognition of its most important

component—that of "a sense of guilt." He borrows his pale clinical examples —dissociated personalities—from the French school of psychiatry (B. Sidis and Morton Prince, its representatives in the U.S.)

31 The "shared superego" I am projecting approximates Freud's formulation of the mutual identifications by members of a group. Examples of shared values in the psychoanalytic situation are the mutually shared ideal of health, the "psychoanalytic contract" with its shared ethics and rituals, mutual obligations regarding time, money, manners, and the ideals of complete candor and scientific truth.

The interplay between the analyst and patient, as it involves moral values in the psychoanalytic situation, is largely a silent process, although it often becomes dynamic under certain conditions. Analysts tend to underestimate their largely nonconscious value system and insufficiently take into account the shared superego with some patients.

32 My caseload is average for a training analyst of the New York Psychoanalytic Institute: educated, intellectual, mostly sophisticated upper and upper middle-class people who are functioning in the world at a high level of adaptation. Three are in psychoanalytic training. Most of the patients are suffering from character disorders; several are borderline. Two are clearly transference neurotics.

33 Winnicott, D. W.: The Use of an Object. Int. J. Psa. L. 1969, pp. 711–719.

34 "Implicit culture. . . is that section of behavior of which members of the group are unaware." Pear, 1950. p. 23. Ref. 7.

35 All of the patients studied, both the more and less mature personalities, lived out a rich variety of social roles, and this raises some very interesting questions.

"We see individuals who are fixated on a very primitive level: they are anal sadists, sometimes they are almost psychotic. We know a great deal about these people; but we are astonished to discover that they are often marvelously adapted in the social situation. They are able to do all sorts of things, presumably without the instinctual personality equipment that more highly developed people have by way of participation or partnership. How does this happen?"

"In some way, a parallel theme to the question I raised before this—that people of a more primitive organization seem to be able to function so very well in the performance of many functions that are expressions of a higher, more mature development. Is it possible to study these matters analytically, through case material?" (From Group Study on Aggression—Discussion by S. Atkin, republished, New York Psychoanalytic Institute.

[36] We here recall that Freud utilizes the church and the army as his examples of Group Psychology.

Another View

Eliezer Ilan

Atkin outlines broadly the problem of psychological motivation for war. He introduces sociological and historical concepts like the War institution, the political unit, the universality of war and he comes to far reaching suggestions through a synthesis of psychoanalytic theory with a specific sociological theory.

As I have no scientific competence as sociologist or historian, I want to express some thoughts as a layman in these fields and as a psychoanalyst.

Atkin gives a psychoanalytic interpretation of war-readiness and of patriotism in psychopathological terms, defining these tendencies as a collective narcissism of megalomanic proportions character-ized by indifference, intolerance and a paranoid attitude (to the outsider) on the verge of the delusional, with a sharp split of ambivalence: All the libido centripetal to the political unit, all the hostility centrifugal. In a later passage Atkin is reluctant to use these psychopathological formulations and he contends that "for most, patriotism—the exaltation of the group—is a legitimate, acceptable, rationalized displacement of the individual's narcis-sism."

I have certain misgivings about these psychoanalytic formula-tions concerning sociological concepts. They bring us too easily into the realm of over-generalizations and inexact interpretation. I wonder whether both the psychological interpretations of patrio-tism are exact. The pathological variety may be characteristic of a certain chauvinistic, totalitarian type of patriotism, but the for-mulation of patriotism as a legitimate displacement of the indivi-dual's narcissism also seems to me questionable. Is not patriotism

defined as the love for one's country and one's people? It has
probably more to do with object relations than with narcissism.

Another point about the sociological formulations: Atkin writes
of the phenomenon of war readiness in the political units today,
examples of which are the democratic modern industrial states. But
is that a justifiable generalization? Do we not live in a world of rather differently structured political units which have a differently
balanced inner equilibrium? This has a bearing on the aggressive
potential inside of the political unit, and dangerously so outside.
I accept Atkins view of the tense, repressed aggression which is
the individual's reaction to the frustrations, the sacrifices, and
the renunciations of narcissistic gratification that are required
for the individual's participation in social life. In this respect there
are vast differences inside the political units of today which make
for a very different aggressive potential toward other units. We
speak easily of paranoid delusion when we describe the distrust
toward the out-group. But let us not forget that every defense
mechanism has its reality adjustment value too, and that *the lack*
of distrust toward the Nazi regime at its beginning had catastrophic
consequences for the world. I doubt very much if we may speak of
war as the same phenomenon with the same meaning at different
developmental points in history, and certainly we cannot characterize the different political units of our times as having the
same dynamics in respect of their aggressive potential.

But now to a more psychoanalytic aspect of Atkin's paper. He
proposes a new model of amalgamation of a psychoanalytic view point with the behavioral sociology of G. M. Mead.
Since I am not familiar with the writings of Mead, I will concentrate
on the psychoanalytic point of view as characterized by Atkin.
He writes of the persistence in psychoanalytic theory of the image
of the "individual" who is confronted or opposed by society, of
the illusion of the individual as someone being apart from society.

Here I feel Atkin did not include the vast contribution of the
development of object-relation theory within the field of psychoanalytic thought. He quotes G.H. Mead: "The 'other' in the dyadic
relationship is the keystone both of the individual psyche and the
social unit; that is essentially the definition of the individual". Is
this not identical with modern psychoanalytic theory which states

that the dyadic relationship between mother and infant, from birth on, is the keystone of the individual psyche? Processes of communication between the infant and his mother who is a part of her social unit, start long before language communication. So do early introjections of parts of the mother and of the mother as a whole, constant, inner object stage. Winnicott speaks of a feeling of concern for the mother as whole object which may form the basis of an attitude to the world, an attitude of ruth, as against ruthlessness and this before the formation of the superego. The internalization of object relations into the inner psychic world is also the basis of an internal relationship to values, ideas, and such abstractions as love for the fatherland, the mother country, the nation. Freud speaks of group formation as the outcome of identification of members sharing a common cherished object. The tie to such objects which are derivatives — one could also say enrichments — of the primary inner objects, is the basis of our social responsibilities. Preparedness to safeguard these cherished objects and the courage to defend them, is a sign of maturely developed object relations and could hardly be understood in terms of narcissism and self-aggrandizement. The problem of narcissism is a very difficult one, and Freud's early formulations should be perhaps revised in the light of our present knowledge of early mother-infant interaction. But this would lead us too far away from the subject. Sublimated object, like others, can he misused through primitive idealizations, and identification with them, for narcissistic self-inhancement by individuals who suffer from a lack of basic security and basic trust. And this makes for proneness to chauvinism and totalitarianism. I would guess that deep psychoanalytic understanding of object dependencies and relations of the individual to his community and its values will have to be arrived at by analyzing our patients on the couch. Atkin's clinical examples are an excellent beginning in this direction, showing that people with basic security and trust do not speak much of their values and their sublimated objects; these are self-understood realities for them.

A dictatorship of reason is certainly a utopia. But in the *Future of an Illusion* Freud speaks of the soft tenacious voice of reason, and in *Civilization and its Discontents* he reminds us that it is Eros who will make a stand against Thanatos when we are faced with total destruction. I dare to translate this into a hope relevant for our times. If people in those political units, which let them voice their opinion, have enough love for their cherished objects—that is enough social responsibility—and enough reality controlled reason, there may be hope, if not for the total abolition of all wars, at least for avoiding total destruction.

Notes on Some Psychic Motives for War

Erich Gumbel

About 2700 years ago the prophet Isaiah proclaimed: "And they shall beat their swords into ploughshares, and their spears into pruning-hooks: nation shall not lift up sword against nation neither shall they learn war any more." Are these the words of an inspired teacher of mankind, or of him who foretells the future or reveals and interprets the will of God? Much, very much has changed over the centuries, with nature's secrets increasingly unravelled and its forces and functions largely controlled by man. Yet war took its toll of every generation.

In the framework of the Israel Defense Forces, there is a special unit of Pioneering Fighting Youth called Nahal, which has simultaneous responsibility for soldiering and farming. At the 20th anniversary of this Nahal, Prime Minister Golda Meir declared: "When I look at today's youth, I have a feeling of guilt and ask myself, why is it that my generation and the ones that followed us, did not manage to create a better world? Why didn't we succeed in giving our youth a world without wars? After all, there is almost nothing impossible in the world nowadays. Only this — that peoples and nations should live in peace — that seems to be impossible...."

"Why War?," the title given to the correspondence between Einstein and Freud 38 years ago, is the age-old question, perennially posed, about what might be done to free mankind from "the curse of war." Must we see in war man's disastrous fate, his fatal destiny? Is it an integral, inevitable part of human life, as are disease and death? It was said indeed: "War is the way of the world, an all pervasive fact." Not only militarists and politicians,

173

but even most historians seem to see in war the essence of human history, as proven by the way they wrote their books and studies. Or is there any justification in looking at war as an abnormal phenomenon of human society which could, possibly, be done away with? Every time another war breaks out, many people appear honestly surprised that this could happen again, as if it were nothing but an unlucky incident.

The world's noblest minds have bent their energies to prevent the outbreak of war, to root out and abolish war once and for all. Freud concluded his letter to Einstein: "it may not be Utopian to hope that these two factors, the cultural attitude and the justified dread of the consequences of a future war, may result in a measurable time in putting an end to the waging of war. By what paths or by what side-tracks this will come about, we cannot guess, but one thing we *can* say: whatever fosters the growth of civilization works at the same time against war."

Such optimistic belief can scarcely be based on historical experience. According to Ashley Montagu, in *The Human Revolution*, "the fact is that as man has advanced in civilization, he has become increasingly, not less, violent and warlike." Even in Freud's own thinking, embedded in psychoanalytic theory, there is many a point which makes the realization of his hope somewhat doubtful. He was of the opinion that civilization progresses by the strengthening of intellectual life and the renunciation of instinct (drives).

Civilization and its Discontents

It is this notion of progress I wish to comment upon. Most scientists: biologists, anthropologists, and psychologists agree that development, evolution, and progress, are essential to the organic world, to living organisms, to life itself. Our understanding of psychic life too is based on these concepts, in phylo-, onto- and microgenesis. In the individual the pleasure principle is modified and superceded by the reality principle. Irrational emotional attitudes become slowly more and more supplanted and controlled by the primacy of the intellect. As Freud said: 'Where id was, there shall ego be." Through differentiation and integration, new higher functions come into being, adaptation to reality increases, and civilized modes and mores are attained.

This developmental process and cultural progress is, however, not achieved by elimination of the earlier, primitive phases and their dominating forces, but by their repression and control within the newly acquired hierarchical organization. They recede into the background and lose their dominance. Their effect diminishes relatively to the growing intellect. But they continue to exist, in force, both virtually and potentially. They feed the psychic organ, even as it functions on higher levels. Without them life would stop. But it is not only a question of energy supply and motivating forces. The primary modalities continue to exert their influence, both dynamically-functionally and structurally, as the newly developed systems which keep them in check are based on them and informed by them, as can be seen in the interaction of primary and secondary process.

Moreover, of no less significance and importance than their subdued presence and activity is their reversal potential. With each further developmental step, with each emergence of a new, higher functional and organizational system, the whole process, or progress, leads to a more delicate, more precarious inner equilibrium and to greater vulnerability. Eternal Eros is forever in struggle with his equally immortal antagonist Thanatos. Their fusion never means that their forces are stably balanced, and it is never exclusively in favor of growth, development, organization, in short, of life. Is this not the meaning of *Civilization and Its Discontents*, i.e., that more pressure must be mobilized and more counterpressure produced, as primitive tendencies and attitudes are increasingly tamed, be it by repression or even by sublimation? There is neither equality nor a static equilibrium between those earlier forms of satisfaction which have to be renounced and those later acquired, as in art, in scientific knowledge, and its technical applications, and in social values and mores. In spite of the vast cultural enrichment, the older pleasures never lose their attraction. The very fact that they had to be given up and are now forbidden, prohibited, taboo, adds to their lure. This too is part of the repetition compulsion in favor of the old. There is a pull from yesterday and a push back, away from today and tomorrow.

There exists an attraction to the known, the familiar, and a repulsion from the unknown. All this facilitates the upsurge, the breakthrough, and the return of the repressed.

Thus the poet, Christopher Fry, asks in his play *A Phoenix Too Frequent:*

"What is your opinion of Progress? Does it, for example,
Exist? Is there ever progression without retrogression?
Therefore is it not true that mankind
Can more justly be said increasingly to Gress?"

Others said, in the same vein: "Progress means going and returning and vice versa without an end. No returning without going and no going without returning. As is said: 'Between Heaven and Earth nothing goes away that does not return'."

We have this to and fro, back and forth in normal everyday life, as in waking and sleeping, in thinking and dreaming. It exists in psychopathology. And it is there, over and beyond the confines of individual life, in social institutions. At all times there were approved arrangements to break the orderly way of life with its cultural achievements, based on a massive array of prohibitions and inhibitions. There are vacations, holidays, to give us respite from the pressure of ἀγάγκη (i.e. life's necessities), both nature's limitations and society's demands. There were the Greek Bacchanalia, the Roman Saturnalia, and there is the Christian Carnival. All of them are upheavals of law and order, an overturning of outer and inner authority. Sexual taboos are shaken, and death is denied. Today there are other institutions which attest to man's overwhelming need to turn the tables and tend to satisfy it. A large part of literature, films, radio and television serve this purpose, as do the amusement parks, providing excitement and thrill, both of a sexual and of an aggressive-destructive character. There is indeed no end to the ways and means intended to shake off the heavily weighing yoke of civilization by regressive expressions of phallic feats, by mastering danger and overcoming the fear of castration and the dread of death.

Such a break with the daily routine of reality adaptation and the drudgery of civilized, moral life, of lawful orderliness, a break in huge dimensions, is the carnival of bloodshed: war. It is the most grandiose return of the repressed, a breakthrough of instinctual drive with all its excitation, flutter and flurry, a reversal of many of our main values whereby the forbidden is bidden and the bad becomes the good, highly estimated and rewarded. There is a fusion of almost uninhibited sexuality and aggression, resulting in the heroism of the victorious Oedipus, the fighting superman, the god-like immortal, denying danger and death. War realizes a general human tendency to "live dangerously" (Nietzsche). It has always been a game, ein *Kampfspiel*, ἀγών, and thence agony. War is the big adventure, the antidote to the tedious, wearisome boredom which civilized life means for many people. They can, they have to take leave of their kin, to leave home, a worn-out security. They can overcome their fears and entertain wild expectations. There is an orgy of destruction in fighting and vanquishing the foe, in subjecting the enemy, in conquering his land, town and countryside, which is woman, mother Earth. Raping and looting accompany the end of every war. In all these respects modern warfare is not basically different from war in ancient times. Technical changes in armament and tactics do not alter its meaning. One may ask, whether the sons kill their fathers and brothers, or whether it is perhaps the other way around: the generation of the fathers sacrificing the sons. In any case, war is an ecstasy of instinctual drive satisfaction, both of Eros and Thanatos. The ego is in firm control of the reality situation. The peace-time conscience is stilled. Fear, guilt, and shame are overcome, and a war-time ego-ideal is installed. The surroundings applaud, exalt and extol the patriotic hero who answers the demand of the hour, the call of duty in the most horrid and destructive carnage. Mysticism and romance have relieved the warrior from his usual socialized self

The Burden of Individuality

This catastrophic regression in war (in the service of the id) seems to fulfill basic human needs. Yet this could not come about without another massive regression, one in the organization of the self.

One developmental feature of human progress, again an outcome of higher differentiation and integration of the personality, is an increase in individuation, in individuality, in personal identity. We are quite proud of this achievement. "*Höchstes Glück der Erdenkinder sei nur die Persönlichkeit*," says Goethe (human beings' highest blessing is but the personality). But really, man is unable to bear and tolerate the essence of individuality, which means being distinct, different from others. Certain animals in a herd all seem to us more or less alike; they feel safe in their togetherness, not troubled by loneliness and not worried by envy. Man, on the other hand, feels single, sole, alone, and insecure. In this respect too he is subjected to a mighty pull back to regress to a state of less differentiated likeness, of being one and the same and so part of a whole. It seems that only then can he feel safe. "He cannot live alone and he cannot leave alone" (Arthur Koestler).

We know the individual is not only appropriately proud of his uniqueness, but is likely to overestimate it, i.e., his own value. This narcissistic attitude is found both in individuals and in groups. All nations tend to see in themselves the culmination of mankind. This is the intrinsic nature of nationalism. We heard it once in the German song: "*Deutschland, Deutschland Über Alles*" and in the saying: "*An Deutschem Wesen soll die Welt genesen*" (by German nature pure, the world should find its cure). It is the same with "La Gloire de la France." Jews have their own, world renowned, old brand of this attitude, as the Chosen People. The same phenomenon is found in all religions and in their subdivisions into innumerable denominations. Each of them is proud of its uniqueness, and vain and thence quarrelsome and pugnacious. Rite, ritual and riot, sacred belief and hatred, sacrifice and the Holy War are all closely connected. Every single and singular feature, be it natural gift or cultural achievement, is a source of pride and of intolerance: the race, the tribe, the clan, the family; city, town, village and hamlet; language, dialect, accent and style. Freud spoke of the narcissism of minor differences." I with my specific features am not only different from you, I am better than you." Yet your being different from me threatens me. "*Und willst du nicht mein Bruder sein, so schlag' ich dir den Schädel ein*" goes the proverb. (If you don't want to be my brother, my buddy, i.e. from the same stock, the

same blood, the same as I am, I shall smash your skull.) The other
one is the stranger, and the stranger is the foe. Thus the word *hostis*
in Latin meant both the stranger and, as such, the enemy. We have
an ambiguous attitude to otherness and strangeness. It can immensely attract us, but at other times we see it as a menace to our
identity. Then xenophobia may get the upper hand. The diver-
gence has to be fought, removed, by death, through war.

But, paradoxically, in order to save ourselves, we have to give up
part of our individuality. We must regress to group identity, to
submerge in a group mentality in which many of our most individual features and values, including our ethical canon, are discarded.
What is felt as a threat to identity, i.e. otherness, distorts the
positive self love and estimation and creates hatred for everything
different. Regressively it leads from an individualistic psychic
stance to group mentality. We know the consequences of this
loss of autonomy: the identification of the members of the group
with their leaders and amongst themselves, the changes in
super-ego and ego-ideal, and the great advantages connected
with this regression.

I want to quote some passages from Alix Strachey's book:
The Unconscious Motives of War to show how this change may contribute to the waging of war. The individual has a need for regressive
groups. "They afford him great relief and pleasure by allowing
his mind to regress to less exacting standards of thought and to
older attitudes of feeling, and they allay his anxiety and sense of
guilt by giving him back an omnipotent, protecting father and
accomplices to aid and to share his dangers; and finally, they
give his ancient megalomania and narcissism room to expand."
And, concerning aggression: "Much of the large amount of libido
which a group-member expends upon his attachment to his leader
and his fellow-members is got by withdrawing it from non-
members, and that makes him not only indifferent to their
welfare and happiness but actually desirous of their destruction and unhappiness.... [the] withdrawal of libido increases
the relative proportion of his destructive and hostile impulses
toward them. ... Members of regressive groups have actually more
destrudo in their mental composition than have individuals in
their private capacity."

In short, to be part of a large uniform whole, to be clad in uniforms as soldiers are, lends the individual grandeur and omnipotence. By a total turning outward of aggression, away from the self and the like, toward the common enemy, danger and death are magically denied. The destruction of the other seems the only way of saving one's own life and limb, personality and identity.

The Bane of Technical Revolution

Finally there seems to be a third factor by which alteration and difference may lead man to war. Sameness, likeness, can after a while create boredom and tediousness, and a change is sought and becomes welcome. But it often also produces uneasiness; it is looked at with suspicion and felt as a menace. A stimulus may be pleasant as well as unpleasant. In any case it requires an effort to adapt to it, to adjust to anything new. Change is always apt to deprive us of a state of equilibrium and of the advantages to which we are accustomed: in short, of the good old times we once hated and are now longing for. The greater the exertions the change demands from us, the more idealized will the past become.

Now change is no less the mark of civilization than tradition. The ascendancy of the intellect, the tremendous progress of science and technology have led to a revolutionary speeding up of the rate of change in our world. This triumphant control of nature, this overwhelming intervention in our material environment, brought about by the rapid progress of our mind, means such enormous changes in the fabric of society in so quick a sequence that almost no time is left to make the necessary emotional adaptations, to acquire a satisfying balance between the individual and his surroundings. With all their advantages these continuous changes are unsettling, unnerving to a high degree. As soon as change acquires too much momentum, adaptation lags behind, and the feeling of identity as well as our self-image vis-à-vis our environment are impaired. We are deprived of the minimal degree of statics which we need to feel safe and secure in life. The very same progress which increases our physical comfort and material security, breeds inner instability, evokes anxiety, and leads to a sense of crisis. And then, sometimes, there seems no other way out than to go backwards, to the good old days, means and ways, to undo the changes and the progress. Often that means war and destruction in order to escape the fear of becoming lost, split off, fragmented.

New technologies, as we read in *War and Peace in the Global Village* by Marshall McLuhan and Quentin Fiore, create new environments which means changes in our sensorium, self-amputation. They shift the order, alter the images which we make of ourselves and our world. They inflict considerable pain on the perceiver, in spite of their advantages. This so much disturbs our inner life that, as misbegotten efforts to recover the old images, wars necessarily result. People are always adjusted to the preceding environment, much as the General Staff is always superbly prepared to fight the last war. All new technologies bring on the cultural blues, just as old ones bring on the phantom pain after they have disappeared. Thus, these authors hold, every new technology necessitates war as an attempt to undo the progress. But since on the other hand, every war leads to new progress, the circle of pro- and regression is permanently kept alive.

Conclusion

It is really a sad comment on humanity that only the instruments of war have changed since Aristophanes expressed its folly in his play Lysistrates. Man is caught in the conflict of his basic instinctual drives, Eros and Thanatos, between movement and standstill. From the plenitude of motives for war, I have singled out only one element: change, and tried to show its role in three configurations.

There is the slow inner change in man's psyche which is the quintessence of cultural evolution: from emotion and magic to logic and science. With every move forward on this road man had to leave something behind. It seems that his need to retrieve what he has lost is so strong that from time to time he has to take recourse to war. The new cultural terrain won by the ego, like the draining of the Zuider Zee, must perforce be given up and is periodically overrun and devoured by the tempestuous sea of our instinctual drives.

Simultaneously there is the change from the undiversified member of a group to the highly differentiated individual with its distinct, unique personality. This change goes hand in hand with a fearful awareness of loneliness, of difference and otherness. It embodies a narcissistic menace which is at times so keenly felt that it can lead to the surrender of the new position, to regression into the masses and the annihilation of all that is different.

Finally, in modern times we have experienced rapid external change of man's physical and social environment. It deprives him of the very ground he is standing upon and thus may force him to massive destruction of the new order of things which impinges on and threatens his self.

In each of these three situations man is ambiguous toward change and difference. He can therefore never enjoy for long the fruits of the victory of his mind over his instinctual drives and over external nature. Torn between neophilia and neophobia, man seems incapable of progressing in a straight line. Einstein wrote to Freud: "Man has within him a lust for hatred and destruction." In *The Future of an Illusion* Freud had expressed himself cautiously: "The voice of the intellect is a soft one, but it does not rest till it has gained a hearing. Finally, after a countless succession of rebuffs, it succeeds. This is one of the few points on which one may be optimistic about the future of mankind... The primacy of the intellect lies, it is true, in a distant, distant future, but probably not in an *infinitely* distant one. "For the present, man's lust seems not sufficiently matched by his intellectual and moral forces. The intellect appears to be more efficient in the control of our natural environment than in the stabilization of our inner world and our interpersonal relationships. In the face of our tremendous tendency toward regression, it finds itself ever so often completely helpless. The loss of primitive satisfaction and inner and outer security is not safely balanced by increasing physical comfort, individuality and higher intelligence. Must we then accept McLuhan's and Fiore's modification of Pope's verse on vice? It runs:

> "War is a monster of so frightful mien,
> As, to be hated, needs but to be seen;
> Yet seen oft, familiar with its face,
> We first endure, then pity, then embrace."

Another View

Louis Linn

It sems to me that in the papers prepared for this volume we have been discussing four distinct issues; namely, aggression violence, fighting, and war. I would like to make the point that these four issues, although related, are in fact separate in terms of their psychic origins, their dynamics, and their adaptational significance. I will discuss them accordingly.

Aggression

The phenomena generally included under the heading of aggression are so numerous and complex that some organizing concept is needed. I propose to discuss aggression developmentally and to describe in temporal sequence the "aggression phenomena" as they make their appearance in the life cycle of the individual.

Let me start with my definition of aggression. To me, aggression is a complex of thoughts, feelings, and actions which make their appearance whenever a drive or a need is obstructed on the way to fulfillment. In accordance with this definition the function of aggression is to remove obstacles and to make drive discharge possible. In this sense, aggression in its primary meaning operates in the service of Eros for the specific purpose of facilitating drive discharge.

I will begin with an example from the earliest stages of development, before distinct object relations have been established and before the rudimentary psychic apparatus has had the opportunity

183

to develop the separate categories of thought and behavior embodied in the terms id, ego and superego. Affect-deprived infants like those classically described by Spitz may be said to experience affect hunger, or a need for sensory input. In an average expected environment this is provided by a suitable mothering person. In the absence of normal external inputs the developing infant improvises his own inputs. In some instances, intensified exploration of the body leads to precocious discovery of the genitalia and early masturbation, or to precocious discovery of the feces and fecal play. With the developing motor skills the affect-deprived infant may add scratching, body rocking, head banging and hair pulling to his repertoire of autonomously available sensory inputs. In short, the aggressive drive makes it possible for the infant literally to tear from his own bodily substance objects with which to interact and which he desperately needs for normal growth and development.

Psychoanalytic literature concerning the outcome of affect-deprivation in infancy has chosen to emphasize anaclitic depression, marasmus and death, which do indeed occur if no rescuing adult appears in time. Nature however provides considerable leeway. Infants do not lapse into marasmus without a struggle; those infants who succeed in maintaining the spark of life by their own efforts often go on to extraordinary feats of growth and development if only the rescuers are sufficiently committed to the infant's welfare.

It is probably unwarranted to say that aggression is the sole key to self-rescue. Masturbation and fecal play do not strike one as examples of aggression. On the other hand, scratching, head banging and hair pulling do qualify for this label as measured by adult stereotypes. The fact is that one cannot at this early pre-object stage separate out aggression as a separate drive from the striving for libidinal gratification. Both drives, if they are indeed separate drives at this phase of development, seem inextricably united in the service of survival.

This paradox presents itself again during adolescence. "Skin slicing" (as contrasted to wrist cutting with clear suicidal intent) often occurs to combat affect hunger. The sting of pain and the sight of bright red blood can have a paradoxically reassuring effect on the youngster who feels "dead" inside. One can say the same of hair pulling, reckless behavior in general, and experimentation with dangerous drugs.

Violence

In the third month of life the capacity for object relationships with adults makes its appearance. This is signaled by the smiling response. Just as the infant can engage adults in loving relationships with a smile and cuddly behavior, so can he express rage or lesser degrees of discontent by screaming, crying and struggling. These expressions of aggression have the effect of signaling to the adults in the environment that the infant is experiencing a need of some kind. The sound, sight and feeling of the unhappy infant can be so distressing to the adult that the latter is often mobilized to act in some purposeful way to reduce the infant's discomfort, thereby reducing his own discomfort.

There are two noteworthy aspects of aggression at this stage of development. First, it is a pattern of behavior displayed by a frustrated individual (in this case the screaming infant) which inflicts pain on another person (in this case the mothering person) in order to coerce the latter to remove the obstruction to drive fulfillment. Henceforth this will be the model for violent behavior. By means of threats, by inflicting pain, injury or death by destructive acts, the frustrated individual strives to remove obstacles to drive fulfillment by coercing others to help him.

Second, like the smiling reaction in the third month of life, this violent behavior is not directed at a specific identifiable human target. It is intended for anyone in the vicinity. For this reason it is a relatively inefficient way of influencing the environment, since it may well represent energy expended at an essentially indifferent target who will not respond in a rescuing manner, or who may react with counter-violence.

Somewhat later in life, violent expressions of aggression not directed at a specific appropriate target may occur during temper tantrums or in adult life as mob violence or in seemingly senseless acts of vandalism.*

Fighting

Around the eighth month of life fateful changes occur. The infant starts to distinguish the special face of the mother from all other faces. His best smiles are for her. Other adults are poor substitutes at best and so often arouse fear and protest that Spitz has called this the period of Eighth Month Anxiety.

Now the key issue is to maintain contact with this most significant of all people, the mother. Just as desperately as he feels his need for her, just so does he come to hate all who obstruct his path to her, or with whom he must share her love. At this point of development, aggression becomes a highly focused instrument. If wishes could kill, this infant would destroy all who deny full and exclusive access to his mother. This encompasses all his siblings. It also encompasses that invincible rival, his father. In each case the hatred for rivals parallels the intensity of mother-love.

Many techniques of group living must be learned within the family. Along with the siblings' need for maternal love and protection there is also a need for freedom. Margaret Mahler has explored this "separation-individuation" problem in great detail, particularly as it must be solved by the individual child in relation to the mother. However, there is also the father to be considered, as well as the other siblings. To achieve peaceful and orderly transactions, a power structure or pecking order must be established within the family. Typically, the father's special privileges cannot be disputed by the siblings. The parents may demand special consideration

---

* In Shakespeare's *Julius Caesar*, Act III, Scene 3, the angry mob comes upon a man named Cinna. They ask him his name. "Truly my name is Cinna," he answers. The mob cries out, "Tear him to pieces, he's a conspirator." In vain he protests, "I am Cinna the poet. I am Cinna the poet." The mob says, "Tear him for his bad verses. Tear him for his bad verses." Once again Cinna appeals, "I am not Cinna the conspirator." "It is no matter," the mob answers, "his name is Cinna, pluck but his name out of his heart and turn him going. Tear him tear him. Come brands, ho! firebrands".

for a youngest, an oldest, or a handicapped child, etc. Within the family enclave law must prevail and parents must be capable of enforcing it. The latter is accomplished by the exercise of parental aggression. This may take the form of physical punishment, withdrawal of love, denial of privileges, and even banishment from the family.

Unless there is an orderly pattern of power-sharing on a parental level it is inevitable that there will be parental dissension from time to time. However well ordered the household with respect to the siblings, it is inevitable that disputes will occur there too because of dissatisfaction with one's position in the family hierarchy. While parental power is totally overwhelming during early childhood, a time comes when the child can protest parental power and fight with increasing effectiveness against unfair decisions. In short, the hierarchical structure of the family is not a stable one. New siblings are born, or weak children grow strong and challenge previous family power arrangements. Each of these power shifts is accomplished by exercising aggression. *Fighting, in the primary sense of the word, may be defined as the use of aggression to advance or defend one's position in the power structure of the family.*

The Vicissitudes of Intrafamilial Aggression

Needless to say, unbridled expressions of childhood aggression cannot be tolerated within the family. To do so would lead to the destruction of the family and for mammals at least, individual survival is impossible without family survival. To insure the latter, devices have been evolved to channel aggression in such a way as to prevent dissolution of the family. The aggression-channeling process becomes part of what is referred to psychoanalytically as superego formation.

At least three separate patterns for channeling intrafamilial aggression can be recognized. The pattern which develops is that which is inculcated and enforced by the parents. The latter in turn is determined by the prevailing culture in which the family lives as well as by the subculture which characterizes the specific family:

(1) This pattern insists unequivocally and without exception "Thou shalt not kill." This may be called the Religious or the Universal Brotherhood of Man pattern. In accordance with this point of view no outward expression of violence is countenanced within the family. With strict enforcement by parents, impending loss of control of hateful impulses causes intolerable feelings of anxiety, guilt and depression. In short, there is no direction for hatred under Pattern One except inward, against onself. This superego structure sees suicide as an ultimate act of morality which prefers one's own death to causing the death of another.

(2) This superego pattern may be called the Scapegoat pattern. This parental injunction reads "Thou shalt not kill any member of the family except the one chosen as the scapegoat or the sacrificial lamb." There is a considerable literature on this subject.

(3) A last pattern reads "Thou shalt not kill any member of your own family. However, individuals who are not members of your own family are fair game."

The three superego patterns enumerated share in common the property of protecting the family from destruction. These same superego patterns will appear in relation to extrafamilial group experiences later in life as transference phenomena. For example, the phenomenon of scapegoating may express itself in the persecution of a specific minority group within a nation. The injunction not to kill any member of one's own family may express itself as an attitude of self-righteous patriotism which justifies any violent act so long as it is directed against the members of an "enemy" nation. The Universal Brotherhood of Man pattern, successfully inculcated by the family during childhood, provides mankind's best hope for the development of a world order in which peace will prevail as a consequence of world law.

War

Just as there are individual needs which can be met only by that group called the family, so there are family needs that can be met only by that group called the community. Here again there must be a power structure. Cooperative relationships must be established between families under the direction of parent-like figures who are the community leaders. When disputes arise between families, these must be mediated in orderly legal transactions. For those who will not abide by the law, aggression must be exerted by the power structure to enforce the law. In situations in which the law is unfair, groups of families may unite to overthrow the existing power structure. This, too, involves the exercise of aggression which may take the form of an election campaign at one extreme or open physical combat, civil war and revolution at the other. And so, by steps, we have come in our discussion to the issue of war.

Whereas civil war is essentially a family matter involving power rearrangements within a given territory, international war introduces competition for new territory or living space. Without exploring this issue in detail it is hypothesized that one's native territory becomes emotionally equivalent to the mother. The need to defend it, the yearning to return to it, are understandable in this one dimension at least in psychoanalytic terms. The poignancy of the Arab-Israeli deadlock becomes evident when that situation is viewed in terms of siblings, each striving to return to his "own soil," a point of view which opens the door to compassion and the recognition that a supranational parent-surrogate's help is needed to mediate this quarrel between brothers. By the same token, the adolescent's drive to acquire a territory of his own may have some relevance for understanding wars of conquest.

These facile and admittedly superficial analogies notwithstanding, the fact of waging war is harder to comprehend than the fact that individual human beings do tend to get into fights. When two adult animals who are strangers to each other are brought together for the first time, one invariably attempts to dominate the other. In the ordinary course of events, dominance is achieved, whether by bluff or by battle, in a few minutes. The ethologists have emphasized the existence of surrender rituals, the primary function of which is to prevent killing in the process of establishing dominance.

Man has surrender rituals and in unarmed fighting he usually respects them as much as do representatives of other species in the animal kingdom. Man went astray, however, when he became a toolmaker and forged weapons or tools for killing. The more lethal the weapon, the more readily available, the easier to use, the swifter and more destructive its effect, the more does this tool rob fighting man of the opportunity either to express surrender rituals himself or to respond to those of a weaker opponent. When large groups of adversaries confront each other with deadly weapons, the cost in human life can become so great that the result of the encounter can no longer serve a useful purpose, and it is precisely for this reason, namely, to decrease the loss of life in armed fighting, that warfare came into existence.

Warfare as a precursor to world law

In its simplest form my thesis is as follows: war is a device to curb man the killer by formalizing, systematizing, controlling, in short, civilizing man's drive to fight with weapons. Many psychoanalysts have posed this paradox. How does it happen that Eros, the very life force which welds individuals into families, and then into still larger groups called communities and nations for the purpose of preserving life and for the purpose of improving the quality of life, can also give rise to war? The answer is simple, because in reality there is no paradox. Eros has given rise to civilization, but it has also given rise to war as a way of protecting civilization.

Warfare creates a new basis for fighting behavior. The soldier fights first and foremost out of a sense of obedience. How does a government mobilize a nation for war? What is the mental set or the war-readiness which makes civilians willing to take up arms and risk their lives in strange places? The answer resides in the concept of Basic Trust. In the case of mobilization for war this is expressed as trust in the leaders of one's nation. When national leaders can convince the individual citizen that his own life and that of his family are in jeopardy so long as the enemy remains unchecked, he becomes willing to take up arms.

The greater the trust, the readier the mobilization, the readier the belief in the need for war. Man mobilizes for war not so much out of a bloodthirsty desire to express aggression as from a desire to limit the consequences of uncontrolled aggression. The wearing of a soldier's uniform is in its very essence an act of passive surrender of one's identity as a free man. The more complicated and technical the tools of war, the more completely one must be willing to obey blindly in order to survive and to win. Once under arms this attitude of trust continues in relation to officers. The soldier becomes convinced that if he trains well and learns to obey, not only will his country emerge victorious, but he as an individual soldier is more likely to return home alive. In a properly run army the soldier is housed, clothed, and fed. If he is injured, every effort is made to keep him alive. And so we can see how far removed are the motivational requirements of a good soldier from those involved in authentic aggression, violence, and fighting.

The classical battles of military history were not massacres. On the contrary, they were distinguished for the fact that whole armies and their equipment were captured intact. Only a few centuries ago battles were decided by encounters between selected champions following which the majority of the others could return to their homes uninjured. Thus it was possible to participate in a battle without fighting, to participate in the carnival and ritual of war without carnage.

War has persisted as a human institution precisely because war, once upon a time, had for the human species a certain survival value. Let us admit at once that war has never functioned efficiently in this respect, and that in modern times it is failing increasingly in this respect. For the major nations war has lost this rational life-sparing function entirely. But it is precisely this fact that provides civilized man with his best hope that the ritual of war, no longer rational, will wither away, and that the international rules of war may yet become the basis for peace through world law.

Motivations for Peace

Jacob A. Arlow

As psychoanalysts we are accustomed to search for meaning and content even in what appears at first glance to be a question of form. When a patient presents us with a dream and makes some comment about its form or structure, if he says, for example, "The dream consists of three parts," or "The last part of the dream seems particularly striking," we suspect that some hidden wish, some concealed meaning may be implied. We feel it proper technique, therefore, to ask the patient to associate to the comments he made about the formal aspects of the dream. What conclusion can I draw then of the intentions of the organizing committee of this volume? The other papers are discussions on the subject of war and aggression, my charge is to write on the subject "Motivations For Peace." Only in this title does the word "peace" appear. Can I do otherwise than to infer an unspoken intention, an unexpressed aspiration, that the tone of my paper shall be a positive one, that this scientific discipline to which we are all so devoted, could be directed in some practical way to solve the most important problem of our age, the problem of war or peace, of life or death?

Such in fact was the spirit of the letters exchanged between Einstein and Freud almost forty years ago. Dangers which at that time they correctly, but only dimly surmised, are in this day as certain as tomorrow's sunrise. In the meantime mankind has learned many distressing and discouraging lessons from the course of history. Forty years ago psychoanalysis was only a very young science. By today our insights have been broadened and deepened in many areas. What have we, as psychoanalysts, learned in the time that has intervened that may shed new light or suggest a brighter vision?

In Freud's essay "Why War?" international conflict is seen as a derivative of the inherent, aggressive drive in man. Freud wrote to Einstein, "... as you yourself have remarked, there is no question of getting rid entirely of human aggressive impulses; it is enough to try to divert them to such an extent that they need not find expression in war." Within the community of individuals the effective threat of imminent force exercised on behalf of the community is augmented by shared interests. The emotional ties which grow out of common interests stabilize the group structure and create feelings which unify the group and constitute the true source of the strength of the community. No society can long be held together by the threat of violence alone. It would be impossible to police even the harshest totalitarian state without the help of some form of ideology. *Ideology and common interest*, however, can unify a group only to the extent that they find some significant basis in the libidinal life of the individuals who comprise the group. This libidinal dynamic may originate in a common instinctual need or it may grow out of the libidinal attachment which ties the members of the group to a common object. In the ideology of the group the libidinal object, aggrandized and idealized, as is the fate of all intensely loved objects, may in time be replaced by the ideals he personifies; unconsciously however the unifying devotion to the cause retains in the minds of the individuals the libidinal cathexis originally attached to the love object. The relationship remains a love relationship and in the process a bond of identification is established among the members of the group. What Freud discovered to be true for the community of individuals, he hoped could be made true for the community of nations. It was this that led him to write:

> "Our mythological theory of instincts makes it easy for us to find a formula for *indirect* methods of combating war. If willingness to engage in war is an effect of the destructive instinct, the most obvious plan will be to bring Eros, its antagonist, into play against it. Anything that encourages the growth of emotional ties between men must operate against

war. These ties may be of two kinds. In the first place they may be relations resembling those towards a loved object, though without having a sexual aim. There is no need for psychoanalysis to be ashamed to speak of love in this connection, for religion itself uses the same words: 'Thou shalt love thy neighbor as thyself.' This, however, is more easily said than done. The second kind of emotional tie is by means of identification. Whatever leads men to share important interests produces this community of feeling, these identifications. And the structure of human society is to a large extent based on them."

Compared to *The Future of an Illusion* and *Civilization and Its Discontents*, "Why War" is, relatively speaking, one of the more optimistic statements to flow from Freud's pen. His hopes sprung from two strongly held convictions. First was the capacity of man in the course of individual development to master his instinctual life, that is, to bring it under the sway of reason. "The ideal condition of things would of course be a community of men who had subordinated their instinctual life to the dictatorship of reason. Nothing else could unite men so completely and so tenaciously even if there were no emotional ties between them." He recognized that this was a Utopian expectation; it was his own ideal. Clearly the Moses of Michelangelo, august and majestic, conquering his wrath and saving the tablets of the law, was never far from his mind.

The other conviction that gave Freud cause for optimism about motivations for peace was his idea concerning the development of the "cultural process." Deeply influenced by Darwinian concepts, Freud regarded the evolution of civilization as analogous to the development of the individual "When... we look at the relation between the process of human civilization and the developmental or educational process of individual human beings, we shall conclude without much hesitation that the two are very similar in nature, if not the same process applied to different kinds of objects." He regarded these processes as organic, that is, biologically determined, sharing the most general characteristics of all life. Accordingly, as individual development tends toward reliable mastery by the ego over the instincts, so cultural evolution tends toward the strengthening of the intellect and the internalization of aggressive impulses. This transformation takes place under the influence of the communal superego. Thus the cultural development of the group and the cultural development of the individual are always interlocked. The reproaches of the individual superego when brought into consciousness coincide with the precepts of the prevailing cultural superego. Using this approach Freud introduced a normative element, and a hopeful one at that, into his concept of the biological developmental process. The mature individual is the cultured, that is, the civilized individual. He reflects the highest precepts of his society. Such a felicitous psychological constitution certainly was true for Freud and for Einstein. They did, in fact, epitomize the finest flowering of the culture of their age. They were, of course, rare and precious examples of the species, hardly the kind of subjects upon which to base valid generalizations concerning the perfectability of human nature or the quest for peace.

In recent years psychoanalysts have learned much about the aspects of mental functioning directly concerned with the problems we are considering. For purposes of convenience these problems can be studied from the point of view of the role of the superego, the significance of identification and of its negative counterpart, alienation, and, finally, the dynamics of the group process.

History and clinical observation have rendered more than ample testimony that the superego, individual and collective, has hardly served as a reliable ally in the quest for peace. Far from being an integrated and consistently functioning mental structure, the superego is fraught with contradictions, less so perhaps than the id, but definitely more so than the ego. The superego is not the precipitate of an identification with one principal morally elevated and feared object. It is, in fact, a jumble of identifications. It reflects in its operation the total complex of human experience, all the influences of education, the vicissitudes of object relations, and the contradictory, inconsistent moral trends of the society in which the individual has been raised. If strong motivations for peace are inculcated into a superego as representatives of the highest values of our civilization, they are at the same time counterbalanced by opposing demands. They are neutralized, if not negated, by considerations of group loyalty, patriotism, manliness, achievement and even libidinal ties to comrades and superiors. Erikson was undoubtedly correct in pointing out that Freud stood for the primacy of insight. He took the state and civilization for granted and faced the specter of totalitarian society only toward the end of his life. Who could have predicted before World War II how ineffectual the conventional morality of the individual and the religious morality of the group would be in the face of the most nightmarish assaults upon the basic values of our culture?

We pass thus from reflecting on the contradictory nature of the superego to considering another of its weaknesses. From developmental psychoanalytic studies we have learned that the superego has its precursors in the pre-phallic phases, and how residues of primitive modes of operation are retained even into adult years. These correspond, in fact, to instinctual fixation. Under conditions of stress and conflict, intrapsychic or international, superego functioning for the individual and the group is remarkably susceptible to regressive reinstinctualization. Primitive forms of its functioning may emerge from the past. Freud alluded to one such mechanism in connection with group psychology. When individuals in a group are united by the love they have in common for the leader, it often happens that the individuals masochistically and submissively surrender the function of moral judgment to this communal ego ideal. Annie Reich has shown that such an ego ideal may be modeled on some aggrandized, pathological, infantile prototype. Thus there comes into being, and history confirms this, a group held together by common but pathological ego ideals and libidinal ties, a group which centers about a prophet of evil. The paranoid and depressive demons, to paraphrase Kleinian concepts, can and do reassert their power over the superego.

We have taken note of the contradictory nature of the superego and of its susceptibility to regression. I will discuss only briefly a third quality of the superego and how it affects motivation for peace. I refer to the unreliability of the superego. To begin with, the categorical demands of the superego do not always correspond to the moral values of the culture. By contrast the quality of the superego may reflect the ideals of a military tradition or the mores of a specific subculture, a criminal subculture. Many of the difficulties which we analysts have in dealing with the concept of the superego stem from the fact that to a very large extent the entire concept has been anthropomorphized. The superego is not the representative of the moral macrocosm of society, implanted by the process of education into the microcosm which is the individual. Concepts, contrary to the official morality, find representation in the superego and operate silently and unobtrusively until a crisis of values supervenes.

But even where the educational process has been successful and there is a confluence of attitude between the cultural idealization of peace and the superego, how strong a positive motivational dynamic for peace may we anticipate? How much moral force can we expect will be expended in behalf of so worthy a cause? Unless connected with some narcissistic or libidinal goal, the idealizing aspect of the superego ordinarily does not seem to be an effective stimulus to action. As a deterrent to antisocial or immoral behavior, fear of conscience, Waelder has shown, plays a minor role so long as conditions remain relatively favorable for the individual. More often it is only when some misfortune or catastrophe has occurred that guilt feelings, according to Waelder, become significant. And, finally, there are those circumstances in which the very operation of the superego works in opposition to the quest for peace. These are circumstances which stimulate intense moral fervor or an outraged sense of justice. Crimes committed in the name of justice outraged confront us almost daily. Moral fervor may take on an aggressive quality hardly distinguishable from the most archaic of id impulses. Id and superego may combine forces to override what is rational and humane, and the extremes of aggression can be readily justified.

Increasing compassion for human suffering is commonly regarded as the measure of progress in moral development. One must face the fact, however, that humanitarian sentiments are selective and discriminating. Especially in connection with political and national conflicts it is possible to observe how men who are aroused by the tribulations, real or imaginary, of some, will remain indifferent toward those of others (Waelder). This moral contradiction is overcome by a combination of denial and rationalization. One closes one's eyes to certain evils and in the name of a political goal justifies others. Since the political goals masquerade as the instrument of an alleged future good, a moral rationalization is added to the mechanism of denial. What one loses in reality testing one gains in simplicity of outlook.

Those with whom we can identify are the principal beneficiaries of the peace-loving aspect of our moral nature. Freud described how peace can often be maintained within the group only through the expedient of a hostile attitude toward outsiders. There is thus the contradiction between the identification among the members of the group and the differentiation and separation from the outsiders. To understand this we must investigate more closely the role of identification in the pursuit of peace.

The struggle to establish one's identity is a long and difficult one. Many influences in psychic life pull regressively towards de-differentiation of the individual identity. The oceanic feeling which has been credited as an expression of the universal love typical of religious feeling is regarded as a manifestation of this process of de-differentiation. Actually, however, such trends do not point in the direction of a diffused, compassionate feeling for the common humanity of all people. On the contrary, they point towards a relationship of a dependent or fusing nature in which the boundaries between the self and a specific infantile object tend to become blurred. The type of non-discriminating identification with all mankind which we posit as the basis for the strongest motivations for peace requires an especially strong sense of individuality alongside of the recognition and appreciation of one's identification with his fellow man.

It is the positively tinged identification with other objects that acts as a deterrent to aggression and leads to a sense of compassion. Compassion is one of the main deterrents to crimes of violence directed against the persons of others. Years ago I was impressed how even the professional murderers who worked for Murder, Inc., had to alienate themselves from their victims in order to be able to commit the crime. What made the situation all the more striking was the fact that these criminals had no acquaintance whatsoever with the intended victim. An investigator connected with the case reported how before a "commercial" murder, the several gunmen designated for the job would get together and study the name and photograph of the intended victim. They would spend some time ridiculing him and fabricating crimes that the victim-to-be supposedly had committed. "He's a wife beater, a cheat and a liar," they would say. "He is cruel to his children. He is not to be trusted. He doesn't deserve to live. Let's wipe him out." Apparently it was necessary even for a group of hardened professional murderers to overcome the inner promptings of whatever superego inhibitions they may have had by a process of alienating themselves from any identification with or feelings of compassion for the victim before they could proceed with the murder.

For a nation to wage war the community, in effect, has to abrogate en masse the lifelong prohibition against murder which it has so painstakingly tried to instill in the mind of each citizen. As in the case of the professional murderers just mentioned, the enemy without has to be alienated from the mass before the criminal act of war can be carried through effectively. Any element that contributes to differentiation, differences of language, culture, skin, race, even the length of one's hair, can be used to break down the sense of identification and with it, the feelings of compassion. This was, in fact, the principal technique used by the Nazis in order to get the German people to participate in mass criminal activity. The Jews, the Slavs, the Gypsies, and others, had to be rendered less than human in the eyes of the German people in order to sanction what was prohibited. The government exercises the supreme authority of the primordial sovereign by suspending the sanctions which it itself has imposed (Brenner). This attitude can be sustained only by the compliance of forces within each individual which reach deep into the childish obedience and fear of the omnipotent parental images. All of these considerations pertain as well to the plight of the black people in America. To continue their subjugation, it is necessary to institutionalize the alienation of the black from the white community about them. Social conventions, biased representations in the mass media and in educational materials structuralize the alienation which makes it possible even for decent citizens to accept without too much protest the fact of inequality before the law.

It is all the more distressing to consider that differentiation and alienation seem to be more acceptable states of mind than identification and compassion. I have often pondered why it is so difficult to motivate people to act together for peace as compared to organizing them for war. It seems easier to teach one to hate his enemy than to love his neighbor. The movements led by Mahatma Gandhi and Martin Luther King, the two greatest proponents of the peace movement in modern times, seem to spring to mind as offering evidence to the contrary, but I doubt if this is really so. Both the movement led by Gandhi and that led by King, non-violent and idealistic as they were, were mounted in the face of an external enemy. The individuals in the group, self-sacrificing and non-hostile as they were in their behavior, nevertheless had a foe in common. In their nonviolent way they sought to bring about the downfall of the enemy, to destroy his power, and we can be certain that for all their passive submission to abuse by the constituted authority, the individual members of the group entertained in their unconscious fantasies hostile and aggressive wishes toward the oppressor. This is not intended to demean the tactics of nonviolence nor the goals of the movement. This comment is only intended to underscore the cohesive activating dynamic which is furnished by a common enemy. The fact is that in the case of Gandhi's movement, the peaceful orientation fell apart once the English enemy removed himself from the scene. And even before the death of Gandhi, the component elements of his party were already beginning to wage war among themselves.

It is one thing to acknowledge that peace is morally desirable and practically advantageous. It is another thing to be motivated to act assiduously and devotedly in the cause of peace. If now we review the psychological analysis we have made to this point, we appear to have reached an unexpected conclusion. Neither the conventional character structure nor conventional morality or religion contribute *effectively* to motivations for peace. It seems entirely paradoxical that the consistent pursuit of peace, a goal which in our technical clichés is ego syntonic, reality oriented and approved by the superego, should have to be studied as if it were for all intents and purposes a psychopathological formation. In the statistical sense the pursuit of peace represents not an aberration but a departure from ordinary behavior. The individual whose major motivation is the pursuit of peace takes his place alongside the prophets and we must remember that prophets are never considered as representing the norm. (Parenthetically and facetiously, if illness is the antithesis of the normal, then we can only hope that this illness attains epidemic proportions and that we cherish every symptom thereof).

Unfortunately we possess very little systematic analytic information about motivations for peace. Since it is a proposition to which most analysts will obviously react in a favorable way, it is possible that the problem has not excited our curiosity till now and that we have not found it necessary to report pertinent findings in detail. Such knowledge as we do have is formulated in terms consistent with our usual model for understanding psychopathology; that is, persistent childhood wishes leading to conflict, defense compromise formation. The themes are familiar enough — saving the world as a derivative of a rescue fantasy, reaction formation against aggression, expiation for guilt from whatever source, etc. These in turn lead to successful resolution in terms of special character formation and/or sublimation. The outstanding analysis of a charismatic personality totally motivated for peace is of course to be found in Erikson's brilliant study of Gandhi. This book illustrates the complex interplay of experience and motivation, conflict and guilt, life cycle and historical development, which go into the fashioning of the unique individual for whom peace is the overwhelming passion. It is difficult however to know what generalizations one can draw from the idiosyncratic phenomenon of a Gandhi.

Up to this point we have considered motivations for peace primarily from the point of view of the psychology of the individual and how he relates to the group, his group and other groups. We have in fact concentrated on the id and the superego aspects of the problem. What of the ego aspect of the question? There are in addition other dimensions to the problem that demand our attention.

War, especially modern war, is a mammoth social enterprise.

In Mussolini's words, it strains the sinews of a nation. More than that, it brings together multitudes of people in ways they had never experienced before. It calls into play diverse and overdetermined group motives, group fantasies and myths, and group patterns of behavior. If we are to understand the effort of war and its opposite, the efforts for peace, one must go beyond individual psychology and vicissitudes of the instinctual drives. One must consider how social and historical forces influence the psychology of the group. One must ask, what determines the option which the group and its individuals exercise in behalf of peace?

In a study of ego psychology and mythology I attempted to demonstrate how group loyalties and ideology receive an affective dynamic impetus from an unconscious fantasy shared in common. The myth represents the group fantasy as transformed by the defensive operations of the ego. Thus groups are held together and propelled into common action not only because they share a common instinctual need but more precisely because they have arrived together at common solutions. In regard to the problem we are considering we may therefore ask, what factors in history and development influenced the ego formation of members of certain groups so that they reordered their psychic life in the direction of seeking peace? This is a complex and challenging area into which few of our colleagues have dared to venture. Several authors have applied psychoanalytic concepts, especially the contributions of developmental and ego psychology, to the understanding of group historical phenomena. The most recent of a series of contributions on such subjects by Wangh deals directly with the motivation for peace in the current student rebellion. Wangh proposes that the dynamic thrust of the student rebellion and its quest for peace stems from a complex of historical and psychological factors which have endowed the ever-recurring conflict between the generations with a specific set of qualities at this time in history. The essential genetic factor resides in the traumatizing effect of recent history on both the older and the younger generation. A sense of abandonment generated by the pervasive effects of unconscious anxiety connected with the threat of nuclear destruction has taught a generation to distrust its elders, not to rely upon them for protection or guidance, and to attempt belated mastery of its traumatization through patterns of alienation, rebellion and withdrawal. Against this background the traditional hostilities between the generations become intensified. The group that is motivated for peace refuses to lend itself as an instrument by which the older generation can work through its own traumatization by war and at the same time express its antagonism to the young.

At best this is only in skeletal form a summary of the illuminating contribution by Wangh, but sufficient I hope to indicate how many different and complex factors were considered at the same time. This is the sophisticated kind of psychoanalytic study which the motivation for peace, regarded as a social as well as an individual phenomenon, requires. It certainly deserves further study along these lines, complemented by workers from disciplines related to psychoanalysis.

The area of psychoanalytic psycho-social history offers much promise for future insights into the affairs of man. The question is, what will be the practical yield and can it come in time to prevent a future holocaust? I stated at the beginning of this paper that I was aware of a charge to culminate our joint reflections on some note of optimism and hope. Perhaps it was all a projection and what I was responding to was a directive with which I have charged myself. In Jerusalem, this eternally embattled city of peace, it is only natural to hope for a prophetic vision. Realist and humanitarian that he was, Freud warned us not to expect this from psychoanalysis. The mills of therapy and the mills of education grind very slowly and each generation of mankind has to be recivilized in its turn. A universal therapy for mankind is far beyond our grasp. We are forced, in fact, to do as Freud said, that is, to make the best with what we have at hand. And this is challenge enough for our common hope for the future of mankind.

Another View

H. Z. Winnik

In the last section of his well-constructed paper, Arlow points to the fact that "a universal therapy for mankind is beyond our grasp," which implies that war and intergroup aggression are to be considered pathological phenomena. Nonetheless, according to Arlow, psychoanalytic psychosocial history extends some promise for the future. But the study of problems tied up with the motivation for peace "must be complemented by workers from other disciplines."

The statement by Jerome Frank that problems of war are "multiple, complex and woven into all aspects of society" is equally valid for those of peace. Their complex and manifold aspects are probably responsible for the fact that relevant literature does not—as far as I know—provide a satisfactory definition of the phenomena of war and peace, as if the authors assume that they are dealing with known and well-defined general concepts. However, the two concepts evidently complement one another and overlap as often happens with concepts in psychological and social sciences, so that eventually *peace* might appear as an extreme case in the complementary series leading to the opposite extreme, the *"absolute war."*

In continuing the discussion of motivations for peace, Arlow outlines briefly the significance of group-binding forces as that of "developmental processes" which, in groups, are analogous to "cultural processes." He proceeds in his discussion according to the model of conclusions by analogy, whereby the mental evolution of the individual, its psychic laws and dynamics serve as a key to conclusions concerning the group; a perfectly legitimate process as long as one is cognizant of its inherent limitations.

Arlow comments that striving for peace might derive from diverse infantile rescue fantasies, with reaction formation against aggression and expiation for guilt feelings. It also follows from his deliberations that peace motivations are ego-syntonic and reality-oriented. Accordingly, it becomes paradoxical to consider active pacifists a "departure from ordinary behavior," since the impression then remains that group allegiance would thrust the individual onto the war path.

As known from psychoanalysis, the superego evolves from the psychic residue of social factors, of objects with their dynamic relations. Therefore, dealing with our problem would imply giving special consideration to the superego. Arlow rightly demonstrates that the superego is controversial, unreliable, with regressive trends. This non-monolithic, split structure is—according to Arlow—one of the reasons for the individual's failure in striving for peace.

The questions emerging from these deliberations would be: Which social tendencies, in their historical evolution and their present structure, influencing the formation of the superego, should be fostered and which should be suppressed so as to reduce, mitigate and finally prevent war among groups?

According to Arlow we would first have to "strengthen the powers which we may most expect to exercise a unifying influence on man." To these belong "insight" and "reason." Arlow speaks here entirely in the spirit of Freud, who in his 35th lecture said: "The common compulsion exercised by such a dominance of reason will prove to be strongest among men and lead the way to further unions" and further: "Our best hope for the future is that intellect—the scientific spirit, reason, may in process of time establish a dictatorship in the mental life of men" (S.E. 22, p. 171).

Arlow then discusses "alienation" as the opposite of "identification," a process leading to negative prejudice and eventually to paranoid attitudes and systems. The significance of those factors in the genesis of confrontations between nations and social groups in general, has been dealt with repeatedly. Some authors see in these *projective* mechanisms a way to strengthen the bonds within by diverting existent tensions to the outside world, thus fostering the group's consolidation. Every endeavor to minimize or inhibit the rising of these negative projective mechanisms would indirectly decrease the danger of intergroup hostilities. Increase of communication between groups, common interests and functions equally serve to prevent arising prejudices and the preparedness to indulge in negative, paranoid projections. The same can be said of relieving tensions inside a group by providing rewarding activities.

Mitscherlich feels that "a change in the mental constitution is needed" in order to strengthen human readiness for peace and he thinks that this could happen through "a new stage in mental evolution expressed by a broadening and deepening consciousness." Even if the reality of such mental development could be accepted, this would be a rather pessimistic outlook since this type of biological evolution proceeds extremely slowly, thus putting off into a very distant future the realization of a general and ultimate peace.

Moreover, does modern social evolution move in this direction? The questions would be: Does modern society make people more or less violent? Is modern society more tolerant toward the violent man, or less so? What is it that enhances violence in social dynamics, or conversely what are the violence-preventing or suppressing factors?

If the thesis of Dollard, for instance, that "aggression is a reaction to frustration" is considered to be right, we should strive for a social order with as little frustration as possible so as to minimize aggressivity.

However, contrary to Dollard and in agreement with Freud, we assume aggressivity to be a natural human drive and—as shown by ethological research—a principal condition promoting social life in animals with social instincts. To prevent aggressive behavior from becoming destructive, there are among other devices, the establishment of socially accepted rituals, competitive sports, games; their highest form is expressed in intellectual competition. There are, furthermore, those rituals—analogous to patterns from the animal kingdom—of which in the course of time we became partially unconscious and which are understood by means of analytical research. Here belong the handshake, the bow, and other ceremonials ruling our social life.

War rituals existed in ancient times. We find in the Bible instructions for behavior in war, for the treatment of the foe and others. It would be superfluous to discuss in detail the war rituals prevalent among primitive peoples, valid during the Middle Ages and still persisting today. These rituals are evidently conditioned by culture; that is to say, they lose their validity when the warring parties belong to different cultures, or in times of cultural disintegration. The omission of these rituals in wars is in fact tied up with an increase of cruelty and wanton destruction. Therefore, the fostering of rituals or of their equivalents, as one way to deprive aggressivity of its destructive character, is frequently recommended.

Another question which often comes up for discussion in the context of our theme is whether the big states are more instrumental in fostering peace, or if smaller ones are to be preferred. Most authors such as Freud, J. Guitton, J. Frank and others consider a planetary state to be the peace-warranting ideal. In his beautiful publication "On transience," Freud expressed the hope that differences among nations would then be overcome and, in a planetary state group loyalty, manliness and patriotism—which Arlow considers contrary to the peace-superego—would tally with it perfectly. These authors also advocate the view that law and order, and through it peace, are best guaranteed by power; and large states are conglomerations of power. In truth, however, the few formations of hyperdimensional states, such as China and for that matter the Roman Empire, did not prove to be particularly encouraging specimens of peace-guarantors, despite the "pax Romana."

Storr contends, in his book on *Human Aggression*, that small communities would offer more opportunities to sublimate aggressive tendencies. By the creation of more responsible roles inside the boundaries of society and by facilitating identification with the group, such states provide greater possibilities for the individual to maintain his self-esteem. The minor differences between such groups would contribute to the diversion of tensions, while major controversies would become deprived of their sting through increased communication, common projects and similar expediencies.

In my own view these varying attitudes are not necessarily contradictory. An ideal peace in a hyperdimensional state must not lead to destruction of units, but rather to an integration of the opposing groups which would in their unification retain their full—and even increased—identity. Peace would thus become the consequence of a co-existence between adversaries, with preservation of their individual characteristics. Individual freedom— as a contradiction of the massive form of social organization— would thereby find a concordant, harmonious solution.

In cultural processes which, despite all "discontent," still represent a positive phenomenon, one can observe a constant striving for the dominance over any destructive tendencies by constructive forces, freed in human mental processes. Eventually a situation would be created in which peace becomes secured through positive elements, construction, creative work, compassion and charity, and not through negative ones as is the present balance of nuclear armament between the great powers.

Today, almost on the eve of a nuclear war, these deliberations may appear unrealistic, utopian. But it should not be forgotten that not so long ago the outlawing of slave labor and the abolition of the caste system were considered equally utopian ideas.

To some extent war can be compared with a bloody, hyperdimensional human sacrifice. Individual human sacrifice was abolished in Israel by Abraham about 3000 years ago. The "collective individuals"—as Freud defines the states—"are perhaps recapitulating the course of individual development and still represent very primitive phases—it may be that only later stages will be able to make some changes in this regrettable state of affairs." I should add, by progressively sublimating aggressive tendencies until the complete abolition of war has been achieved.

Some Aspects of Children's Aggressive Behavior During States of Illness and Recovery*

Albert J. Solnit

" — man has within him a lust for hatred and destruction. In normal times this passion exists in a latent state, it emerges only in unusual circumstances; but it is a comparatively easy task to call it into play and raise it to the power of a collective psychosis." (Albert Einstein July 30, 1932) This was a central statement in Albert Einstein's letter to Sigmund Freud to contribute his insight and understanding to the Symposium, "Why War". Freud's studies on instinctual drive theory in man had already been underway for more than 35 years. In 1893 in his report "On The Psychical Mechanism of Hysterical Phenomenon" Freud said, "But as an English writer has wittily remarked, 'The man who first flung a word of abuse at his enemy instead of a spear was the founder of civilization.' "

We are in a period of our history when the concern for man's capacity for destruction has given a sense of urgency to the search for knowledge about the tendency to aggression as an innate independent, instinctual disposition in man (Freud 1930). Few will doubt that the adult human being's destructive behavior is unique and a characteristic that distinguishes him from the other animals. ". . . When terrible things, cruelties hardly conceivable, occur among men, many speak thoughtlessly of 'brutality,' of bestiality, or a return to animal levels. . .as if there were animals

---

* Some aspects of this study have been reported elsewhere (Solnit, 1966).

which inflict on their own kind what man can do to man. Just at this point the zoologist has to draw a clear line: these evil, horrible things are no animal survival that happened to be carried along in the imperceptible transition from animal to man; this evil belongs entirely on this side of the dividing line, it is purely human..." (Adolf Portmann, quoted by Waelder, 1960). As one index of this power of destructive aggression, which is very likely an underestimate, it has been calculated that 59 million human beings were killed in wars, assaults and other deadly quarrels between the years 1820 and 1945 (Richardson, 1960). In man the use of aggressive drives against the self can be seen in earliest childhood, especially in connection with the loss of, or deficiency of, care by the love object.

Our strong tendency to equate aggressiveness and aggression with anger, hatred and hostile behavior is often apparent even in those who have stated their intellectual conviction that aggressive behavior can be constructive, productive and peaceful. Perhaps, this is a deeply embedded and early learned defensive attitude, which asserts itself despite a theoretical conviction that aggression is an instinctual drive. The derivatives of aggression as an instinctual drive can be hostile and destructive or productive and peaceful depending on how they are related to libidinal and ego influences.

All theory is to some extent a fiction, the utility of which is based on its explanatory and predictive value. In our studies of the developing child, the explanatory and predictive value of the instinctual drive theory of aggression has been centered on object loss and states of illness and recovery in early childhood.

In this paper, I shall report observations of a small number of critically ill, hospitalized infants for whom modern biochemical medicine had provided life-saving physiological therapy, but whose recovery was initially blocked by reactions to being separated from their mothers. Certain aspects of these observations have been reported and discussed elsewhere (Solnit, 1966). Also, I shall present briefly the observations of children attempting to recover from maternal deprivation and the implications of these observations based on an elaboration of instinct drive theory, in particular the aggressive drives.

Rene Spitz (1965) has pointed out:

"Anaclitic depression and hospitalism demonstrate that a gross deficiency in object relations leads to an arrest in the development of all sectors of the personality. These two disturbances highlight the cardinal role of object relations in the infant's development. More specifically, the catamnesis of our subjects affected by these two disturbances suggests a revision of our assumptions about the role of the aggressive drive in infantile development. The manifestations of aggression* common in the normal child after the eighth month, such as hitting, biting, chewing, etc., are conspicuously absent in the children suffering from either anaclitic depression or hospitalism. I have pointed out earlier in this study that the development of the drives, both libidinal and aggressive, is closely linked to the infant's relation to his libidinal object. The infant's relation with the love object provides an outlet for his aggressive drive in the activities provoked by the object. At the stage of infantile ambivalence (that is, the second half of the first year) the normal infant makes no difference between the discharge of the aggressive or the libidinal object drives; both are deprived of their target. This is what happened to the infants affected with anaclitic depression."

Continuing his formulations about maternally deprived infants, Spitz said,

"Now the drives hang in mid-air, so to speak. If we follow the fate of the aggressive drive, we find the infant turning aggression back onto himself, onto the only object remaining. Clinically, these infants become incapable of assimilating

---

* Spitz states, "My usage of the terms "aggression" and "aggressive drive" has nothing to do with the popular meaning of the word "aggressive". The aggressive drive, "aggression" for short, designates one of the two fundamental instinctual drives operating in the psyche, as postulated by Freud (1920) — and referred to by some authors as "aggressive instinct". Accordingly, when I speak of "aggression," I do not imply hostility or destructiveness, although at times these also may be among the manifestations of the drive."

foods; they become insomniac; later these infants may actively
attack themselves, banging their heads against the side of
the cot, hitting their heads with their fists, tearing their hair
out by the fistful. If the deprivation becomes total, the condition turns into hospitalism; deterioration progresses inex-
orably, leading to marasmus and death."

"As long as the infants were deprived of their libidinal
object, they became increasingly unable to direct outward,
not only libido, but *also* aggression. The vicissitudes of the
instinctual drives are, of course, not accessible to direct
observation. But one may infer from the symptomatology
of anaclitic depression that the pressure (impetus, Freud,
1915) of the aggressive drive is the carrier, as it were, not
only of itself, but also of the libidinal drive. If we assume
that in the normal child of that age (that is, the second half
of the first year) the two drives are being fused, we may also
postulate that in the deprived infant, a defusion of drives
occurs." (pp. 285–286.)

He continues (1965, p. 288):

"The infants suffering from marasmus had been deprived of
the opportunity to form object relations. Consequently they
had not been able to direct the libidinal drive and the aggressive drive onto one and the same object — the indispensable
prerequisite toward achieving the fusion of the two drives.
Deprived of an object in the external world, the unfused
drives were turned against their own person, which they took
as object. The consequence of turning nonfused aggression
against their own person became manifest in the destructive effects of deterioration of the infant, in the form of
marasmus."

Rene Spitz's contributions (1945, 1946a, 1946b) along these
lines were of critical assistance in successfully treating four infants
reported in this paper, who appeared doomed to the ravages of
post-infectious diarrhea. His continuing work (1950a, 1950b, 1951,

1953 and 1956) and that of Hartmann (1939, 1950, 1952 and 1953) of Hartmann, Kris and Loewenstein (1948) and of Schur (1958, 1962, 1963, and 1966) enabled us to articulate the theoretical implications of the observations of the illness and successful treatment of the four infants.

Aggressive behavior is often mistaken as a threat to socialization or to survival. In this paper, it is assumed contrariwise, that in the infant and in older children recovering from maternal deprivation it often should be viewed as providing a basis for contacting the object world and holding onto it. From our observations, aggressive behavior can be understood as the revitalization and redirecting of the drive energies that had been dampened or deprived of attachment to and investment in the world of love objects. The critical question is to what degree and in what way do the aggressive strivings indicate turning toward health and in what way do they indicate a turning toward illness? In the first year of life, what promotes the clinging attachment to the crucial human objects and the binding of instinctual striving elicited and directed toward those objects which are essential in creating this environment?

A seven-months-old hospitalized infant died despite the appropriate physiological and antibiotic treatment of post-infectious diarrhea. Although the diarrhea had been viral in origin and the infection had yielded to the classical treatment (replacement of fluids and electrolytes while relieving the gastrointestinal system of unnecessary stress), the child's post-infectious diarrhea continued. The baby died despite the biochemical replacements and despite the detailed attention to his physical condition. As we reviewed the death of this unfortunate child, questions about his emotional needs were raised. However, these questions were put aside for a few days when in rapid succession four more infants, five to twelve months of age, were admitted to the hospital with the same condition; an infectious diarrhea in which the infection had yielded to the treatment, but the continuing diarrhea and apathy indicated a life-threatening course for each child. Our study did not suggest alterations in the physiological-biochemical treatment, which included electrolyte and fluid replacements as indicated by a careful monitoring of sodium, chloride and potassium levels.

We made the assumption that emotional replacements would be essential if these children were to recover. It was assumed that the hospitalization was accompanied by a severe deprivation of essential mothering care, crucial libidinal supplies for young children who had a dawning or well-developed specific awareness of their respective mothers. It was inferred that the physiological depletion caused by the infectious diarrhea had magnified this emotional maternal deprivation not only by sapping the strength and resilience of the babies, but by requiring initial hospitalization on an isolation ward because of the infectious process. Isolation techniques by their precautionary content tend to discourage and decrease physical contact with the young patient. The children were transferred to general pediatrics when they were no longer infectious, and it was at this point that our responsibility began.

Since a rooming in arrangement for the mothers was not feasible at that time, we decided to arrange for emotional replacements by providing substitute maternal supplies as closely as we could for four infants. A unit system of nursing was instituted in which each of the four children had the same student nurse for each of the eight-hour shifts. Each nurse had sufficient time to provide total care, essential physical and psychological care (libidinal nutrients), for the children to whom she was assigned. The nurses were encouraged to hold, cuddle, talk to and be very visible to each of the children for whom they were caring. Brightly colored suitable toys were offered in an appropriately playful manner. Monitoring and replacing physiological and biochemical ingredients continued in a vigorous and detailed manner.

Each of these four children recovered completely. From the observations of their recovery, it appeared that irritable activity initiated the recovery process and implied that this was based on a restoration of instinctual drive energy. Such manifestations not only suggested derivatives of a qualitatively different instinctual drive activity but also indicated a change in the direction of the drive activity discharge. Each of the infants was washed out, limp, apathetic, and reduced to a whimper by the time they were transferred from the contagious disease section to the pediatric unit in the same hospital. The infectious process had subsided, but the diarrhea persisted. In each case, the return of interest in sucking and in food was preceded by evidence of more body tone, kicking and flailing activities of the extremities and the expression of a vigorous angry or irritable cry. These activities were assumed to represent manifestations of aggression or aggressive activities.

The nurses initially were alarmed when the children sounded angry and irritable. They fearfully wondered if they were not caring for the children correctly and tried desperately to soothe them, since they were aware of our consternation and anxiety about the death of the first child. However, reassured by our knowledge that recovery is often accompanied by irritable disagreeable behavior, the nurses were encouraged to maintain their care. Soon thereafter, the infants again showed interest in sucking when food appeared, the diarrhea began to abate, and the nurses could tell us that the children were now responding in the expected manner and that they were recovering.

The washing out effects of the diarrhea appeared to have been heightened to an alarming degree by the child's reactions to the loss of mothering attention, a fusion of libidinal and aggressive investments. These children, 5, 6, 7, and 12 months of age, were being deprived of maternal care, which in our later thinking we formulated as the loss of the emotional nourishment that can be provided by a need-satisfying figure who had begun to become specific, i. e., constant, in many significant and expectable ways as their mother. This vital relationship was seriously compromised by the hospitalization that was otherwise so crucial for the recognition and effective treatment designed to promote the healing and recovery of the insulted body. However, the infants' capacity to use this treatment regime was seriously hampered by the accompanying effects of maternal deprivation. The individualized need-satisfying nursing care enabled each child to have a substitute or replacement maternal presence, and to retain and benefit from the medical treatment and replacements he was given. One could say that critical libidinal nutriments were required before essential mineral and caloric replacements could be retained and assimilated.

During the acute physical illness, the dawning ego capacities of the infants were overwhelmed by the physiological depletion, as well as by the loss of and unavailability of the maternal love object, the child's auxiliary ego. Thus, even those external and internal capacities for modifying, channeling and discharging the available drive energies were impaired and unavailable.

Why did irritable behavior appear first; rather than behavior that signified the usual evidence of satisfaction and contentment when the nurse played with and cared for her patient as she provided him with loving attention, i.e., libidinal supplies? Probably because the child generally and physically felt irritable and somatically uncomfortable, but also because there was a need-satisfying object, a detectable presence who stimulated and evoked his fussy behavior and its discharge. The student nurse actively cared for the child and provided him with meaningful stimulation and with a target for his feelings and behavior. She coaxed the child to pay attention to her and was the person to whom the child could relate. She enabled the baby to feel loving attention and provided him with a person against whom to discharge those irritable feelings that are the forerunners to later aggressive activity. One could say that otherwise such psychic energies remain attached to and destructive of the self. In the infant, the mental or psychic self and the body are one and the same until shortly before the second half of the first year of life; that is, in the first months of life the child's psychological functioning is represented by the child's physiology.

Hartmann's views provide a further theoretical understanding of these phenomena. He said:

> "Neutralization of energy is clearly to be postulated from the time at which the ego evolves as a more or less demarcated substructure of personality. And viewed from another angle, we might expect that the formation of constant object relationship presupposes some degree of neutralization. But it is not unlikely that the use of this form of energy starts much earlier and that already the primordial forms of postponement and inhibition of discharge are fed by energy that

is partly neutralized. Some countercathectic energy distributions probably arise in infancy. Again, these and related phenomena seem easier to understand if one accepts the hypothesis of gradations of neutralization as just outlined." (1952, p. 171f).

Earlier, Hartmann (1950) had declared:

"To take again an example from the field of 'narcissism': it is of paramount importance for our understanding of the various forms of 'withdrawal of libido from reality,' in terms of their effects on ego functions, to see clearly whether the part of the resulting self-cathexes localized in the ego is still close to sexuality or has undergone a thorough process of neutralization. An increase in the ego's neutralized cathexes is not likely to cause pathological phenomena; but its being swamped by insufficiently neutralized instinctual energy may have effects (under certain conditions). In this connection, the ego's capacity for neutralization becomes relevant and, in the case of pathological development, the degree to which this capacity has been interfered with as a consequence of ego regression. What I just said about the bearing of neutralization on the outcome of libido withdrawal is equally true where not libidinal but aggressive cathexes are being turned back from the objects upon the self and in part upon the ego." (p. 129f).

In these children, recovering from a post-infectious diarrhea, the physical illness compounded by the loss of the mother had a retarding and regressive influence on the processes of drive differentiation and the differentiation of the self and the body. This speculation further suggests that the maternal deprivation caused by the hospitalization is experienced as a loss of the need-satisfying object that was also beginning to be perceived as a dependable-expectable-constant love object. This loss has an impact that can be formulated energetically as the infant's instinctual drive elements remaining relatively undifferentiated and unneutralized. These archaic drive elements are retained by the body and one might say that they have the effect of a catabolic force. Rather than being discharged in a health-promoting interaction toward the mother and other figures in the environment, the deprived convalescing child's interests and energies were withdrawn from the outside world. This withdrawal further deprived the weakened child of libidinal nutrients that were available.

Spitz's observations, though concentrating on the psychological and physical impairments caused by object loss, have implications for the pathological reinforcement that results when physical illness in infancy is compounded by object loss. In his study of the role of aggression (Spitz, 1953), he stated:

"How does this come about? When the separated infant cannot find a target for the discharge of its drive, the infant first becomes weepy, demanding and clinging to everybody who approaches it; it looks as though attempts are made by these infants to regain the lost object with the help of their aggressive drive. Later on, visible manifestations of the aggressive drive decrease; and after two months of uninterrupted separation the first definite somatic symptoms are manifested by the infant. These consist of sleeplessness, loss of appetite, loss of weight."

Presumably, physical illness, such as an infectious diarrhea could bring about an acceleration of this process, the child's resources being exhausted by the combined physiological and psychological insults. Spitz continued his formulation (1953):

"Some light is thrown on this question by our observations on infants suffering from hospitalism: they present a tangible demonstration of the defusion of the two drives. It can be observed in the unchecked progression of deterioration in these children who were subjected to long-term deprivation of emotional supplies. The result is a progressive destruction of the infant itself, eventually leading to death." (p. 134)
"Theoretically we may posit that in these children the aggression has been turned against the self, resulting in the shockingly high percentage of deaths. . ." (p. 135)

In commenting on the contributions of Hartmann, Kris and Loewenstein (1949) to the theory of aggression, Spitz further increases our understanding of the process involved in the illness and recovery of these infants. He stated (Spitz, 1953):

"This approach resulted in several conclusions, one of which is that .... the internalization, without neutralization, of aggressive energy in the ego must lead to some kind of self-destruction. The authors (Hartmann, Kris and Loewenstein, 1949) suggest further that 'internalized aggression plays a relevant role in the etiology of illness.' " (p. 126)

Recapitulating, we can say that in this group of hospitalized infants, recovery from a post-infectious diarrhea was hindered dangerously because biochemical replacements could not be retained in the absence of the love object. The body's capacity to respond to the biochemical and fluid infusions was restricted until libidinal replacements could be infused at the same time. The nurse, as a substitute love object, provided libidinal infusions, enabling the child to retain the biochemical and fluid infusions. Lacking the libidinal supplies, the child also lacked sufficient neutralized energies to deal with aggression directed against the self and to respond to external nutrients.

Further, I would hypothesize that a deficit of neutralized energy hinders the body's capacity to retain and assimilate physiological replacements. To put it in another way, the retention of physiological replacements requires a degree of physiological inhibition — a capacity to store and hold against developing pressure — that may be the equivalent of the psychological capacity to postpone or wait. This psychological capacity is dependent on the presence of a countercathectic influence or force (Hartmann, 1950), which is directed against the instinctual drives pressing for immediate discharge. To follow this analogy (with all of its risks) of physiological and psychological explanations, just as a child cannot develop if he cannot wait, a child who cannot retain physiological pressure may suffer from a chronic diarrhea that does not respond to biochemical replacement therapy.

The relationship to the active, loving maternal figure is, as studies of the marasmic, institutionalized, affect-deprived child have suggested, a vital and essential protective and nurturing influence on the young child. This formulation is now elaborated to suggest the further consideration that a child's irritable, aggressive reaction may be his first response of recovery and adaptation when psychological and physiological replacements are made available. In such a situation the aggressive energies destructively contained within or directed against the self are now redirected to the external object as the influence of the libidinally invested nurse vigorously stimulated, soothed and cared for these ailing infants. In this manner, the nurse as an auxiliary ego aided each child's capacity to neutralize instinctual energies, bringing into effect the counter-cathexes and postponing, inhibiting capabilities. Without these capabilities the children would have been unable to retain stimuli and eventually to utilize the gratifying libidinal relationship as discharging, relieving, soothing, pleasurable experiences. In turn, these processes provided the conditions for continued object relatedness and a neutralization of instinctual drive energies so necessary for ego development and functioning.

In life threatening situations, the first defense against an external or internal danger is flight or fight. Flight is maturationally not available in infancy or for that matter in any physical illness. The capacity to fight or actively to express aggressive outer-directed behavior requires an object, an auxiliary ego to facilitate the neutralization of instinctual energies and to provide a target against which the infant can discharge his feelings and behavior. Thus, the child is encouraged — in fact, coaxed to respond in an object-related manner. The maternal object provides the helpless infant on the one side with a target against which libidinal and aggressive drive derivatives can be directed; and on the other side with the neutralizing, countercathectic influences of the auxiliary ego.

The need-satisfying mothering object carries out those ego functions that provide the expectable or required adaptive influences necessary for preservation of life and promotion of growth and development. In the case of the hospitalized infants with post-infectious diarrhea and their recovery described above, it is assumed that with the replacement of the need-satisfying object and the biochemical deficits the child regained the capacity to complain, to engage in defensive behavior, and to develop that physiological and psychological tone compatible with adaptive responses.

In our studies of children who failed to thrive due to under-stimulation and neglect, provocative poorly-controlled behavior often appears as restitutive survival and socialization phenomena presenting a paradox of bewildering proportions. These phenomena have been observed in children recovering from relative maternal deprivation in the home, and in those who were placed in a foster home after living in an institution. As the individual child recovered from the disadvantage of understimulation, his pathway to recovery appeared to be characterized by aggressive behavior. This pattern of recovery, namely aggressive provocative behavior was often misperceived as undesirable wildness. What could be regarded as the child "coming alive" as his drives were awakened by affection and a responsive environment, was often reacted to by parents and foster parents as unacceptable, undesirable and rejecting of the adults. What the psychologically educated observer might view as tumultuous desirable unfolding behavior is usually experienced by parental persons as intolerable.

I have assumed that this "coming alive" or activation of dor-mant and often stunted drive capacities produces a disharmony or dissynchronization of impulsive energies and regulative capa-cities in the individual child. Viewed in this way, the recovering deprived child's drives and his capacities to transform, channel or ward off the pressures and demands of his revitalized drive energies are out of phase. Ironically, just as some of these children begin to respond, to "come alive," the (foster) parents feel over-whelmed by their behavior, which is often misperceived as a lack of grace and gratitude as well as a rejection of the parents. In these instances, the foster parents, feeling let down, often bitterly invoke the explanation of the bad seed in these children whose background may represent evidences of unacceptable social values for these parents. The natural parents also usually reject such behavior as the reason they neglected or could not take adequate care of the child in the first place. This latter rationalization is one of many defensive, protective reactions by these parents in their efforts to ward off their own fearful or guilty feeling about their abused or neglected children.

In their follow-up study of institutionalized children placed in foster homes, *Infants in Institutions* (1962, p. 148), Provence and Lipton state,

> "As time passed the beneficial influence of maternal care, family life, and the enrichment of experience in many areas was increasingly manifest in all aspects of development. The children became more lively, more active, began to learn to play, and to solve everyday problems. They increasingly made relationships with each other. In addition, there were signs of improvement that were not always universally recognized by the parents as signs of growth: they began now to show some provocative, negativistic and aggressive behavior. This was a time of crisis for some of the parents and children. If the parents saw this behavior as bad or as indicating that they were failing as parents or if they felt rejected by the child, some either gave up in actuality and asked that the child be removed from the home, or withdrew some of the emotional investment and interest that were so important to his improvement. Others realized that such behavior was a necessary step in the child's progress and were able to react to it in a helpful way."

Socializing is a broad concept. It deals with people living together, forming a unit in which the whole is greater than the sum of the parts, embracing considerations as widely separated as social values and biological adaptations. The infant will die or suffer severe developmental impairments if the mother does not feed, stimulate and protect him in the context of affectionate expectations.

Recent studies of deprived children (Powell, et al., 1967) strongly suggest that the biological forces that are associated with skeletal growth are significantly influenced by maternal deprivation. There is a parallel effect on instinctual drive development; the phase specific unfolding and organizing of psycho-sexual and psycho-aggressive energies are muted and in severe cases seem to be unavailable for involvement with people and human situations outside of the child himself. Failure to thrive is a term that often describes the effect of maternal deprivation on both physical and psychological development. Such paradoxes as temper tantrums representing recovery and easy adaptation to changes in the environment representing illness are clarified by assumptions provided by psychoanalytic instinct theory, especially by Schur's recent work, *The Id and The Regulatory Principles of Mental Functioning*. (Schur, 1966) The maturation of instinctual drives, not only in the differentiation of libidinal and aggressive drives, but also in other characteristics, is a productive theory building assumption in that it classifies the reactions to object loss and the restitutive phenomena of recovery states.

Emotional deficiency, as in institutionalization, can and often does lead to nutritional deficiency and failure to grow, with permanent residual impairments of physical, social, mental and emotional capacities. The earliest observation of this fact is recorded in the famous experiment in education by Emperor Frederick the Second, in the Thirteenth Century. Curious about what language a child would first speak if he were untaught — whether it would be the classic languages, Latin, Greek, Hebrew or his own mother tongue, the Emperor instructed the nurses of newborn homeless babies to provide all necessary physical care but never to speak to the children or show any signs of affection. The infants all died at an early age, and the Emperor stated that they could not live without the demonstrated affection and friendliness of their nurses.

Conversely, when a child has suffered such deprivation and replacements of continuing affectionate care are made available, the recovery often manifests itself by behavior that is derivative of the activation and freeing-up of instinctual drive energies. Initially the behavior suggests that the drives are poorly fused and not influenced in a sustained manner by ego functions that are also being restored and unfolded in this restitutive or recovery process.

In considering the implications of such observations, it becomes clear that the maturational vitality of the instinctual drives is a critical dimension of the reversibility or permanence of the impairment of development caused by maternal deprivation. Paradoxically, the provocative or demanding qualities of this restitutive behavior are associated with and characterize recovery of drive energy available for survival, biologically and socially.

As has been pointed out by Hartmann (1950) and Schur (1966) as well as others (Provence and Lipton, 1962), the maturational unfolding of psychic capacities and structures, including id and ego functions tends to follow the patterning characteristic of the species, man. When there are conditions of deprivation, these functions may be lost, stunted or distorted. In providing conditions that promote recovery from these deprivational states, we may expect to see phenomena in which id and ego are dissynchronous and in which id-ego relationships are conflicted and distorted.

Summary and Conclusions

The study of a group of infants recovering from diarrhea and of children recovering from institutional maternal deprivation enables us to elaborate the hypothesis that aggressive behavior may be adaptive, and to suggest that the absence of aggressive behavior may be an alarming evidence of maladaptation. Aggressive behavior in such instances may be viewed as the return of drive energies available for relating to love objects and life in the external world. However, such recovery often proceeds with the return of externally directed drive activity followed by ego development that enables the child to fuse and neutralize drive energies necessary for the recovery and progressive development.

In the first part of this study, maladaptation involved a debilitating physical illness magnified by the persistent loss of the constant love object, the auxiliary ego. With this loss the infant may be said to have a decreased capacity to form countercathexes necessary for curbing and channeling the instinctual drives and their derivatives. The regressed helpless state of these infants suggests that the relatively unmodified drives were discharged within the body with the aggressive components unbound and destructive.

In the study of older children recovering from the affect deprivation that commonly is associated with institutionalization, the rate of recovery and characteristics of the ego and id functions during the recovery period may be uneven and poorly synchronized. This is often misperceived as undesirable provocative behavior which can result in a damaging rejection of the child just when he has expressed his trusting and restitutive responses to the adults who have provided him with the beginning basis for recovery.

REFERENCES

Einstein, A. (1932) Letter to S. Freud *Standard Edition*, 22*, 1932–1936 London, Hogarth Press & The Institute of Psycho-Analysis, 1964.

Freud, S. (1893–1899) On The Psychical Mechanism of Hysterical Phenomena, *Standard Edition*, 3*, pp. 36

——— (1915), The Unconscious. *Standard Edition*. 14*

——— (1920), Beyond the Pleasure Principle, *Standard Edition*. 18*

——— (1930), Civilization and its Discontents. *Standard Edition*, 21*
Hartman, H. (1939), *Ego Psychology and the Problem of Adaptation*. New York: International Universities Press, 1958, pp. 119–126.

——— (1950), Comments on the Psychoanalytic Theory of the Ego. *The Psychoanalytic Study of the Child*, 5.

——— (1952), The Mutual Influences in the Development of Ego and Id. *The Psychoanalytic Study of the Child*, 7.

——— (1953), Contribution to the Metapsychology of Schizophrenia. *The Psychoanalytic Study of the Child*, 8.

——— Kris, E., and Loewenstein, R. M. (1949), Notes on the Theory of Aggression. *The Psychoanalytic Study of the Child*, 3/4.

Powell, G. F., Brasel, J. A., and Blizzard, R. M. (1967) Emotional Deprivation and Growth Retardation Simulating Ideopathic Hypopituitarism

I. Clinical Evaluation of the Syndrome *The New England Journal of Medicine*, June 8, 1967, Vol. 276, No. 23, pp. 1271–1278.

* *The Standard Edition of the Complete Psychological Works of Sigmund Freud*, 24 Vols., translated and edited by James Strachey. London: Hogarth Press and the Institute of Psycho-Analysis, 1963.

Powell, G. F., Brasel, J. A., Raiti, S., and Blizzard, R. H. (1967) Emotional Deprivation and Growth Retardation Simulating Ideopathic Hypopituitarism. II. Endocrinological Evaluation of the Syndrome *The New England Journal of Medicine*, June 8, 1967, Vol. 276, No. 23, pp. 1279–1283.

Provence, S. and Lipton, R. C. (1962), *Infants in Institutions.* New York: International Universities Press.

Ribble, M. A. (1943), *The Rights of Infants.* New York: Columbia University Press.

Richardson, Lewis (1960), *Statistics of Deadly Quarrels.* London: Stevens and Son.

Schur, Max (1966), *The Id and the Regulatory Principles of Mental Functioning*, pp. 51–76. New York: International Universities Press, (Journal of the American Psychoanalytic Association, Monograph Series Number Four).

Solnit, Albert J. (1966), Some Adaptive Functions of Aggressive Behavior. In *Psychoanalysis — A General Psychology*, ed. R. M. Loewenstein, L. Newman, M. Schur & A. J. Solnit. New York: International Universities Press.

Spitz, Rene (1945) Hospitalism: An Inquiry into the Genesis of Psychiatric Conditions in Early Childhood. *The Psychoanalytic Study of the Child*, 1.

——— (1946a), Hospitalism: A Follow-Up Report. *The Psychoanalytic Study of the Child*, 2.

——— (1946b), Anaclitic Depression: An Inquiry into the Genesis of Psychiatric Conditions in Early Childhood, II. *The Psychoanalytic Study of the Child*, 2.

——— (1950a) Psychiatric Therapy in Infancy. *American Journal of Orthopsychiatry*, 20.

——— (1950b), Anxiety in Infancy: A Study of Its Manifestations in the First Year of Life. *Int. J. Psycho-Anal.*, 31.

——— (1951), The Psychogenic Diseases in Infancy: An Attempt at Their Etiologic Classification. *The Psychoanalytic Study of the Child*, 6.

——— (1953), Aggression: Its Role in the Establishment of Object Relations, in: *Drives, Affects, Behavior*, ed. R. M. Loewenstein. New York: International Universities Press.

——— (1956), Some Observations on Psychiatric Stress in Infancy. In: *Fifth Annual Report on Stress*, ed. H. Selye & G. Heuser. New York: M. D. Publications.

——— (1965), *The First Year of Life*. In collaboration with W. Godfrey Cobliner. New York: International Universities Press.

Waelder, R. (1960), *Basic Theory of Psychoanalysis*, New York: International Universities Press.

Another View

Naomi Glucksohn-Weiss

Dr. Solnit's thought provoking paper touches upon many problems which have occupied us for no less than three decades: the problem of an infant's reaction to lengthy separation from his mother; the process of recovery when a substitute is found; the way the process of recovery and return of vitality is accompanied by outbursts of aggression as well as all the theoretical implications deriving from the observations.

I would like to react to some of the points Dr. Solnit touches upon in a free and personal way. First of all I was struck by the similarity of this phenomenon of the outburst of aggression of Dr. Solnit's convalescent infants with what happens in psychotherapy of youngsters, when the child patient, in the transference situation, attacks the therapist. I was wondering whether we can do justice to this problem without paying attention to the experiencing side of these children. Could closer observation of the individual children, especially the older ones among them, give us any hint as to how the child felt, how the new maternal figure looked to him, and how he interpreted his pain and discomfort in relation to the person who nursed him.

One of Dr. Solnit's main ideas is that aggression need not necessarily be an expression of anger, hatred, destructiveness, but that aggressive behavior can be adaptive, and that its manifestations during recovery from illness and states of acute maternal deprivation might be a sign of returning vitality, while its absence might be an alarming evidence of maladaptation.

I can quite agree with this statement as, like so many analysts today, I have come to regard aggression not as a "death instinct," or a destructive force per se, but as a vital force in the emotional equipment of man. Since the work of Hartman, Kris and Loewenstein, we have also come to accept the theory of neutralized aggression which supplies the energy for so many ego functions, as well as the idea of an early undifferentiated state, when libido and aggression are part of a general drive energy at the beginning hardly distinguishable from each other. Spitz — as quoted by Dr. Solnit — expresses the idea that the pressure of the aggressive drive is the carrier not only of itself, but also of the libidinal drive. Winnicott goes one step further in regarding aggression at the beginning, as the motility aspect of every libidinal drive, the force that makes the neonate and even the foetus reach out into the environment. Far from equating aggression with the death instinct, he calls it "life force."

Returning to the subject "Why War," why hatred, why destruction? — I would raise the question: At what point and under what circumstances does this force which in itself can be beneficial and productive assume hateful, destructive aspects. Further, does the behavior of the four children in Dr. Solnit's study already entail elements of hostility, over and above its beneficial function, and if so, can we detect the cause of such hostility?

I think that Dr. Solnit himself gives us a partial answer when he says; "In man, the use of aggressive drives against the self can be seen in earliest childhood, especially in *connection with the loss of, or deficiency of, care by the love object.*"

While Dr. Solnit here speaks of aggression turned against the self, I think that this point of the loss of the love object is crucial and has also a bearing upon the problem of pathological destructiveness in general. Since the work of Bowlby in England we have come to recognize the close link between antisocial, destructive behavior and early maternal deprivation. As we all know, maternal deprivation, with all its implications, lies at the root of many forms of pathology and we know how great a pathogenic role aggression plays in these states.

I think it may help our understanding of the problem a little further if we look into some of Winnicott's ideas on the subject.

Briefly, though this might oversimplify matters to a certain extent, Winnicott regards aggression at the beginning of life as the motility aspect of every libidinal drive. Every primitive lidibinal drive has a powerful motility component which causes it to reach out into the environment, hit against is, and thus gradually get an awareness of its existence, as well as of the boundaries of the self. Any harm caused in this way is purely accidental. That is what Winnicott calls the "preruth" stage. Later, however, things start to change, and further development depends on what environment the baby has. If there is "good enough mothering" the baby learns more and more about self and environment, his aggressive drives develop through dealing with normal opposition, and he starts looking for opposition in order to exercise his strength. When ties to the libidinal object strengthen he starts being concerned about possible harm caused. With the less lucky cases there are gradations from not so good to positively bad mothering. Here it is not the baby who, through his own impulses, reaches out and hits against the environment, but the environment impinges upon the baby. The baby's behavior now consists not of genuine impulses belonging to his true self, but a series of reactions to impingement. As the environment impinges upon the baby, the baby withdraws, and when impingement is persistent, even that is impossible. The world looks hostile, full of persecutors, and the baby may react with anxiety or violent outbursts of aggression.

Now returning to Dr. Solnit's four little patients, I would like to suggest that while their aggressive behavior in fact was a sign of returning vitality — libidinal and aggressive alike — yet there was still enough suffering (results of physical illness as well as separation from real mothers) — so that the babies may have felt maltreated, and reacted with a good deal of anger.

This brings me back to my first point, that of the experiencing side of what happens. You will remember that in her paper on "The Role of Bodily Illness in the Mental Life of Children," Miss Freud makes the important point that different children give different interpretations to what happens to them during illness. I am quoting now: "The analytic study of such behavior reveals as different not the actual bodily experience of pain but the degree to which the pain is charged with psychic meaning. Children are apt to ascribe to outside agencies whatever painful process inside the body. . ." further: "So far as his own interpretation is concerned, the child in pain is a child maltreated, harmed, punished, threatened by annihilation." Admittedly Miss Freud talks of children older than those of Dr. Solnit's study. Yet the latter, in the second half of their first year of life, assuming they have developed normally prior to their hospitalization, may be conceived to be emerging from the symbiosis with their mothers, or — to use Winnicott's expression again — they are now whole persons relating to whole subjects. Most likely they already have some feeling, and fantasies in relation to the central figures around them. While we canot ask them what they feel and think, we might try and observe whether, e. g. when they hit the nurse, they look frightened, angry, pleased or concerned. We also might listen to slightly older children. I happened to hear a little 18 month old normal girl, who while suffering from sore throat shouted at her mother: "Stop! Stop!" Another similar incident was reported to me by a mother of a twenty months old normal child, who under similar circumstances kept on complaining "Enough, enough!" Obviously both children assumed that their mothers were hurting them and that it was in their power to relieve the pain, if they so wished. Their anger was an appropriate reaction under the circumstances. The four hospitalized children might have had similar fantasies. Also, those of them who might have had a memory of their mothers, might have resented the nurses for not being the mother they miss, assuming that the nurses caused their mothers to disappear.

To understand the problem better, we have to take the information gained through such research as Bowlby's and Solnit's and try to enrich and deepen the understanding by studies of the type of Miss Freud and Winnicott, in an attempt to get some insight into the inner life of the child.

To sum up: My assumption would be that anger, hatred and the wish to destroy become more and more closely and inseparably linked to normal aggressiveness as a function of the deficiency of good mothering.

Outlook: An American View

Mortimer Ostow

In the letter which we chose as the point of departure for this volume. Freud wrote: "Why do you and I and so many other people rebel so violently against war? Why do we not accept it as another of the many painful calamities of life? After all, it seems to be quite a natural thing, to have a good biological basis and in practice to be scarcely avoidable."

My interest — and I assume the interest of all of the contributors to this volume—in the subject of war, is the hope that psychoanalysts might be able to make some contribution to an understanding of the psychological basis for war, and the hope that we might then be in a position to suggest some measures which might help to prevent or even to deter war. If one asks why do we have such an interest, one seems to be asking a foolish question. The answer is self-evident. We wish to avoid the possibility that we, our children, our families of friends might be hurt or killed. We wish to hold onto the culture and community within which we live. Gumbel describes the interplay between our conscious attraction to these, and our unconscious rejection of them.

In 1932, Freud gave an additional answer, namely, that the "process of civilzation" has wrought an organic change in some individuals so that they can no longer "put up with it." He compared the evolution of this "constitutional intolerance" of war to the progressive refinement of our esthetic sensitivities. Here one misses Freud's usual cynicism, which is better reflected in the statement I quoted first. One suspects that Freud might have hesitated to suggest the existence of a constitutional growing and transmitted aversion to savagery in western civilization in the light of the events of the subsequent fifteen years. I then asked myself the following questions: (1) Is the nature of the human propensity for making war properly a subject for psychoanalytic study? (2) What happens in the area of psychic function to the citizens of a country at war, and to the soldiers? (3) What is the nature of the struggle against war? (4) What can we hope for? (5) What recommendations can we make?

Is war properly a subject for psychoanalytic study? From a practical point of view one suspects that the answer is No. I say that first, because there has been so little psychoanalyitc study of the subject of war despite ample opportunity: and second, because although Freud himself was in a position to make studies, I know of no data that he published. Making war is an activity of the community rather than of the individual, as both Atkin and Wedge observed. The individual participates in the warring community or in the fighting itself, but he does not make war or terminate it. The war, and the war-preparedness of his community, constitute a portion of the individual's reality. The patient's attitude toward war comes to the psychoanalyst's attention when it carries a projection of the patient's unconscious wishes: when it deviates significantly from the attitude of the community or the government; or when the psychoanalyst himself is not a member of the warring community. Otherwise, as Atkin tells us, the patient's attitude towards war remains invisible to the analyst.

I have had only one occasion to observe analytically the effect of a crisis of threatening war. That was in October 1962, at the time of the Cuban missile affair. There were two kinds of response. Some patients talked about plans for the remote future, mentioning nothing of the immediate threat. That is, they denied the threat. Other patients spoke only of their wish to be with their families at the time of the anticipated holocaust. Death seemed to be feared less if the family was together at the time. I did not see any concern with the enemy, or any question about the stand of the government. In other words, at a moment of sudden and real war peril, the only phenomena that were visible in analysis were emergency responses to the threat of personal annihilation. The phenomenon of being at war, of being arrayed against an enemy, of accepting leadership did not present itself for examination.

War is made by the community, but the community does not come under psychoanalytic scrutiny. Aggression toward another member of the group becomes visible in analysis as a miscarriage of object love, as a consequence of frustration, in negative transference, as an expression of repetition compulsion, or as a defiance of the superego or the community. But participation in the aggressiveness of the group is not visible as an individual phenomenon, certainly not to an analyst who is a member of the same group. If one regards was as a natural phenomenon, as a biologic property of the human community, then one would expect the readiness for war to be as inaccessible to clinical psychoanalytic study as the biology of the instincts or the biologic basis of group psychology. The psychologic basis of the readiness for war would become visible when the individual, because of his own idiosyncrasies; cannot permit himself to be incorporated into the group and to identify with its other members.

But we do know something about the psychology of the citizens of a country at war, and about the psychology of the fighting man. The papers of both Bental and Jaffe are instructive. We have read several versions of the thesis that intergroup hostility is derived from intragroup hostility by displacement and projection. Noy, as well as a number of others, describes this phenomenon clearly. This is a process which we can see in analysis, though usually with respect to visible and proximal objects of hostility, rather than remote enemies. It can also be inferred from the striking reduction of intragroup and even intrapersonal hostility in wartime. Jaffe describes the separate but coordinate roles of the fighting man's affection for his comrades and his hostliity towards his enemy. However, understanding the subjective experience does not mean that we understand how the phenomenon of war comes about, the mechansim, the dynamic process.

I have proposed that a special instinctual disposition is called into play on the occasion of war. One sees in it almost pure culture in the fighting men themselves and to a somewhat lesser degree in noncombatant civilians. It consists of two elements, a weakening of narcissistic and object-directed drives, and an overwhelming tendency to subordinate oneself to the needs of the community. This means that the individual becomes eager to expose himself to danger in the interest of defending the community, In the service of these tendencies, sensitivity to pain is markedly diminished. Danger, though still appreciated intellectually, becomes less threatening. Perhaps at the peak of belligerent excitement, the prospect of injury may seem sensually inviting in the same way that it does to the wrist-cutting adolescent. These changes seem to create an illusion of omnipotence and invulnerability. Jaffe described this remarkable focusing of attention on the task at hand to the point of derealization and depersonalization.

I have also suggested that this disposition, which makes war possible, is identical with, or related to, other and similar dispositions which promote self-sacrifice in the service of the welfare of the group. One thinks here of the mother in the process of parturition, the parent endangering himself to rescue a child in trouble, the angry adult who turns his anger back upon himself to protect the love object. Reflection of anger back upon oneself is commonly encountered in cases of psychosis, melancholic depression or suicide.

Similar to this pattern is one which we see earlier in life. The infant's hostility to his parent is often transformed into a masochistic perversion. The hostile impulse is turned back against the self and libidinized at the same time. But here the need to reflect aggression back against the self arises not from the need to protect the vulnerable object, but as a result of the inability to attack, that is, out of impotent rage. In all instances but the last, one exposes oneself to pain or danger to protect the vulnerable object. At the same time one experiences an illusion of omnipotence and indifference to, or welcoming of, danger and pain. The danger against which the object is protected may be one's own anger, some environmental threat, or any enemy.

Ordinarily one would not expect an enemy to be "hated" any more than any other threat, fire, flood or famine. But the hatred phenomenon is probably to be understood as a projection of one's own hostility toward the vulnerable object who is being protected. This notion is supported by Jaffe's observation that a soldier began to "hate" the enemy only after his comrade was killed.

But here again, even if we assume that this thesis is correct, it provides us only with the mechanism by which the individual accommodates himself to the community eneavour. It does not help us to understand how this community endeavour is initiated.

Yet, we ought to give serious thought to the proposition that when we find a biologic mechanism we may anticipate that it *stands ready*, and in a sense *strives* for activation. In this case, this proposition would mean that the availability of a biologic mechanism which provides for individual participation in the community war-making endeavour, actually encourages the community to utilize that mechanism.

I propose that the state of mind of the fighting man at the height of his involvement is a different state of mind from that which we ordinarily expect to encounter. It is characterized by the features which we have mentioned, namely, hyper-attention to the task at hand, an absence of fear, detachment from the rest of reality, a sense of invulnerability, and exhilaration to the point of omnipotence. While the incipience of this state of mind is not marked by any psychic experience, its termination is. I refer here to the sense of let-down and depression which Jaffe describes and attributes primarily to the separation from the group.

After the battle is over, the soldier asks, "How could I have done that?" I attribute this question to the fact that in one state of mind, the individual cannot comprehend or identify with his own subjective experience in the other state of mind. In the same way the depressive cannot understand how he could have been manic, and the manic cannot understand how he could have been depressed. Again, the schizophrenic in remission tries to understand what had happened to him in his state of relapse, but cannot understand it.

The spirit of self-sacrifice probably prevails widely through the entire army and probably through the entire nation in wartime. The further the individual is from the front lines, however, the less developed is this mental state.

If, as I contend, war is a natural function of the human species, embedded in its biology, then we must ask, "Why do we protest against and try to combat war?" (Notice how naturally one uses military concepts even in the cause of peace.) In short, what are we doing here?

We may divide opposition to war into two categories. Opposition to war arises among those individuals like us who deplore the loss of life, the pain, the suffering and the destruction which war brings, and yet who recognize that war may be inevitable, at least in the world as we know it today. We participate in investigations such as this, we work to promote international understanding and cooperation, and we are even willing to make certain sacrifices if we feel that they will prevent or deter fighting. However, we do not really expect that war will disappear from the face of the earth, at least not in our time.

Opposition to war arises also among individuals who are persuaded that wars *can* be stopped and prevented. What is required, they contend, is only that one's own government make whatever concessions to the enemy that may be demanded, or that one's own government disarm unilaterally in the expectation that this act will deter any potential enemy from attacking. When one attempts to argue against such a program on the basis of history, human nature, or logic, one encounters a surprising intransigence. The conviction of the antiwar idealist is maintained and proclaimed in the face of all contrary evidence and arguments. From such unreasonable behavior, the psychoanalyst might infer that the position is held in support of another, undisclosed and perhaps unconscious purpose. In this respect the position may resemble a delusion.

Like a delusion, this contention rests upon a nucleus of reality. There is a mechanism which operates among members of certain species of animals which prevents intra-specific murder. During territorial or courtship fighting, when the animal which is being overcome surrenders to the victor by exposing a vulnerable part, the victor is prevented from pressing his victory further and he must allow his victim to escape. Lorenz has proposed that the fragment of this mechanism which obtains among humans forms the basis of the Christian teaching that one should "turn the other cheek." But this mechanism seems to operate rather feebly among humans. Even that rudiment that may occasionally deter some individuals from cold-blooded murder, becomes inoperative when one's *society* is arrayed against another.

Second, a society which feels threatened by its neighbor may be discouraged from making war if the neighbor demonstrates in a realistic and meaningful way his disinclination to attack. But consider another case. Consider a society which, for entirely internal reasons, is impelled to take up arms against its neighbor. It will project its own hostility and see its neighbor as a threat. Should the neighbor now attempt to reassure the aggressor of his peaceful intentions, he will stand no more chance of succeeding than the victim of a paranoiac's delusional system will be able to persuade the patient of his good wishes. If the neighbor in a sincere, concilatory move, begins to disarm, his growing vulnerability is apt to motivate the aggressor to press his attack. It is not the projection which causes the hostility: it is the hostility which causes the projection.

There is little doubt that unilateral disarmament and generous concessions in the presence of a militant, expansionist, and unscrupulous enemy will only facilitate one's own downfall. We must conclude that those who press such measures unconsciously know their outcome, and that their unconscious desire is to see the downfall of their own society and of their families and themselves with it. I think of such unrealistic antiwar movements as forms of utopian antinomianism, in most of which one easily detects a suicidal and antisocial tendency. Atkin suggested that in some instances, peace-mindedness may be a reaction formation against war-mindedness. One of my patients who is especially active in the peace movement in the United States, enjoyed sadistic masturbation fantasies. She recently dreamed that someone's face was being branded with the peace symbol.

If these considerations are correct, we arrive at the paradoxic conclusion that antiwar zealots are no less—and perhaps more— carried away by the aggressiveness which prevails in their societies. They differ from their fellow citizens in that they refuse to divert hostility from self, family and friends to strangers. They therefore come to serve the interest of the enemy-stranger. In this way they try to satisfy directly their hostility toward their loved ones. Why these individuals turn against their parent society has not been satisfactorily studied, nor why such antisocial attitudes become more prevalent in different groups at different times. However, to the extent that these antiwar zealots weaken the parent society and make it hesitant, weak, fumbling and vulnerable, they invite attack by its enemies. The existence of the fifth column may encourage an enemy and itself become a cause of war or at least an invitation to it.

It is interesting parenthetically to note that by turning away from the causes of war to a study of its enemies, we learn something more about its causes.

Yet our hope for an extended spell of peace is encouraged by the fact that in many instances, contiguous societies dwell in peace and amity for generations. One could explain these instances by a similarity — or in some cases a dissimilarity of interests, or by adequacy of territory and resources, so that the material basis for rivalry does not exist. Such instances also occur when the two neighbors are threatened by a common enemy or a common natural problem. Yet no such theory explaining the occasional prevalence of protracted peaceful relations is cogent enough to have predictive value. The Arab states on the one hand and Israel on the other certainly possess much in the way of common history and tradition, many similar interests, material resources adequate for all, and some say even common enemies. Yet these reasons for peace cannot overcome the motivation for war. We note too that the efforts of the "haves" to share their resources with the "have nots" aggravate rather than attenuate hostility. After all such historical, sentimental, economic and territorial considerations, we must still explain the fact that at certain periods of history, certain people are more bellicose, more aggressive, or more fierce than at others.

I should like to propose for consideration a comparison which seems to me of some interest.

Just as Freud related the triumph of the sons over the fathers to regular festivals, and the latter ro recurrent mania, I should like to suggest another comparison relating individual illness to social behavior. I am impressed by Atkin's suggestion that one may consider that the social unit is more basic biologically than the individual. In that case the shift from independent psychic function to state of mind characteristic of being a member of a group would constitute a regression.

My comparison relates to mania too. It is my impression that manic behavior is to be compared not so much with behavior of a victor, as with the behavior of an individual in a mood to make

war. I speak not of the mood of the individual who fights merely
to defend himself against attack, but the mood of the belligerent
aggressor. The manic is an aggressive individual in the sense that
he presses campaigns with intensity and vigor. He becomes literally
belligerent if he is opposed, frustrated or merely unsuccessful. Like
the manic, the warrior nation is ambitious, and self-confident to the
point of feeling omnipotent. Wedge quotes from White a list of
six characteristics of the state of mind of the peoples of nations in
conflict. These include over-confidence, absence of empathy,
selective inattention, self-righteousness and projection of one's
own hostile imlpuses. These characteristics apply to the individual
manic as well. The attitude and behavior of the depressed individual on the other hand suggests that of a defeated community.

When I review the clinical characteristics of my own manic depressive patients, I find that indeed they all attempt to assume a
dominant role as they become manic and subside into an attitude
of surrender and subjugation as they become depressed. For example, one of my patients in his hypermanic attitude has been
called a "little Hitler" by his associates. Another only half jokingly
insisted upon being called El Supremo.

If such a comparison can be considered more than suggestive,
than it might be inferred that just as mania is a pathologic condition
of the individual, so war readiness may be considered a pathologic
condition of the society. However I prefer to think of manic-
depressive behavior as a pathologic variant of normal social
attitudes. In other words, in a state of pathologic degeneration
the attitude which the individual, as a member of his society,
assumes toward other societies, may become that of the manic
depressive. The manic depressive individual exploits and adapts, for
the needs of his own illness, a propensity which he possesses as a
member of a group.

Is anything to be learned from this comparison? The manic
depressive individual is one who cannot relate to other individuals
simply by mutual exchange of affection. In his relation to others
he must either dominate or submit. On the one hand the difficulty
of changing this characteristic of the manic depressive discourages
hope for decreasing war readiness. On the other hand, however,
one wonders why some nations are content with the role of one

among equals, while others insist on domination, and how rapidly and under what circumstances a nation will change from the latter state to the former. Finally, if nations *can* change, is it totally unrealistic to hope that at some time all significantly strong nations will accept the role of one among many equals?

Let me conclude with the following proposals: That psychoanalysts take an interest and promote research, together with historians and sociologists, into those historical circumstances under which belligerent nations become pacific ones and pacific nations become belligerent. Let us study not only the economic and material circumstances, but also the nature of the society residing in that country at that time. This research can be undertaken individually, or under institutional sponsorship. That as analysts we make continuing and intense efforts to "see beyond our patients' neuroses," so as to discover their perception of international, national, and local events, how they respond to them and participate in community responses. That we engage as individuals and in organizations in a major public education project. We can act alone as analysts, or cooperatively with other serious, scholarly organizations who are interested in world affairs. We can ascertain whether and when we can apply psychoanalytic understanding to analysis of propaganda, social behavior and government activity. In other words, we can constitute ourselves a kind of institute for propaganda analysis. Perhaps this would be most effectively done by a committee of the International Psychoanalytic Association.

Outlook: An Israeli View

Rafael Moses

Rather than attempt to summarize the points of view presented in this volume, I will present some personal reactions and thoughts on the problems discussed. Let me begin with some remarks on the problem of subjectivity on the part of Israelis. The danger in our dealing with our subjectivity seems to be mainly twofold: I think we are trying to steer our way between the Scylla of a patriotic nationalism which sees war as forced upon us entirely against our will and the Charybdis embodied in that self-critical attitude which is beginning to be heard a little more in Israel these days, of blaming ourselves for the absence of peace, and ignoring the responsibility of the "other side." I think the third danger of reacting to subjectivity—that of being pseudo-detached and pseudo-objective—is much less present among psychoanalysts. It seems to me that these three maladaptive ways of dealing with our subjective reaction to being involved in an ongoing war, represent three main pathological patterns of dealing with aggression by the individual which have emerged in this volume. In being patriotic and blaming the other side for their aggressiveness, we use the mechanisms of displacement and projection, as outlined, among others, by Atkin and Noy. In holding our own side responsible, we use a mechanism of turning against the self akin to that described by Solnit. Were we to detach ourselves and pretend to be 'objective,' we would use the third mechanism—which Atkin writes of as dehumanization, which is part of Jaffe's analysis of the mechanisms of war and which is related to isolation and intellectualization.

There is no question in my mind that the greatest temptation is to turn chauvinistic, to displace our individual narcissism onto the Jewish nation and the State of Israel and not least among them to the Israel Defense Forces. Perhaps our army makes it easiest for us to succumb to the regressive pull towards an omnipotent stance, to become identified with that superman of which Gumbel speaks, that virile phallic anthropomorphized group, which leads us out of the fear, the anxiety and helplessness which repeatedly threaten us. It is very difficult for us, in the existing political and military situation in Israel, to work realistically for the peace which we all want and are so sorely in need of; a peace we desperately want to come about in our lifetime and in that of our children—and which yet seems so disappointingly out of reach. The everyday events of soldiers and civilians killed and wounded, of planes shot down in the "war of attrition," tend to puncture our phallic narcissistic omnipotence and return us—each time anew—to more realistic evaluations and to castration fears. I wonder whether this is one explanation for the individual narcissistic hurt which each one of us felt when there was bad military news.

Since I believe that subjectivity has advantages as well as disadvantages—as we well know from our therapeutic work—I will try to evaluate my own measure of subjectivity. Having been able to fulfill a psychiatric-medical role prior to and during the Six-Day War impressed me again with the importance of mastery through activity.

Those around us who had no clear-cut task to fulfill were considerably more anxious and afraid than those of us who did. I felt the same urge to do something after the Six-Day War and as a result spent some two and a half years in trying to establish contact with Palestinian Arabs and with the world in which they live. There may have been small effects of those contacts on outside events, but certainly the attempt to act in a way compatible both with my wish to bring about some meaningful communication and with my professional know-how, in a situation of acute and violent conflict, made me personally feel a little more comfortable about what seemed at times an intolerable situation. One of my co-workers * used the apt phrase of "colleagues and enemies" to

---

* Jona M. Rosenfeld, Ph. D.

describe the feeling engendered by our endeavor to collaborate with Arab professionals. My professional activity with wounded soldiers after the Six-Day War also gave me some feeling of mastery vis-à-vis the physical injuries of war. All these activities, then, provided me with three psychological assets: a feeling of mastery through activity, a feeling of participation in what were central events of the times and third, it increased my knowledge: of the reactions of myself and others—friends and enemies—and of some of the psychological processes taking place in times of violent conflict of which, nolens volens, I am a part. It is some of these items of knowledge which I want to describe — knowledge which comes both from within and without. Perhaps for this reason it is as yet less organized and crystallized than I would like it to be. This is the price which I think we pay for our subjectivity: our knowledge is still more intuitive than cognitive.

It is not surprising that I was impressed mainly with the vicissitudes of hostility, aggression, fear, blame and guilt, as well as a strengthening of bonds with some of those near us. Let me start with this last point. Ruth Jaffe describes the strong mutual libidinal ties in army units, the atmosphere of brotherhood and parental leadership which helps the soldier master his fear and carry out his duties. I was specially impressed with this bond in a soldier who, on the third day of the war, passed the wreckage of an Israeli plane and the mutilated body of its pilot. Although he knew the area was mined, he went to extricate the pilot's body. In the process he stepped on a mine and lost one of his legs. Although he had not known this pilot, he spoke of him in loving and personal terms, as of a lost brother. He felt a much stronger bond with the dead pilot than with the soldier of his unit with whom he went to extricate the pilot and who subsequently extricated him from the minefield. The reasons appeared too complex to allow for a simple explanation.

I have personally experienced the ego-strengthening effect of such a bond. On visiting a United Nations Works and Relief Agency Headquarters a week after the war with a colleague, where the two of us passed through a large crowd of Arabs, my acute fear was mitigated only because we were two, joined in a common purpose. When, later, we visited many Arab refugee camps and met with professionals and notables who unanimously and ubiquitously attacked Israel and its policy in vituperative terms, I again felt that I would not have been able to go through such visits and meetings successfully by myself. We needed to be at least two to feel strong and effective enough. Interestingly enough, I remember walking in one of the towns of the Gaza strip—at a time when terrorist acts were already part of the scene—and feeling completely unafraid because of a bond that had by now been formed with the Palestinian Arab who arranged these meetings for us—a bond with one of the opposing camp. In organizing psychological civil defense in Jerusalem, too, we learnt quickly that people were best sent out in twos—rather than alone. Such a bond must be engendered as a result of a degree of regression; it clearly can be in the service of the ego.

When I began a study of the mechanism of projection some three years ago, I soon became aware of one reason for my using this particular defense mechanism as a vehicle for the study of psychoanalytic theory. Projection was widely prevalent all around us and seemed to be an integral part of the psychological scene of the Israel-Arab conflict. The fear of disfigurement of wounded soldiers was projected onto their relatives. A soldier with an amputated leg did not want to "frighten his daughter" by having her see his stump; another did not want to frighten his wife by having her see his amputated arm. A woman whose husband was killed by Arabs, after the Six-Day-War, did not want her daughter to know that her father had been killed by an Arab, because she, the mother, did not want her daughter to grow up to hate the Arabs. These are clear-cut examples of the projection of fear, castration fear, and a special form of the projection of aggression. "It is not I who would be shocked by the sight of a stump—it is he or she." Or, "It is not I who would hate the Arabs, it is my daughter." Both forms of projection are formed as a response to an acute trauma not only on the basis of personality make-up, but also involve a varying degree of participation in the group bond.

We are all familiar with the reactions of guilt to the death of those around us; in contrast to Jaffe I firmly believe that there were and are many such reactions in Israel. I will quote just one example to show that these reactions are little different in war-time from those known to psychoanalysts otherwise: A medical orderly was hit in the arm during a battle. He was bleeding profusely but had run out of tourniquets. He asked a friend to bring him a tourniquet, which the latter did, thereby saving his life, though not his arm. The friend was killed shortly thereafter—and our medical orderly was seriously plagued by feelings of guilt and hostility with which he tried to deal in different ways in accord with his basic conflicts.

More dramatic examples of the confrontation with hostility and aggression toward the Arab enemy could be seen in Israeli hospitals during and directly after the Six-Day War. When the first wounded Arab prisoners-of-war arrived, some of the medical staff experienced a violent internal conflict: should they medically treat and take care of the enemy? Should they leave their own wounded temporarily to take care of enemy wounded, who were in more dire straits? An emotional reaction ran through the hospital when it was learnt that one ward was filled with prisoners-of-war. The evil enemy was there, right there in our midst. There was an implication that this should not be allowed. A nurse on duty in that special ward could not cope with her conflicted impulses; her fear that the prisoners would physically harm her—projected aggression at least in part—was her most immediate response. Israeli wounded soldiers on an orthopedic ward wanted to do violence to an Arab armed infiltrator who was rumored to have wounded an Israeli soldier and was admitted to the same ward. They talked to the doctors, and as a result, managed to handle their feelings more directly.

I hope I have been able to convey some of the feeling qualities, the atmosphere, the human interactions which I perceived, and to which I reacted, in these different environments—all related to the Arab-Israeli conflict. Let me oversimplify at this point, by saying that one of the adaptive tasks set by a country for its citizens in time of war, is that of maintaining a projective stance which I would formulate as "I will kill you in order to stop you from killing me." This, after all, is the rationale—or rationalization—of all wars, and of all fights just like those of children, where we are told "He started the fight, not I." As in all projections, there is some basis of truth in these formulations. Some paranoid patients also say: "I will kill him so that he won't kill me." Paranoid patients,

as Freud (1911, 1922) told us, and as has been considerably elaborated since, base their delusions on the *reality* of the *unconscious* aggressive impulses of the other. Among children, too, there is a reality basis for the accusation "He started it." Indeed, it is often hard to
decide "who started the fight", among children as well as among
peoples and nations. "It takes two to tangle," it takes two to
project, and it takes two to make war. Furthermore, the more
one side is convinced that the other is out to destroy it, the more
basis the first provides by its 'defensive' moves for the second to
feel that it is about to be attacked. In other words, as the intensity
of projection increases, so—in this mechanism—does outer reality
change, so as to augment the reality basis for the projection. This
is in addition to the actual readiness to be aggressive by each side
which surely exists from the outset. Then, as both sides ready themselves more and more against the other, a situation arises which
may from now on *itself* tend toward the discharge of war.
At such a time more momentum seems to be required to lead
away from war than toward war. Somewhere along the line, a
"shift," a "flash" takes place (cf. Atkin), where psychological
resistance to change shifts from a peace-time footing to a war-time
footing. Then war seems to be perceived almost as a relief from
tension, rather than as the shocking catastrophe it had represented
a short while ago.

I am aware that I here extrapolate from the individual to the
group as though they were alike, and that this has its dangers and
limitations. This is a problem which has been brought to our
attention by several contributors to this volume—Neubauer,
Rosenberger, Jaffe, Noy, Atkin, and Gumbel. I will return to
this point later.

I would like to stay now for a while, with the defense mechanism of projection, as it is prevalent in and related to violent conflict and to war. In our study of projection,* it has been our impression that the projection of aggression is more ubiquitous than
the projection of libido; and that we tend to project active drives
more than passive ones. While both of these findings would indeed

* I have been engaged in a study of projection with Mr. Hai Halevi supported by the Foundations' Fund for Research in Psychiatry. Grant G 68–425.

tend to connect projection with aggression, we also know that it is the passive drive of wanting to be loved by a person of the same sex—homosexuality—which is at the root of the most widely found instance of projection: when we ascribe to the other that aggressive drive which we cannot bear to find in ourselves. This transformation, was formulated by Freud (1911, 1922) and Fenichel, as "I love him–I hate him–He hates me." The 'I' here is of course a man. Although much has been written about the intimate connection between homosexuality and paranoia, I think that there is much yet to be understood in this area. This question has been touched upon by Neubauer, Jaffe, Noy, Gumbel and Atkin. What seems to me most unclear is the reason for, and the detailed process of, the affect reversal—from "I love" to "I hate." In fact, the reversal goes from 'I (a man) want *to be loved* by him'—a passive wish—to 'I hate him,' which is a double reversal, both of passive into active drive, and of libido into aggression. Here we encounter the question whether the 'I hate him' is primarily a result of the frustration of not being loved; or whether it is dominantly an affect reversal. If the latter, then it is so because the passive libidinal wish is even less acceptable than the active aggressive wish. It might also be a mixture of both. All this in addition to the fact that the active aggressive wish is still so unacceptable as to require being transformed into the projection "He hates me." We encounter here the question which was raised by several of the papers in this book: To what extent is aggressive drive the result of frustration—or an innate independent drive? This question is posed by Solnit's fascinating paper: to what extent is the aggression—so life-saving when expressed—related to the frustration dammed up as a result of the removal of the love object? One way of solving this problem is to say that the affect reversal stems from the previous basic ambivalence. This is Spitz's solution. Freud, (1922), compares the affect reversal of the paranoid person — from love to hate — to that of the early homosexual phase, where the hate for the rival is reversed by reaction formation into love for him, the negative Oedipus complex; and sees in this same affect reversal both the process which leads to socialization of the aggressive drive and the basis for the subsequent reversal of the paranoid. This would then be a regressive phenomenon — retracing a previous developmental step. The wish to be loved by the person of the same sex would now become again what it once was—the wish to remove the rival. Socialized aggression would thus be regressively defused and released in part.

We do not know enough about the specific processes and steps which lead from homosexuality to certain projective mechanisms; though we do know that one of the steps must be the affect reversal, since later regression leads back to it. In effect projective mechanisms, like all defense mechanisms, are much more widely used than is apparent from a study of gross pathological reactions. There is a range of projective mechanisms which do not assume psychotic proportions and thus form a part of everyday psychopathology. In a projection, there are two main ways of diluting, of weakening, the drive which encounters resistance from the superego and the ego—two ways in addition to the projection itself, which ascribes the drive to another. The first mode of diluting the 'drive event' is to vary the distance from the subject:—a close relative who is believed to want to kill one poses a greater threat than a distant stranger or an abstract idea, or an inanimate object. The second mode of diluting affects the intensity of the drive itself. The unconscious wish to kill may be ascribed to another as a plain wish to kill, or only to harm unspecifically, or even only to hinder. Now, in violent inter-group conflict today, the object is more distant than the immediate family; we speak of a depersonalized war (Jaffe, Wedge). However, the drive is diluted not at all—as evidenced in the violence and brutality of war. Yet projections in times of violent conflict, have a considerable basis in outer reality. Furthermore, such projections tend to mould the outer reality in accordance with the inner regressive one. The majority of psychotic projections, though at times as undiluted as to the drive, and somewhat less diluted as to the object of the drive, do not tend to mould external reality, and have no objective basis in reality, but base themselves on the reality of the other's unconscious drives. The third group—projections that are not psychotic and not related to violent conflict—are more under ego control than either of the other groups. They show a considerable dilution of the drive as well as a fair amount of dilution through distancing from the love object. At the same time they retain more of a reality basis and also involve a better testing of reality, and furthermore mould this reality less.

These four attributes of projection then—dilution of drive, distancing from the love object, degree of reality basis, and amount of influence on outer reality—allow for some differentiation of types of projection and for assessment of the amount of ego control. As Gumbel points out, war involves a regression in the service of the id; ego control over inner processes diminishes as regressive influences increase.

If we go back to the most common type of projection: "I don't hate you; you hate me," we find that two variations on this theme are of interest: First, "It is not only I who wants or does this bad thing; they, too, wish it or do it." This mechanism is described by Fenichel as characterizing the artist, for whom acceptance of his work means that the public shares his guilt related to oedipal wishes, and thus relieves him of his guilt feelings (cf. Hanns Sachs, Rank). Here too, there is a reality basis related to unconscious wishes and their expression, though one subsequent to artistic creation, in this case the real acclaim of a work of art. This mechanism — albeit with much less diluted drive — is part of mass and mob psychology (cf Freud 1921) and thus serves to allay the superego pressures in times of war; and similarly to further regressive pulls. But it is also used as a partial projection onto the other, the stranger, the enemy, and then serves as a rationalization for all the 'bad' acts committed by "me" or by "my side." In the case of Israel, one of the often repeated formulas is: "We all know what the Arabs would have done to us, had they won the war." It is felt that the conquering Arab armies would have raped and killed with a vengeance; consequently, so the reasoning goes, there is no need, or less need, to criticize ourselves for deeds of needless violence committed by our side. We thus alleviate our feelings of guilt, our superego, by ascribing aggression to the other — with a varying basis in reality.

The second variation of the more widely used category of projection ("I don't hate him; he hates me") is: "It is my people who are doing this evil thing; but it is not I," to which at times may be added: "I will therefore go against my own people." One can readily recognize this formulation as characterizing certain splinter groups in Israel and in the United States. We thus see that there are three possible variations, which form a continuum. Some use the simple, direct form of projection — "We have to attack them, or else they will attack us." An in-between form is to say: "We are not so bad after all — look how much worse they are." And the extremists of the other side say: "It is my brethren, my kinfolk who are evil — and not I. I will use all my energies to fight them and right the wrongs they have committed." In other words, the first group justifies their own aggressive acts by projecting their aggression onto the enemy and thus justify its expression; whereas those on the other extreme justify their hostility or their aggressive acts by projecting their aggression onto their own people, thus rationalizing the need to attack their own side. The in-between projection limits itself to alleviating guilt over aggressive acts already committed. It is clear, I think, that those who project onto their own kin are much less successful in repressing their guilt, than those who project onto the more distant enemy. I have been able to confirm this impression in clinical work with patients. And yet, we see here two sides of the same coin — two extreme ways of dealing with internal aggression, expressing it and justifying its expression. As Neubauer, Atkin and others have pointed out, Freud tells us that the hostility to the stranger derives from narcissism, including the collective narcissism, sometimes of megalomanic proportions (cf. also Gumbel) which makes for patriotism; while the hostility towards the loved ones derives from the ambivalence toward them. Yet the stranger and the enemy are often close and even kindred. Arabs repeatedly tell Jews that "after all, we are brothers and should therefore get along" or that "Jews and Arabs are cousins and could have lived on good terms, had it not been for the British who tried to rule by dividing us." (Wedge's superordinate intervention). Many Israelis refer to Arabs, half jokingly, as "our cousins." This supports what Noy stresses, that it is close neighbors, blood relatives who fight with each other; whereas only the strangers who are far away can be more safely hated from a distance without too much physical aggression. It seems to me that here there is an interplay of distance and closeness — of relating to stranger and relative — of narcissism and ambivalence — which deserves closer scrutiny.

There is one further impression about the Arab-Israeli conflict which I want to mention. It is what seems to me and some others a dominant and highly prevalent attitude — reciprocal and complementary, though more distinct at first from our side. On a visit with us to the Gaza strip, a sociologist*, referred to this phenomenon as 'the culture of contempt' — an Israeli culture of contempt towards the Arab. You meet it in many areas and walks of life. Israelis at times refer to bad workmanship contemptuously as 'Arab workmanship.' Arab military actions are passed off as 'bad jobs;' the Arab terrorists are talked about as impotent or at best inept. Changes in Arab military capability are discounted contemptuously. Israeli technology is seen as so obviously superior to what the Arabs do, that the latter cannot possibly pose a serious threat. Similarly, Israeli intellect is seen as inordinately superior to that of the Arabs. In other words, Israeli physical prowess, courage, knowhow, skill and intelligence are all seen on an unconscious level as narcissistically phallic omnipotent attributes which turn the Israelis into natural victors over our Arab rivals. This is seen both as masculine prowess on the phallic level, and as the same phallic omnipotence displaced upward to the intellectual sphere. This attitude clearly possesses a markedly irrational quality. The very real dangers inherent in such a distortion of reality are obvious.

We can observe the complementary attribute on the Arab side. The Arab perceives the Israeli as a threat to him, as alien, as an agent of change, as stronger, as more capable technically, economically, militarily, perhaps also intellectually. On an unconscious level, the Arab seems to feel castrated as compared to the phallic potent Israeli, and I think this also tends to invite the use of magical thinking. Here, too, there is some reality basis as well as a marked irrational exaggeration. What is striking is the complementarity of the attitudes and roles, although the reverse also exists.

There is, however, more to the "culture of contempt" than can be understood on the phallic level alone. Many Israelis look on the

---

* Morris Schwartz, Brandeis University, Boston, Mass.

Arab as dirty. As we know, such an attitude involves a projection of 'unclean' and uncontrolled drives onto the other. The Arab in this sense can be compared to the Negro in the United States. They are both seen as the incarnation of unmastered pregenital sexuality and aggressivity, and are, at times, avoided accordingly. There are some people who found it impossible for long months after the Six-Day War to venture into areas inhabited by Arabs. They gave as reasons both the fear of the dirt and the fear of what might be done to them. This attitude, then, has an anal, pregenital aspect to it — anal dirt, anal sadism, and pregenital, perverted sexuality seem to be involved. There is the clear-cut split of the ambivalence mentioned by Atkin and Neubauer. The attitudes of Israelis of Western descent to those of Asian and African origin, and vice versa, are basically similar to those of Israelis and Arabs, although — in line again with what Noy has told us — these differences tend to disappear in times of violent conflict with the outer Arab world. On the Arab side, the Israeli seems very much the alien stranger, who threatens to upset the existing way of life. This is reminiscent of the way in which Neubauer talks of stranger anxiety in the 8-month old child serving to protect against the danger of the unknown. It is important to remember that Israelis and Arabs are not as distant as Americans and Russians, but — especially since the Six-Day War — meet each other frequently.

It seems to me that aspects of the contempt, the looking down that have to do both with the castration complex—denied or fear-ed—and with regressions to the narcissistic anal level, with a split of the ambivalence, lead us back to unconscious, repressed homosexuality—and, through it, once more, to projection. We assume, as I have said previously, that the original impulse is: "I, a man, want to be loved by another man;" that this then becomes converted into "I do not love him, I hate him"—showing a reversal of passive into active drive, and of libido into aggression; and that the final change is "It is not I who hate him; it is he who hates me." In fact, the projection 'He hates me and wants to harm me" also carries with it an implied, fantasized gratification of passive wishes. If the projector will be assaulted, some of his passive—libidinal and/or aggressive—wishes will be gratified, albeit against his will, i. e., without his responsibility. In the same vein, if the projector attacks the other, with the projective rationalization that he thus avoids the other's attack, he will thereby also gratify his fused libidinal and aggressive wishes toward another male. War, after all, is fought by men against men. In other words, the projection shows clear traces of the original— passive or active—unconscious wish.

Let me now turn to the outlook for the future. One criterion for the outlook is the degree of ego control over our drives as opposed to their regressive pull in the individual as well as in the group. Gumbel has sketched a frighteningly realistic picture of the strength of our regressive pulls, and of the inevitability in the foreseeable future of violent conflicts. Arlow reminds us similarly of our very realistic limitations. Little has changed in this respect since Freud and Einstein corresponded in 1932; the outlook is at least as grim, in fact more so. Both the United States and Israel, amongst others, have been engaged in violent conflict for most of the past 20 years at least, and this after the holocaust of the Second World War. We have thus less cause for optimisim than did Freud in 1932.

What are the factors that might encourage optimism? Enhanced ego control, both in the individual and in the group for one; and a muting and individualizing of the superego, that unreliable ally—in Arlow's words. This would show itself in a variety of ego activities on the one hand—among which I would list an increase of the quest for knowledge and insight. The muted, more individualized superego should, among other things, lead to an increasingly personal and realistic quest for peace. A minor product is the search for more meaningful communication between disparate groups; be they in conflict—as Arabs and Jews—or merely distant from each other — like American and Israeli psychoanalysts. The curiosity to come to know the strange and the stranger, related to the wish to master, is a positive factor here.

A number of participants in the conference leading to this volume have reminded us that we have no developmental theory of the aggressive drive to match our developmental theory of the sexual drive. We are not unanimous in deciding to what extent aggressive behavior results from the frustration of the quest for gratification, and to what extent from an aggressive drive per se. Freud's theory of the death instinct has not found many adherents. Yet, as Arlow also suggests, aggression dealt with inwardly prevents, or at least minimizes, destructive aggression turned outward. Similarly, outward expression of constructive aggression minimizes that of destructive aggression. Arlow has reminded us that even non-violence requires an external enemy; therefore non-violent outlets for aggression spare us violent ones. Yet we are not clear in differentiating hostility from aggression, aggressive from destructive behavior. Even the constructive effects of aggressive behavior in infants tend at times to lead the caretaking figures to react with counteraggression, thereby negating the constructive effect of the original aggressive behavior. Clearly there is much yet to be learnt, much to be done. Perhaps the considerable changes wrought in dealing with the sexual drive since Freud gave us its developmental theory, will allow us to hope for similar changes if we address ourselves to the developmental theory of aggression in the decades to come.

Aggression is related to mastery and to activity. To the extent that mastering activity increases, destructive channelization of aggression decreases. Yet we know little about how to help bring this about. Certainly, the developments of the past fifty years have brought about much additional mastery of the environment, yet it seems to have brought little additional mastery of inner forces. We know that mastery and activity decrease fear and thus decrease the need to project—and to move from a war institution to war-mindedness, in Atkin's terms. Yet much of the mastering of the enviroment has led to an increased —and realistic— fear of the tools in the hands of man.

One of the problems approached again and again in this volume is the shift from the individual to the group. As psychoanalysts, we deal with individuals rather than with groups. Yet all of us live within groups, and many of us extend our professional interest to group phenomena. We are experts at increasing the control of the ego in the individual, yet we know little about how to bring about a similar change in the group. Even in the individual, an enormous effort is required, a great investment of time and energy, of scrutiny of the other and of the self, of compassion and identification, of frustration tolerance in many forms. Is it conceivable that we might transfer such efforts to the group, the community, the nation, the state. Furthermore, while our patients are motivated to seek help through the pressure of their suffering, large groups have easier ways of dealing with their hardships than to seek the help of our kind of professionals.

The two main ways open to us to improve the outlook for peace—understanding and activity leading to constructive change— seem to leave us far behind. And yet human nature does not tend to give up, to relinquish optimism. Each of us continues in his own way to seek his gratification—gratifications both directly for himself, through attempts to help others, and to improve what is happening around us. In these areas, I think we must continue and shall continue, both to increase our knowledge and our insight, to learn more about the vicissitudes and the genetics of aggression. In short, to be active, each in our own way, to continue to stress those human and humanistic aspects in life which oppose mechanization and dehumanization.

And here we have some points to our credit. Each of our groups in its country strives toward the increase of knowledge about psychic processes; and each has something to show for its efforts. The understanding of human relations has become more important in Israel, too, in the past ten years. We are part and parcel of an over-all process of change, which we try to influence in the direction which seems best to us. We do so professionally and also as citizens, and as members of our families. In the long run, we throw our lot in with our group, our country and—while continuing our activity to the best of our abilities and ideals—take our chances with our friends and neighbors. As Freud said: "And now it may be expected that the other of the two 'heavenly forces', eternal Eros, will put forth his strength so as to maintain himself alongside of his equally immortal adversary." (1930)

REFERENCES

FREUD, S. (1911), Psychoanalytic Notes on an Autobiographical Account of a Case of Paranoia, S.E. 12, 3.

FREUD, S. (1915), A case of paranoia running counter to the psychoanalytic theory of the disease, S.E. 14, 263.

FREUD, S. (1922) Some Neurotic Mechanisms in Jealousy, Paranoia and Homo-sexuality, S.E. 18, 223.

FREUD, S. (1921) Group Psychology and the Analysis of the Ego, S.E. 18, 69

FREUD, S. (1930) Civilization and its discontents, S.E. 21.

FREUD, S. (1932) Why War? S.E. 22.

FENICHEL, O., *The Psychoanalytic Theory of Neurosis*, Norton, N.Y. 1945, pp. 428, 498.

RANK, O., *Der Kuenstler*, Hugo Heller, Vienna, 1907.

SACHS, H., The Community of Day Dreams. In: *The Creative Unconscious*, Sci-Art Publ., Cambridge, Mass., 1942.

CONTRIBUTORS

ALEKSANDROWICZ, DOV, M. D. Psychoanalyst; A. Member, The Israel Psychoanalytic Society; Visiting Staff Member, The Menninger Clinic, Topeka, Kansas.

ARLOW, JACOB A. M. D. Clinical Professor of Psychiatry, State University of New York; Faculty Member, New York Psychoanalytic Institute.

ATKIN, SAMUEL, M. D. Faculty Member and former President, New York Psychoanalytic Institute; former President, New York Psychoanalytic Society; Associate Professor, Albert Einstein College of Medicine; Consultant, Hillside Hospital.

BENTAL, VICKY, M. D. Training and Supervisory Analyst; Member, Israel Psychoanalytic Institute; President, Israel Psychoanalytic Society.

BUXBAUM, EDITH, M. D. Child analyst, training and supervisory analyst, Seattle, Washington.

GUMBEL, ERICH, M. D. Training and supervisory analyst; Director, Israel Psychoanalytic Institute; Past President, Israel Psychoanalytic Society.

ILAN, ELIEZER M. A. Child Guidance Clinic, Ministry of Health, Jerusalem; Senior Teacher in Psychology, Hebrew University; Training and Supervisory Analyst, Israel Psychoanalytic Institute.

JAFFE, RUTH, M. D. Director, Shalvata Psychiatric Hospital; Associate Professor of Psychiatry, Tel Aviv University Medical School; Training and Supervisory Analyst, Israel Psychoanalytic Institute.

KESTENBERG, JUDITH S., M. D. Lecturer, Division of Psychoanalytic Education and Lecturer in Child Analysis, State University, Downstate Medical Center, New York.

LINN, LOUIS, M. D. Clinical Professor, Mount Sinai School of Medicine, City University of New York; Attending Psychiatrist, Mount Sinai Hospital; most recent books: *Handbook of Hospital Psychiatry* and *Frontiers of General Hospital Psychiatry*.

MOSES, RAFAEL, M. D. Visiting Professor in Psychiatry, Hebrew University; Training and Supervisory Analyst, Israel Psychoanalytic Institute; President-Elect, Israel Psychoanalytic Society.

NEUBAUER, PETER, B., M. D. Associate Clinical Professor of Psychiatry and Chairman, Child Psychiatric Section, Division of Psychoanalytic Education, Downstate Medical Center, State University of New York; Training and Supervisory Analyst; Director, Child Development Study Center, New York.

NOY, PINCHAS, M. D. Visiting Lecturer in Psychiatry, Hebrew University of Jerusalem; Training and Supervisory Analyst, Israel Psychoanalytic Institute.

OSTOW, MORTIMER, M. D. Visiting Professor of Pastoral Psychiatry, Jewish Theological Seminary of America; Director, Bernstein Counseling Center; recent President, Psychoanalytic Research and Development Fund, Chairman of its Study Groups on Sexual Perversion and Studies in Drug Therapy.

PERES, SHIMON Cabinet Minister, Israel Government.

ROGOW, ARNOLD, Ph. D. Graduate Professor of Political Science, City College of New York; Visiting Professor, Hebrew University of Jerusalem.

ROSENBERGER, LIZZIE, M. D. Psychoanalyst, Consultant in Child Psychiatry, Shalvata Hospital; Teacher, Postgraduate Institute for Psychotherapy, Tel Aviv University.

SCHOSSBERGER, JANOS, M. D. Psychoanalyst; Director, Kfar Shaul Work Village, Jerusalem.

SOLNIT, A., M. D. Professor of Pediatrics and Psychiatry; Director, Yale Child Study Center; Chairman, Committee on Child Analysis of the American Psychoanalytic Association; Former President, Western New England Institute for Psychoanalysis; Former President, International Association of Child Psychiatry.

WALLERSTEIN, ROBERT S., M. D. Director of Department of Psychiatry, Mt. Sion Hospital, California; Training and Supervisory Analyst; Former President, American Psychoanalytical Association.

WEDGE, BRYANT, M. D. Director, Institute for the Study of National Behavior, Inc., San Diego, California.

WEISS-GLICKSON, NAOMI, M. A. Training and Supervisory Analyst, Israel Psychoanalytic Institute.

WINNIK, H. Z., M. D., M. R. C. Psych. Professor of Psychiatry, Hebrew University of Jerusalem; Training Analyst, Israel Psychoanalytic Institute; Former President, Israel Psychoanalytic Society; Editor-in-Chief, *Israel Annals of Psychiatry and Related Disciplines;* Director Talbieh Psychiatric Hospital, Jerusalem.